Haiti
A Slave Revolution

❧❧

200 years after 1804

Edited and Compiled by
Pat Chin, Greg Dunkel, Sara Flounders and Kim Ives

International Action Center
New York

2004

Haiti: A Slave Revolution
200 years after 2004

© Copyright 2004
ISBN 0-974751-0-X

International Action Center
39 W. 14th St, Suite 206, New York, NY, 10011
Phone: 212 633-6646; Fax: 212 633-2889
Website: www.iacenter.org
E-mail: iacenter@action-mail.org

Cover Design: Katharine Kean **Cover lithograph:** Ambush at Ravine aux Couleuvres, designed by Karl Giradet, engraved by Outwaite. **Back Cover photo:** Haitians at a pro-Aristide rally in Kenscoff on December 6, 1990 by Carol Halebian.

Cataloging Data

Haiti: a slave revolution: 200 years after 1804/ edited by Pat Chin, Greg Dunkel, Sara Flounders, and Kim Ives.—1st ed.

p. cm.

Includes bibliographic references and index.

ISBN 0-974751-0-X (pbk.: alk. paper)

1. Haiti—History—Revolution, 1791-1804. 2. Haiti—History—American intervention, 1994-1995. 3. Haiti—Relations—United States. I. Title.

F1923.H3 2004

972.94'03

TABLE OF CONTENTS

PREFACE: WHY THIS BOOK

Editors

This book is a joint project of the Haiti Support Network (HSN) and the International Action Center (IAC). Both organizations since their founding have tried to promote solidarity with the continuing Haitian Revolution.

As the bicentennial of Haiti's independence approached, we considered how to commemorate this singular event in the history of the world, the successful revolution in Haiti against the French slave owners. Just holding a meeting or a series of meetings didn't seem to be enough. So we decided to compile a book to mark Haiti's 200 years of struggle against racism and colonialism, to mark the only time slaves managed to rise up, break their chains and set up a new state and social order that reflected some of their aspirations and hopes.

The mainstream press and politicians say they celebrate the bicentennial of the world's first Black republic and its achievements. But they explain its poverty and political instability by pointing to "poor leadership," a lack of "democratic traditions" and isolation due to geography and language.

This book is going to combat 200 years of racist indoctrination and propaganda about the Haitian Revolution. It is essential to challenge these stereotypes in order to build true, informed solidarity with Haiti.

Chapters in this book point out how the United States and other imperialist powers like France and Germany have persecuted, exploited and from time to time, occupied Haiti and how the Haitian people have resisted by any means possible.

At least half of Haiti's population in 1790 were killed before 1802 and still the Haitian people won. They crushed France's genocidal attempt to re-enslave them by crushing Napoleon's army. This hard-won victory meant Haiti was a beacon of hope and inspiration to enslaved African people of the United States, even after they obtained their freedom. Frederick Douglass, the famous Black abolitionist who was the U.S. consul in Port-au-Prince in the 1880s, expressed this clearly in a speech, included in this book.

This book is not a traditional history of Haiti. It's a people's history. We link historical events to current realities and show a continuity of oppression and resistance.

This book exposes some little known and carefully hidden history. For example, how the slave-owning George Washington got his slave-owning secretary of state Thomas Jefferson to send $400,000 — a vast sum at the time — to support the slave-owners of Haiti in their vain attempt to put down the revolt. We connect this, the first significant foreign aid the United States ever granted, to the millions the U.S. gave Marc Bazin, a former World Bank Official, to run against Aristide in his first campaign.

The Jefferson-Washington grant and the money granted to Bazin are the historical precedents for the funds the International Republican Institute gives to fund the so-called Democratic Convergence, which opposes the current Aristide government.

We include the explanation given by Ben Dupuy, the leader of the National Popular Party, of why the United States invaded Haiti in 1994. We have an analysis of the huge demonstrations that the Haitian community in the United States held to protest the coup against Aristide, police brutality and how they were stigmatized using the AIDS hysteria. These were not just demonstrations, they were also one-day strikes.

Since this is a people's history, we have a diversity of voices. Edwidge Danticat, a well-respected Haitian-American author, has a chapter on how Haitian refugees are detained in Florida. Stan Goff, who served in the U.S. Army's Special Forces during the 1994 occupation of Haiti and was moved to condemn this occupation in his book *Hideous Dream*. We selected a chapter.

Fleurimond W. Kerns, a columnist for Haïti-Progrès, points out in his chapter on the birth of the Haitian flag that the Congress of Arcahaie in 1803 was the occasion when the more privileged sectors in the Haitian revolution put themselves under the command of the most oppressed. Former U.S. Attorney-General Ramsey Clark, who is the founder of the IAC and investigated the 1991 coup as a member of the Haiti Commission, has an overview of Haitian history.

We were very happy when Local USWA 8751, representing Boston school bus drivers, a union which is 75% Haitian, asked to contribute a chapter. The struggle that the Haitian working class in the diaspora has waged against racism and U.S. neocolonialism has been part and parcel of the local's daily activity.

We hope the translations from two of Haiti's most celebrated poets

– Paul Laraque and the late Félix Morisseau-Leroy – will give the reader an impression of the Creole language's beauty and imagery and how Haitian poets raise political themes.

We could not cover every aspect of Haitian history we would have liked: for example, Haiti's intervention in the Dominican Republic, which ended slavery there; the *cacos'* struggle against the U.S. occupation from 1916 to 1922; the mass uprisings against the U.S. occupation in the late '20s and early '30s. We wanted to focus on the impact Haiti has and has had on the United States.

We hope this book builds a better understanding of Haiti's importance in the history of this hemisphere, and indeed, the world.

Pat Chin, Greg Dunkel, Sara Flounders, Kim Ives

Notes

If a chapter appeared earlier in another publication, we put the date when it appeared at the beginning of the chapter and the publication where it appeared at the end. We indicate the translator for chapters that earlier appeared in French or Creole.

We spell the last name of Toussaint Louverture the way he did; a common alternative is L'Ouverture. We italicize all the quotes from Creole that are used in this book. We use the word "voodoo" to refer to a religion in Haiti that is called and spelled "vodou" in Creole because we want to examine the contexts in which this word is used in North American English.

Here are some terms that are used in the book:

Cacos were armed peasants, who fought under the leadership of Charlmeagne Péralte and then Benoît Batraville against the first U.S. occupation;

affranchis were slaves who bought or were granted their legal freedom under French rule, or the children of colonists and enslaved mothers freed at birth; often they had significant wealth and were slave owners;

putsch is a sudden political uprising, almost a synonym for coup d'état;

Lavalas, what Aristide called his movement, is a Creole word meaning sudden flood;

Macoutes or *Tonton Macoutes,* formally the Volunteers for National Security, were a paramilitary organization that François Duvalier set up to neutralize the Haitian Army and terrorize the Haitian people.

Tenth Department is the popular term for Haitians living outside of Haiti, which has nine Departments (provinces or regions).

ACKNOWLEDGMENTS

Every book is a collective effort. For one to be produced, the talents, skills, dedication and time of many people are vital, especially when a book like *Haiti: A Slave Revolution* is produced on a compressed schedule. We want to thank all the writers and activists who contributed to this book and made it possible to present a people's history of Haiti.

Alana Salcer and Katharine Kean of Crowing Rooster Arts put a great deal of effort into designing and implementing the striking cover. Daniel Simidor graciously helped us find a cover graphic. We also want to thank photographer Carol Halebian for contributing one of her remarkable photographs for the back cover. Margarita Aguilar designed and typeset the inside of the book.

The staff and editors of Haïti-Progrès went out of their way to make their indispensable archives available; in particular, Berthony Dupont, Melissa Jerome and Jill Ives were very helpful. Joanne Spadaro and Elisa Chavez of the Haiti Support Network helped with the fact checking, proofreading and sending out the oh-so necessary fundraising mailings.

Janet Mayes and Paddy Colligan of the IAC did the proofreading. Colligan also carefully checked most of the translations and translated a chapter herself. Lal Rookh and Deirdre Griswold helped with technical and editorial work on the photo section.

Paddy Colligan, Joanne Spadaro, Josina Dunkel, Ed Lewinson and Marie Jay were stalwarts in getting out the large mailings we used to pay for this book. Kathy Durkin helped with finding funding for this effort and promoting it. We also want to thank the volunteer staff at the International Action Center national office for their efforts in promoting and distributing all of the International Actions Center's publications. They have done much to help on this work, from mailings to answering the phone and from processing the orders and donations to doing the shipments. They include: Marie Jay, Carol Holland, Kadouri Al-Kaysi, William Mason and Henri Nereaux. Deirdre Sinnott provides the daily organizational guidance in the office.

Acknowledgments to Donors

We acknowledge and thank all of the donors whose generosity enabled the publication of this highly significant and needed book. This is a concrete way in which contributors can show their support for the heroic and victorious struggles of the Haitian people both historically and today We also recognize the financial assistance of those who gave anonymously, but whose donations nevertheless have helped to make this important book possible.

We give a special thanks to the People's Rights Fund for its support throughout this book's production from start to finish, and for its commitment to its promotion and distribution.

We appreciate the financial support of those listed below:

Sponsor: Greg Dunkel, in memory of Key Martin, Barbara S. Jones

Supporters: Al Appel, Charlotte Appel, Boston Labor's ANSWER (Act Now to Stop War and End Racism), Progress Unity Fund

Donors: Gray Anderson, Ken Bann, Regina Bann, Hillel Cohen, Irwin Corey, Leslie Feinberg, Sara Flounders, Harlan Girard, Gloria K. Hannas, Nina Howes, Michael Kramer, Dominique Ledan, Bob McCubbin, Balquis Muhammad, Shooks Munroe, Laurent Pierre-Philippe, M.D., Minnie Bruce Pratt, Abdul R. Rasheed, Lee Steinberg, Al Strasburger, Carol Thomas, Gloria Verdieu, Joe Yuskaitis

Friends: Mary E. Ayers, Bernel Company, Barbara Boyd, William E. Brown, Olga Z. Emmel, C. Steven Fate, Carol E. Gay, Frances Goldin, Tika Jankovic, Lionel Jacque Jean, Marie C. Jean, Merle G. Krause, B. Sam Lacy, Rev. Lawrence E. Lucas, Steffan J. Manno, Linden P. Martineau, Cecile Meyer, David Meyerhof, Monica Moorehead, Alfred Olivi, William Peery, Tina Rhoades, Sarah Ringler, Dagny Rodriguez, Mike Shaw, Donald O. Sheppard, Donna Sinetar, Lois Singer, Deirdre Sinnott, Jeanne A. Smith, Doug Thompson, Richard Vanden Heuvel, Radmila Veselinovic, Laurence Wallace, Mary Jane Wallace, Portia Waldon, Laverne Williams

Also, the following chapters of the International Action Center: Baltimore, with the All-Peoples Congress, Boston, Detroit, Houston, Los Angeles, Philadelphia, Providence, San Diego, San Francisco.

Timeline

1492 Christopher Columbus lands near today's city of Cap Haïtien and claims the island of Hispaniola for Spain. The western third of the island is now Haiti and the rest of the island is the Dominican Republic.

1625 First French settlements on Tortuga Island, off the northwest coast, are established.

mid-1600s French settlements and plantations are established in coastal areas on the western third of the island.

1697 Under the terms of the Treaty of Ryswick, Spain cedes the western third of Hispaniola to France.

1700s The French colony of Saint Domingue is the most lucrative colony in the world, at this time, more lucrative than the 13 Colonies. Its slave-produced tropical crops—sugar, rum, cotton, tobacco, and indigo—generated great wealth. Near the end of the 18th century, 500,000 to 700,000 people, mainly of western African origin, were enslaved by the French.

1791 The Haitian Revolution begins when a group of slaves gather at Bois-Caïman in the northern part of the colony. Jamaican-born Dutty Boukman holds a voodoo ceremony that launches the struggle.

1803 The Haitian blue-and-red flag is adopted at the Congress of Arcahaie. The Battle of Vertières is the last victory of the Haitians over the French.

1804 Jean-Jacques Dessalines declared Haiti independent on January 1, after crushing the French army sent to re-enslave Haiti. Over half the people in Haiti die before the struggle has run its course.

1806 Jean-Jacques Dessalines is assassinated at Pont-Rouge.

1815-1816 Simón Bolívar gets asylum in Haiti twice and also receives military assistance to liberate South America from Spain.

1822 Haiti invades the Spanish colony of Santo Domingo (today's Dominican Republic), and ends slavery there.

1838 France fully and unconditionally recognizes Haiti's independence. It had given Haiti "conditional" recognition in 1825 after Haiti promised to pay 150 million gold francs as "compensation" for its "losses."

1844 The Haitian occupation of Santo Domingo ends.

1862 The United States recognizes Haiti.

1889 Frederick Douglass is appointed as U.S. Minister and Consul General to Haiti.

1915 United States Marines invade Haiti and occupy it. A largely peasant guerrilla army, known as the *cacos*, resists the occupiers under the leadership of Charlemagne Péralte, who is betrayed and assassinated by Marines in 1919.

1934 As popular resistance grows stronger, the nineteen-year U.S. occupation ends.

1937 Between 17,000 to 35,000 Haitians living in the Dominican Republic are massacred by the Dominican armed forces on the orders of President Rafael Trujillo. U.S. Secretary of State Cordell Hull subsequently declared "President Trujillo is one of the greatest men in Central America and in most of South America."

1957 François "Papa Doc" Duvalier becomes President of Haiti.

1958-1964 Duvalier attacks his opponents violently, driving many of them into exile.

1964 Papa Doc declares himself "President-for-Life."

1971 François Duvalier dies and is succeeded by his son, Jean-Claude "Baby Doc" Duvalier.

1970s-1980s Thousands of Haitians flee poverty and repression in Haiti by boat, often arriving in South Florida.

1982-1984 The U.S. State Department's Agency for International Development and the Organization of American States (OAS) oversee the slaughter of Haiti's "creole pigs," accused of being carriers of African Swine Fever. This is a major blow to the peasant economy.

1986 Widespread protests against repression force Baby Doc to flee Haiti on February 7th. The U.S. Air Force flies him to exile in France. A military junta, headed by Gens. Henri Namphy and Williams Regala, takes power.

1987 In July, big landowners (*grandons*) massacre hundreds of peasants demanding land in Jean-Rabel. In November, presidential elections are canceled after Army soldiers and former Tonton Macoutes massacre dozens of would-be voters.

1988 In January Christian Democrat Leslie Manigat is elected in military-run elections boycotted by the Haitian people and most candidates. In June he is overthrown in military coup by Gen. Namphy. In September Namphy is overthrown by Gen. Prosper Avril.

1990 President/General Prosper Avril declares a state of siege in January. Rising protests convince Avril to resign in March. A Provisional Government led by Supreme Court Justice Ertha Pascal-Trouillot is formed. Democratic elections take place on December 16, 1990. Father Jean-Bertrand Aristide, well known throughout the country for his support of the poor, is elected president with 67.5% of the counted popular vote. The "U.S. favorite" Marc Bazin finishes a distant second with 14.2% .

1991 In January, a coup by former Tonton Macoutes head Roger Lafontant is foiled after tens of thousands pour into the streets of the capital, surrounding the National Palace. Aristide is sworn in as president February 7. On September 30, a military coup deposes Aristide, who goes into exile first in Venezuela, then in the United States.

1991-1994 Thousands of Haitians flee violence and repression in Haiti by boat. Although most are repatriated to Haiti by the U.S. government, many enter the United States as refugees.

1994 The de facto military government resigns at the request of the United States in September, which then sends in troops to occupy Haiti. This occupation is sanctioned by the United Nations in violation of its own charter. The U.S. returns Aristide as president October 15.

1995 The U.S. nominally hands over military authority to the United Nations but maintains effective control of the occupation. Aristide dissolves the Haitian army. In December, former prime minister René Préval is elected president.

1996 Aristide leaves office on February 7th and is succeeded by René Préval.

2000 Legislative, municipal and local elections are held in May. The OAS disputes how the sovereign electoral council calculates the run-offs for eight Senate seats. In November, Aristide is reelected for a second five-year term with 92% of the vote in elections boycotted by the opposition. The last UN peacekeeping forces withdraw from Haiti.

2001 Aristide succeeds Préval for a second five-year term.

2001-2003 With Washington's support, Aristide's bourgeois opponents use the OAS challenge to the 2000 elections to increase economic and political instability. Former Haitian soldiers carry out guerrilla attacks, primarily along the Dominican border and in the capital.

2004 January 1. Haiti's 200th anniversary of independence.

Haiti's Agonies and Exaltations

Ramsey Clark

The history of Haiti will break your heart. Knowing it, the weak will despair, but the caring will strive to break the chains of tragedy.

When Columbus landed on the island in December 1492, he found a native Arawak, or Taino, population of three million people or more, well fed, with cultivated fields, lots of children, living in peace. It had by far the largest population of any island in the Caribbean. Twenty-two years later, there were fewer than 27,000 who had not fallen victim to the sword, the ravages of forced labor, and diseases heretofore unknown to them. The Spaniards called the island La Ysla Española, which in use became Hispaniola.

The native people called the island Haiti, a word that three hundred years after the Europeans arrived would strike fear throughout the empires of the hemisphere built on slave labor and societies that accepted its practice, but bring hope to slaves as they heard of it.

Only a few who came with the Conquistadors dared, or cared, to speak out against the genocide. The historic exception was the priest and later Bishop of Chiapas, Bartolome de Las Casas. For his only briefly successful efforts to persuade Charles V and the Pope to protect the peoples of "India" from slavery and abuse, Las Casas became "the most hated man in the Americas" among the violent, rich rulers of New Spain. In a census Las Casas conducted in 1542, only 200 Taino were found. The soil of Haiti was already red with human blood.

Slowly the population of Hispaniola was replenished, the slaughtered Indians replaced primarily by the importation of Africans in chains who rarely knew, but never forgot, those who perished first at the hands of their masters.

Few Spaniards settled in far western Hispaniola. By the mid-17th century, French buccaneers gained footholds on its coast. In 1697, France was recognized as sovereign over the western third of the island in a minor concession from Spain by the treaty of Ryswick, which ended the war of the Grand Alliance and resettled the map of western Europe. France called its new colony St. Domingue.

By the 1750s, St. Domingue was France's richest colony, rich from the sweat of slave labor's brow.

Hispaniola declined in importance as Spanish colonies in Mexico, Peru and the Caribbean spread through South, Central and North America.

On the eve of the revolution in France, St. Domingue had a population of about 32,000 from France, 24,000 freedmen of mixed blood, and nearly 500,000 African slaves. The native population was extinct.

The Creole language found birth in the slave quarters and secret places slaves could meet as their need to support each other and to resist grew. African languages permeated the French with African melody and African drums. English, Spanish and occasional Indian words were gathered into it by chance and attraction. Creole became the heart of Haitian culture, shared with others who were torn out of Africa and carried to European colonies in the Caribbean.

In trials of Haitian-Americans charged with planning to overthrow Jean-Claude "Baby Doc" Duvalier in the mid-1980s, the most skilled French-English translators and professors of French in the universities of New Orleans could not translate Creole into English for the Court. It is a beautiful, separate language born from the suffering of African slaves of French masters and their determination to maintain their own identity.

In Paris, the philosophers of the Enlightenment condemned slavery. Diderot wrote that slavery contradicts nature. Montesquieu observed that when we admit that Africans are human, we confess what poor Christians we are. Abbé Reynal proclaimed that any religion that condones slavery deserves to be prohibited. Rousseau confessed that the existence of slavery made him ashamed to be a man. Helvetius observed that every barrel of sugar reaching Europe is stained with blood. Voltaire's adventurous hero, Candide, meets a slave whose hand was ground off in a sugar mill and leg was cut off for attempting to escape and proclaims, "At this price you eat sugar in Europe."

Few periods in history have given rise to more intense thought and concern about freedom and the rights of humanity, but St. Domingue was a long way away and the wealth of France and its slave masters were not impressed.

Unaware, or contemptuous, of the enlightened views of France's philosophers, "His Majesty" in 1771 considered requests for the emancipation of mulatto slaves in Haiti and other French colonies and authorized his Minister of Colonies to explain his views:

> ...such a favor would tend to destroy the differences that nature has placed between whites and blacks, and that political prejudice has been careful to maintain as a distance which people of color and their descendants will never be able to bridge; finally, that it is in the interest of good order not to weaken the state of humiliation congenital to the species, in whatever degree it may perpetuate itself; a prejudice all the more useful for being in the very heart of the slaves and contributing in a major way to the due peace of the colonies...

Within two decades the people of France and Haiti would provide Louis XVI a clearer understanding of what was in their heart.

In Léogâne in 1772, a Haitian woman named Zabeth, her story recorded, lived a not uncommon life and death. Rebellious, like many, from childhood, she was chained for years when not working, chased and attacked by dogs when she escaped, her cheek branded with a fleur de lis. Zabeth was locked up in a sugar mill for punishment. She stuck her fingers in the grinder, then later bit off the bandages which stopped the flow of blood. She was then tied, her open wounds against the grinder, where particles of iron dust poisoned her blood before she died. Her owner lived unconcerned across the sea in Nantes.

For five years, the French Revolution, consumed with the struggle for human rights ignored the slaves of Haiti even over the protests of Marat and Robespierre and the words of the Declaration of the Rights of Man.

On August 14, 1791, the slaves of St. Domingue rebelled. News of the insurrection sent electrifying waves of fear throughout the hemisphere. The slave states and slave owners in all parts of the U.S. and elsewhere in the Americas were forced to face what they had long dreaded, that the cruelty of their deeds would turn on them in violent slave rebellions. Their fear produced hatred and greater cruelty toward the slaves that led to the barbarity of lynchings in the late 19th and early decades of the 20th centuries and the excessive force employed with zeal by police in race riots into the 1960s in the U.S.

The struggle of the Haitian slaves for freedom dragged on for more than a decade, the French army caring less and less about the destructiveness of their arms and about the lives of the Haitian people.

President George Washington and Secretary of State Thomas Jefferson, both slave owners, supported France in its efforts to suppress the slaves of St. Domingue. Their successors have consistently acted against the rights and well-being of Haitians ever since.

In 1794, after fighting both Spain and Great Britain to control St. Domingue, harassed by the slave insurrection led by Pierre-Dominique Toussaint Louverture, and in need of troops easily recruited from freedman before the rebellion, France declared the abolition of slavery in its colonies.

Frightened by the freedom of slaves in Haiti, the next year the King of Spain ceded the rest of the island, Spain's first colony in America, to France. The island was once again, temporarily, united.

By 1801, Toussaint Louverture, a slave himself before the insurrection, proclaimed a constitution for Haiti, which named him governor-general for life. Napoleon was not consulted.

Later that year, Bonaparte sent General Charles Leclerc with a veteran force of 20,000 trained soldiers, including Haitian military officers, among them Alexandre Pétion, to crush the "First of the Blacks." In 1802, Napoleon ordered the reinstatement of slavery. Toussaint was captured by ruse and sent to France where he died a prisoner on April 7, 1803. Fearful that Napoleon would succeed in restoring slavery, African and mulatto generals in the French Army joined the bitter revolt against France. U.S. merchants sold arms and supplies to the former slave forces, while the U.S. government supported France.

The French army of Napoleon Bonaparte was defeated by Haitian former slaves. It surrendered in November 1803 and agreed to a complete withdrawal.

Haiti lay in ruins, nearly half its population lost. The African slaves of Haiti had defeated the army of Napoleon Bonaparte. The 12-year war for liberation had destroyed most of the irrigation systems and machinery that, with slave labor, had created France's richest colony and were the foundation of the island's economy.

On January 1, 1804, independence was declared for the entire island in the aboriginal name preferred by the former slaves: Haiti. In September 1804, Dessalines was proclaimed Emperor Jacques I.

Nearly all whites who survived the long violence fled the island before, or with, the departing French army.

Profound fear spread among white peoples throughout the Americas wherever Africans were held in slavery. In the U.S. slave states, news from Haiti of the slave rebellion, the emancipation, the imprisonment and death of Toussaint Louverture in France, the failure of Napoleon's effort to reestablish slavery after sending 20,000 professional soldiers for the task, and their final defeat sent shock waves infinitely greater than those of 9-11-2001 two centuries later. Years before Nat Turner and the even earlier slave rebellions in the United States, the fear of slave rebellion became a brooding omnipresence.

As word spread among slave populations, exaltation embraced its people who could now believe their day of freedom too would come. The conflict between fear and newborn faith sharpened the edge of hostility that separated slave and master, creating greater tension and more violence.

Dessalines' nationalization and democratic distribution of land led to his assassination in 1806 by jealous elements of a new ruling class, both black and mulatto, emerging from the ranks of the Haitian generals. The alliance between the formerly freed—the freedmen or affranchis—and the newly freed—the former slaves—was dissolved with Dessalines' murder. A new ruling class of big landowners and a merchant bourgeoisie supplanted their colonialist predecessors. There ensued civil war primarily between the mulatto Pétion, who was elected president in Port-au-Prince over the south, and Christophe, a full-blooded African, who was proclaimed King Henry I in the north. Christophe committed suicide in 1820 after a major revolt against his rule. Jean Pierre Boyer, who had succeeded Pétion in the South in 1818, then became president of a united Haiti.

Haiti was reviled and feared by all the rich nations of the world precisely for its successful slave revolt which represented a threat not only in nations where slavery was legal, but in all countries, because of their large under-classes living in economic servitude. The strategy of the nations primarily affected, including the U.S., was to further impoverish Haiti, to make it an example. Racism in the hemisphere added a painful edge to the treatment of Haiti, which has remained the poorest country, with the darkest skin, the most isolated nation in the Americas. Even its language, spoken by so few beyond its borders, made Haiti the least accessible of countries and peoples.

In one grand commitment, Haiti, through President Pétion, contributed more to the liberation of the Americans from European colonial powers than any other nation. Twice Haiti, poor as it was, provided Simon Bolívar with men, arms and supplies that enabled the Great Liberator to free half the nations of South America from the Spanish yoke. On New Year's Day 1816, Pétion, his country still in ruins, blockaded by France and isolated from all rich nations, met with Bolívar, who had sold even his watch in Jamaica, seeking funds. He promised seven ships, 250 of his best soldiers, muskets, powder, provisions, funds, and even a printing press. Haiti asked only one act in repayment: Free the slaves.

Bolívar surely intended to fulfill his promise and achieved some proclamations of emancipation, but at the time of his death in 1831, not even his own Venezuela had achieved de facto freedom for all of its slaves.

Thus Haiti had achieved the first successful slave rebellion of an entire colony, the defeat of veterans of Europe's most effective fighting force at the time—Napoleon's legions—and made perhaps the decisive contribution to the liberation from European colonial governments of six nations, all larger and with more people than Haiti. Each act was a sin for which there would be no forgiveness.

Spain retained effective control over the eastern part of the island after its concession to France in 1795. The Dominicans revolted against Spain in 1822, joining nearly all the Spanish colonies in the Americas. President Boyer blocked Europe's counter-revolutionary designs against Haiti by laying claim to the Spanish lands where he abolished slavery, but Haitian control was never consolidated. The Dominicans declared independence in 1844 which, after a decade of continuing struggle, was finally achieved.

In 1825, France was the first nation to recognize Haiti, from which it had profited so richly, but at a huge expense to Haiti through a more sophisticated form of exploitation. Haiti agreed to pay France 150,000,000 gold francs in "indemnity." The U.S. permitted limited trade with Haiti, but did not recognize it until 1862, the second year of the U.S. Civil War.

Haiti, true to its struggle against slavery, permitted Union warships to refuel and repair in its harbors during the Civil War. In 1891, the U.S. sought to obtain Môle Saint-Nicolas on the northwest tip of Haiti as a coaling station by force, but failed. A decade later, the U.S. obtained Guantanamo Bay from Cuba after the Spanish-American war. Môle Saint-Nicolas and Guantanamo are strategically located on the Windward Passage between Haiti and Cuba, the best route from the Atlantic to the Panama Canal. First France, then the U.S., coveted the notion of a base at Môle Saint-Nicolas.

Between 1843 and 1911, sixteen persons held the highest government office in Haiti, an average of four years, three months each, but eleven were removed by force and its threat from a still revolutionary people.

During the period from August 1911 to July 1915, in which many Haitians believed their country was being taken over by U.S. capital, one president was blown up in the Presidential Palace, another died of poison, three were forced out by revolution, and on July 27, 1915, President Vilbrun Guillaume Sam was taken by force from the French legation where he had sought sanctuary and killed.

The next day U.S. Marines landed in Haiti and began an occupation that lasted nineteen years. The U.S. invoked the Monroe Doctrine and humanitarianism to justify a criminal occupation. Haiti was forced to sign a ten-year treaty, later extended, which made Haiti a U.S. political and financial protectorate.

Shortly before World War I, U.S. bankers, in the most debilitating form of intervention, obtained shares in the Haitian Bank which controlled the government's fiscal policies and participated in a huge loan to the Haitian government, again placing the people in servitude to a foreign master. U.S. capitalists were quickly given concessions to build a railroad and develop plantations. As the Panama Canal neared completion, U.S. interests in Haiti grew.

Franklin D. Roosevelt, than assistant secretary of the Navy, drafted a constitution for Haiti, something Toussaint Louverture had been capable of one hundred and fourteen years earlier. In 1920, while campaigning for the vice-presidency, Roosevelt boasted of his authorship accomplished on the deck of a U.S. Navy destroyer off the coast of Cap Haïtien. Such is the certainty of the U.S. in its natural superiority and right in matters of governance.

In 1918, US Marines supervised a "farcical" plebiscite for the new constitution. Among other new rights, it permitted aliens for the first time to own land in Haiti.

Haiti paid dearly. U.S. intervention in education emphasized vocational training at the expense of the French intellectual tradition. The racist implications were clear to the people. The national debt was funded with expensive U.S. loans. The occupying force imposed harsh police practices to protect property and maintain order, but with little concern for injuries it inflicted, or protection for the public. In the spirit of democracy, Haitians were virtually excluded from the government of their own people.

Over the years, opposition to the occupation grew, and slowly Americans joined Haitians in protest against it. In 1930, after student and peasant uprisings, President Hoover sent missions to study ending the occupation and improving the education system. The first election of a national assembly since the occupation was permitted that year. In turn, it elected Stenio Joseph Vincent president. Vincent opposed the occupation, and Haitians quickly took control of public works, public health, and agricultural services.

In August 1934, Franklin Roosevelt, now president of the U.S., to confirm his celebrated Good Neighbor Policy, ended the occupation and withdrew the Marines. When the occupation was over, Haiti was as poor as ever and deep in debt. The U.S. continued its direct control of fiscal affairs in Haiti until 1941, and indirect control until 1947, to protect its loans and business interests.

Among accomplishments the U.S. proclaimed for its long governance was a unified, organized, trained and militarized police force. Called the Garde d'Haïti, it guarded Haitians less than it guarded over them.

In 1937, Haiti was weakened by nearly two decades of foreign occupation and subjugation and a huge part of its unemployed work force was in the Dominican Republic laboring under cruel conditions at subsistence wages. The Dominican dictator, President Rafael Trujillo, directed the purge of Haitian farm workers and laborers in an overtly racist campaign of government violence to keep his country "white." As many as 40,000 Haitians were killed. The Organization of American States interceded and forced the Dominican Republic to acknowledge 18,000 deaths for which it paid $522,000 in restitution with no other consequence than an angry neighbor. A Haitian life was worth $29 to the OAS, with most lives unrecognized.

Art flourished in Haiti in the late 1930s. By the mid-1940s, there was a "Renaissance in Haiti." Artists painted furiously on any surface that offered the opportunity. Haitian artists gained international reputations and fame: Philomé Obin, André Pierre, Castera Bazile, Wilson Bigaud, Rigaud Benoit, Hector Hippolyte, and others. Their work commanded prices unimaginable to the poor of Haiti. With the painting, the richness of Haitian culture burst out in music, poetry, literature and cuisine. But more tragedy lay ahead.

Vincent served until 1939 when, under U.S. pressure, he retired in favor of Elie Lescot. When he sought to run for a second term, Lescot was forced from office by student strikes and ultimately mob violence in 1946. A military triumvirate directed a new election of the National Assembly in 1946. The Assembly elected Dumarsais Estimé president.

Near the end of his term in 1950, the same military triumvirate seized power, forcing Estimé to leave Haiti. Col. Paul E. Magloire, a member of the triumvirate, was then chosen to direct public elections as president. Magloire was in turn forced to resign and leave the country as his term expired in December 1956.

After a period of turmoil, strikes and mob violence, during which several men, then an Executive Council and an Army commander served briefly as provisional leadership, François Duvalier, a physician, was elected president, with Army approval, on September 22, 1957.

The brutality, capriciousness, and arbitrary exercise of power and violence by Duvalier provides a classic study of dictatorship in poor countries.

In 1960, he forced the Catholic Archbishop François Poirier into exile to prevent interference and opposition by the Church of Haiti's official religion. Duvalier organized and licensed the notorious Tonton Macoutes from among his core supporters to terrorize the people to accept his rule.

The terror of Duvalier's long reign is described nowhere better for non-Haitians than in Graham Greene's classic, *The Comedians*, published in 1966. Greene knew Haiti before Duvalier. He loved the people. He thought they were beautiful. When he returned in 1963, he found the Tonton Macoutes, searches, road blocks, a place where "terror rides and death comes at night." Rebels were in the hills.

He stayed long enough to develop material for a book. Before he could return for a last impression, he was warned he should not. He had written a harsh profile of Duvalier in the English press.

Instead he flew to the Dominican Republic, traveled to the border to observe and walked "along the edge of the country we loved and exchanged hopes for a happier future." *The Comedians* ends on the border, but it contains a testament to the misery and the beauty of the Haitian people and the power of the committed among them.

In 1964, Duvalier imposed a new constitution on Haiti which made him president-for-life. To please the U.S., show he knew how to handle problems, and unintentionally confirm the accuracy of the sobriquet Comedians, the death penalty was decreed in 1969 for the "propagation of communist or anarchist doctrines through lectures, speeches, or conversations" and for accomplices in such propagation and persons who merely received or listened to such doctrines.

In 1971, "Papa Doc" Duvalier caused the constitution to be amended to empower him to name his successor and lower the age requirement for the presidency to age 18. He named his son, Jean-Claude, then 19, and died, having extended his dynasty by another 15 years.

Baby Doc's regime was as brutal as his father's, if somewhat more subtle. When President Carter criticized Haiti's human rights record in 1977, a few token prisoners were released. But arrests and disappearances continued. A young Haitian-American, the son of a former officer in Papa Doc's air force who had fled into exile, was arrested for public criticism of the Duvalier dynasty and held in cells under the Presidential Palace where the president could witness the discomfort of people he did not like. A barrage of entreaties for his release were ignored until the eve of the first visit in 1983 of a pope to Haiti. The prisoner was released, taken to the airport with his lawyer, provided first-class seats on an Air France flight to Miami without explanation, or apology.

By 1980, there was a mass exodus from Haiti by sea. The U.S. Coast Guard policy was to interdict boatloads of Haitians fleeing at great risk toward freedom. When it caught boats close to Haiti, it forced them back to what could be death for some. Others caught in the Windward Passage were taken to prison at the U.S. Naval Base at Guantanamo, where they were held as early patrons of a cruel experience which was later refined for Muslims, usually never named or charged, but treated with a cruelty that would make Baby Doc blush.

Other Haitians reached Florida's waters. The bodies of some washed up in the surf on Ft. Lauderdale beaches. Local residents were outraged, or horrified, depending on their character. Other Haitians caught on land or sea were taken to the Krome Avenue Detention Center in Miami. The treatment they endured there caused many Haitians to yearn for the free, if impoverished life, of Cité Soleil or Haiti's northwest, from which they had fled.

As opposition to Baby Doc grew and his hold on power weakened, vibrations of rebellion in Brooklyn, Queens, Miami, and other Haitian communities in the U.S., resonant with those throughout Haiti, rose and fell with conditions in the beloved country.

The Duvalier signature means of intimidation—bodies of its most recent victims left casually in the streets and byways to remind the people the next morning of the price of disobedience—became daily fare.

The U.S., to defuse outcry and support for revolution, sent recruiters—agents provocateurs—house-to-house and through the streets, to find and recruit young men identified by U.S. intelligence as hostile to the Duvalier regime. Many were escorted to an airfield on Long Island to see a plane without markings loaded with guns to be used, they were told, in the overthrow of the Duvalier regime. A planeload of eager recruits was flown to New Orleans. They were promised training to participate in an invasion of Haiti.

Among these was the youngest son of fourteen children in the Perpignon family, who escaped separately with their mother from Haiti after their father, a prominent lawyer, was murdered by Duvalier in his first days as President. Duvalier had his body dragged through the streets of Port-au-Prince behind a mule for a week.

The men were set up in rooms in a motel and questioned in front of a concealed camera. They were asked why they wanted to overthrow the government of Haiti and encouraged to boast about what they would do when they captured Duvalier.

More than 40 Haitians and Haitian-Americans were then arrested in New Orleans, far from their homes, and charged with violations of the Neutrality Act of 1797, an act U.S. agents and paid assets violate every day. Most were released within a few days when lawyers retained by their families showed up to meet with them. Despite the criminality of the entrapment, and the fact that all freely admitted they were not in condition to capture a Boy Scout camp, some remained in jail for several months. This was late 1985: The last year for Duvalier.

Within the U.S., editors in the flourishing Haitian exile media, risked assassination as befell the courageous anti-Duvalierist Firmin Joseph, a founder of Haïti Progrès, in front of his home in Brooklyn in 1983. Thirteen years later, Emmanuel "Toto" Constant, who headed a U.S.-supported death-squad called FRAPH before and after the U.S. invasion in 1994, found asylum in New York. For other leaders of the 1991-94 coup d'état in Haiti, Washington arranged golden exiles in countries like Panama, Honduras, and the Dominican Republic.

Finally, after nearly 30 years under the heel of the Duvaliers, condoned, if not protected, by the U.S. government, the end had come. On February 7, 1986, Jean-Claude Duvalier and his family, with most of their possessions, flew on a U.S. Air Force C-130 cargo plane to France, where he has lived safe and comforted by the spoils from the toils of countless Haitians he abused so badly.

The question must be asked: how could the heirs of slaves who defeated Napoleon and who founded freedom in the hemisphere be subjugated to such petit tyranny? This book will help find the answer and the means of ending its furtherance.

A liberation theology priest, Jean-Bertrand Aristide, trusted because the people had witnessed him share their danger and privation, ran for President in the first real post-Duvalier elections in 1990 over the muted but fierce opposition of the U.S. The U.S. choice, Marc Bazin, who had served at the World Bank in Washington, was provided millions of dollars in direct support and assistance and highly touted in the subservient U.S. media. Aristide with no resources, soft-spoken, but honest, won by a huge margin, with some 67% of the vote. Bazin, who came in second, bought 14% of the vote.

Aristide, despite support from the overwhelming majority of the people of Haiti was driven from office within nine months by the U.S. organized, armed and trained military and police. At least twice he had escaped attempts on his life. Finally on September 30, 1991, with only a handful of Haitian security officers, bearing just side arms and rifles, President Aristide was trapped inside the Presidential Palace. Outside thousands of loyal supporters, a huge Haitian throng, unarmed but offering their bodies as protection, faced an army with overwhelming firepower. The dreaded Colonel Michel François in his red jeep led his police force in assaulting the Palace and the crowd. President Aristide faced the end.

Hundreds of Tonton Macoutes long alleged to have been disbanded, could be seen in their blue jeans and red bandannas milling about the center of the city, a warning to the wary.

President Aristide was saved by the intrepid ambassador of France, Rafael Dufour, who with perfect timing drove to the Presidential Palace, placed President Aristide in his limousine, drove to the diplomatic departures area at the international airport, and escorted the president to a plane ready to depart for Venezuela.

Duvalier was flown to life on the French Riviera by the U.S. Air Force. The U.S., fully aware of Aristide's peril, did nothing to protect him.

Within a year, Marc Bazin was Haiti's de facto prime minister. And that is about how long he lasted. Popular protest forced his resignation. The U.S. could install him in office, but for all its power, it could not keep him there.

The richness of Haitian culture and character has survived all these centuries of suffering. The "Renaissance in Haiti" in the 1940s was forced into exile for its open expression, but it was never silenced. Haitian authors and poets like Félix Morisseau-Leroy, Paul Laraque, Edwidge Danticat, Patrick Sylvain, Danielle Georges, artists and intellectuals, musicians and singers carried the torch of Haitian culture and truth abroad. They knew

> you say democracy
> and it's the annexation of Texas
> the hold-up of the Panama Canal
> the occupation of Haiti
> the colonization of Puerto Rico
> the bombing of Guatemala

from "Reign of a Human Race" by Paul Laraque. (The full poem is included in this book.)

In September 1994, to "stop brutal atrocities" and "restore President Aristide to office," the U.S., having secured United Nations approval, landed a 20,000 troop, high-tech military force in Haiti, accepted, if at the last moment, by the military government of Haiti. It was an army of the same size as that led by General Leclerc who came to destroy the "First of the Blacks." It was called "Operation Restore Democracy." It met no armed resistance, suffered no casualties, but managed to kill several dozen Haitians.

In 1915, an excuse for U.S. intervention had been the slaughter of some 200 political prisoners at the National Penitentiary in Port-au-Prince.

This time, the U.S. priority was "force protection," the security of its own men. It made no plans or efforts to protect political prisoners, or other Haitians. Once again, Haiti suffered under a U.S. occupation.

A lone U.S. Army captain, Lawrence Rockwood, assigned to counter-intelligence and aware of the danger faced by political prisoners held by the FADH, the Armed Forces of Haiti, made a valiant effort to persuade the military command to take quick and easy action to protect prisoners at the National Penitentiary, to no avail. The FADH, generally supported by the U.S., represented the spirit of militarism that had contributed so much to death and human suffering over five centuries in Haiti. The prisoners were not seen as friends of the United States.

Rockwood went alone, over the wall of the military compound at the airport, found his way to the National Penitentiary, succeeded in gaining entry, and secured the facility. He observed a hundred or more prisoners, several score in conditions as bad as those in any prison of Duvalier, and by his mere presence protected the others. For his effort, though a fourth generation officer in the U.S. Army, he was court-marshaled, threatened with seven years imprisonment, and finally separated from the service as a danger to the morale of the military. He is the perfect military officer for a free and democratic nation and for international peacekeeping. For these reasons, he was no longer acceptable to the U.S. Army.

The U.S. had waited out three years of Aristide's presidency. With most of his term stolen, President Aristide returned to Haiti and served the final year. Although most Haitians called for Aristide to serve out the three years he spent in exile, Washington forbade it. He stepped down. But he did not run from the people of Haiti, and after five years he was elected to his second term at the beginning of the second millennium.

With the steady opposition of the U.S., and we know not what acts of subversion by it, the provocateurs of the old establishment seeking to return to the past, and the ever present poverty, progress has not been easy.

But a new day for Haiti is essential if the world is to address its greatest challenge: to end the exploitation of the growing masses of poor everywhere in the face of greater concentration of wealth and power in the few who have in their control armies with the capacity of omnicide and media that can veil the truth and mislead the poor to self-destruction.

The challenge for all who seek peace and freedom and economic justice, a decent standard of life for all, and believe the cycle of tragedy and misery for Haiti and all the poor nations and peoples of earth must be broken is to unite in a vision of peace and compassion and persevere until they prevail.

There is no other way to fulfill the promised legacy of Toussaint Louverture as written by William Wordsworth, deeply troubled by Toussaint's imprisonment two hundred years ago. It is the legacy we must promise all Haitians.

TO TOUSSAINT LOUVERTURE

Toussaint, the most unhappy man of men!
Whether the whistling rustic tend his plough
Within thy hearing, or thy head be now
Pillowed in some deep dungeon's earless den-
O miserable Chieftain! where and when

Wilt thou find patience! Yet die not; do thou
Wear rather in thy bonds a cheerful brow:
Though fallen thyself, never to rise again,
Live, and take comfort. Thou hast left behind
Powers that will work for thee; air, earth, and skies.
There's not a breathing of the common wind
That will forget thee; thou hast great allies;
Thy friends are exaltations, agonies,
And love, and man's unconquerable mind.

AND NOW—TO ALL HAITIANS

Photo Essay
on Haiti

⤬

Selected by Pat Chin

Heroes of Haiti

Haitian revolutionaries Toussaint Louverture,
top right and Jean-Jacques Dessalines, above.
Lower right, Charlemagne Peralte, leader
of the peasant guerrilla resistance
to the 1915 United States invasion
and occupation.

New York City, November 23, 1979, top.

New York City, August 1987, left.

President Francois Duvalier
and U.S. Gov. Nelson Rockefeller
in Port-au-Prince, bottom.

aitian Rebellion, 1986."

Haiti is the poorest country in the Western Hemisphere. Port-au-Prince, August 1974.

New York City, November 1987.

Joyce Chec

Fort Dimanche had been a prison and torture center
under the U.S.-backed Duvaliers.

Pat C

owds greet President Aristide at inauguration of Ft. Dimanche as a museum, bruary 1991.

Pat Chin

On the campaign trail, December 1990.

Aristide supporters.

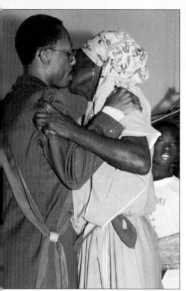

Pat Chin, above and right

n-Bertrand Aristide inaugurated
February 1991. Peasant woman
ces sash on new Haitian leader.

itians greet Aristide, December 1990.

Deirdre Griswold

Kim

National Popular Party (PPN) May Day 2002. Their shirts say "National Production = Agrarian Reform." If Haiti wants to have its own food, it must give the land to the peasants.

Pat

Cuban sports trainers now teach young Haitians at this former Duvalier ranch.

PPN Secretary-General
Ben Dupuy, right.
Cuban and Haitian flags
hang from podium.

Ben Dupuy and Pat Chin
with a security officer at
the April 1999 Congress
of the National Popular
Assembly (APN), left.
Delegates voted to
transform the APN
into the PPN.

Below, delegates to
the 5th Congress of
the PPN, 2003.

Haitian Women in the Struggle

Maude Le Blanc, PPN leader.
Peoples Video Network/Key Martin

APN Congresses, April 1999, below; May 1995, bottom.
Pat Chin

San Francisco,
September 21, 1994.

Bill Hackwell

The U.S. murdered
Charlemagne
Peralte in 1919
and put his body
on display.

Greg Dunkel

w York City, August 1978.

re Haitians in New York City honor their revolutionary history in a protest
President Ronald Reagan's support for the Duvalier dictatorship.

San Francisco, October 4, 1993.   Boston, July 29, 2002.

Ray LaForest speaking at a rally agair
illegal detentions, 2001.

Springfield, Mass., October 15, 1994, le

Boston demonstration against the U.S. Food and Drug Administration
over scapegoating of Haitian community at beginning of AIDS epidemic.

San Francisco, September 21, 1994.

Bill Hackwell

Haitians and Greg Dunkel at massive labor rally
for immigrants' rights, Queens, New York, October 4, 2003.

Pat Chin

Greg Du

Demonstration against U.S. asylu for FRAPH death squad leader "Toto" Constant, Queens, New Yor August 16, 2000.

Diallo
Louima
Huang
Rosario
Baez
Bumpers
ENOUGH!

Haitian woman holds photo and list of New York police brutality victims at Patrick Dorismond's funeral.

Pat Chin

Pat Chin above and right

Brooklyn protest
against the police
torture of Abner
Louima, 1997.

Right and below, New
York Haitians demand
justice for police killing
of Patrick Dorismond.
June 26, 2000, right.
Below, April 20, 2000.

G. Dunkel

Painting by Fritz M. Joseph on album cover of recording by Atis Indepandan / Paredon Records,

"Haiti, what is to be done, Ki sa pou-n fe?"

Part I

Haiti in History

Thank You Dessalines

Félix Morriseau-Leroy
Translation by Marie-Marcelle B. Racine

Thank you, Dessalines
Papa Dessalines, thank you
Every time I think of who I am
I say thank you, Dessalines
Every time I hear a black man
Who is still under the white man's rule
A black man who is not free to talk
I say: Dessalines, thank you
I alone know what you mean to me
Thank you, Papa Dessalines
If I am a man
I must say: Thank you, Dessalines
If I open my eyes to look
It is thanks to you, Dessalines
If I raise my head to walk
It is thanks to you, Dessalines
Every time I look at other negroes
I say: Thank you, Dessalines
When I see what's happening in other lands
I say: Thank you, Dessalines
When I hear white people talk
I say: Papa Dessalines, thank you
When I hear some negroes like me talk
I say: Thank you, Papa Dessalines
Only I know what you are for me
Dessalines, my bull
Dessalines, my blood
Dessalines, my two eyes
Dessalines, my guts
Only I know
All negroes must say:

Thank you, Dessalines
You are the one who showed us the way
Thank you, Dessalines
You are our guiding light
Dessalines
You gave us the land on which we walk
The sky over our heads
The trees, the rivers
The sea, the lake, it is you
Dessalines, you gave us the sun
You gave us the moon
You gave us our sisters, our brothers
Our mothers, our fathers, our children
You made us who we are
You made us kind of different
From the other negroes

If I look everyone straight in the eye
It is you looking at them, Dessalines
You gave us the water we drink
You gave us the food we eat
Thank you, Papa Dessalines
You also gave us the house in which we live
You gave us the land we plant
You taught us how to sing
You taught us to say: No
We are told some negroes say: Yes, Yes
Some others say: Yes, sir *(in English in the original)*
You taught us to say: No
Dessalines, please teach all black people
All blacks on this earth to say: No
Thank you Papa Dessalines
Some negroes want to explain:
"What we know today is not
What we experienced in the past
And of course, nowadays
Human fraternity,
Humanity, Civilization…"
All of this is just French talk
The only thing I know is you, Dessalines

I say: Thank you, Papa Dessalines
You made me who I am
My mother is your daughter
My son, my daughter are your children
Thank you, Dessalines
My grandchildren are your children
Dessalines, my king, thank you
No need to talk about the flag
No need to talk about Arcahaie
Or Gonaïves!
That's been said already
And who's going to hear that again?
The Requiem Mass on October 17th?
Who will go to the Cathedral?
The Minister's speech?
Who will listen to that?
But, what I am telling you now?
Only two words: thank you
Thank You, Papa Dessalines
So, be done with that Pater noster
Monsignor, Dessalines is not dead
Cut out that French speech, Minister
Dessalines will never die
Dessalines is right here
This man could never die!
Dessalines lives in my heart
Standing at attention
Dessalines is watching
One day, Dessalines will rise
That day, we will all know
We'll know if 1804
We'll know if Arcahaie
We'll know if La Crête-à-Pierrot
We'll know if Vertières
We'll know if Dessalines did all that
For small boy to write poem
For politicians to make speeches
For priest to sing TeDeum
For bishops to give absolution
Dessalines does not need your pardon

Everything Dessalines does is right
One day Dessalines will rise
You will hear throughout the Caribbean Sea
Voices shouting: Where is he, where did he go?
Dessalines took up arms
Arrest him
At that time you will hear his thundering voice:
All black folks, cut their heads, burn their houses
You'll hear throughout the Americas
Voices shouting: Stop him
But Dessalines' voice is already on the radio:
Cut heads, burn houses
Throughout Harlem, Dessalines is putting things in order
You'll hear: Stop Dessalines
All the way to Dakar
All the way to Johannesburg
You'll hear: Where did Dessalines go?
Cut their heads, burn their houses
Dessalines does not need your absolution
Does not need God's pardon
On the contrary: Dessalines is God's arm
Dessalines is God's justice
No need for that Pater noster, monsignor
No need for black men's apologies to white men
Dessalines does not need that
For everything he did I say: Papa Dessalines, thank you
For everything he will do
I say, Thank you, papa Dessalines.

Haiti Needs Reparations, Not Sanctions

July 17, 2003

Pat Chin

The Republic of Haiti will mark the 200th anniversary of its independence on Jan. 1, 2004. Preparations for celebrating the bicentennial are being made against the backdrop of a deepening economic crisis in that oppressed country, exacerbated by economic sanctions.

"For over two years," reported the May 23 (2003) Inter Press Service, "the United States, the European Union, and multilateral lenders have been holding up some $500 million in aid and loans because they say Aristide's government and Lavalas Family party have failed to reach a compromise with opposition parties, which boycotted the 2000 Presidential race after protesting allegedly fraudulent parliamentary contests in 2000."

The Washington-backed "Democratic Convergence" is made up of 15 tiny, bourgeois opposition parties, ranging from hard-core Duvalierists to Social Democrats, with no real support in the popular masses. The group is similar to the U.S.-backed "Democratic Coordination" in Venezuela that has unsuccessfully tried to oust progressive Venezuelan President Hugo Chavez. The Convergence has reportedly received some $120 million from the U.S.-based right-wing National Endowment for Democracy. In response to the imperialist maneuver to force a "regime change" by tightening the economic squeeze, Haitian President Jean-Bertrand Aristide has called on France—the original colonial power—to make restitution for an indemnity Haiti was forced to pay after militarily defeating the French, forcing slavery's end and declaring independence.

The French government in 1825 demanded 150 million gold francs, and eventually collected 90 million, to "compensate" white planters for property loss due to the revolutionary war in return for diplomatic relations and trade with France. It was decades later, however, that the United States recognized Haitian independence and lifted its crippling sanctions. The Aristide administration calculates the sum owed Haiti by France, including interest, to be well over $21 billion.

The indemnity insured that Haiti would remain in debt to French financiers for most of the 1800s.

Reparations for hundreds of years of forced labor are also being demanded. This call is supported by African-American organizations that have launched a movement for reparations in the U.S.

Aristide first sounded the call on April 7, 2003, at a massive gathering in front of the National Palace marking the 200th anniversary of the death, in a French prison, of revolutionary leader Toussaint Louverture. Almost two months later, at a June 3 press conference during the G-8 summit of capitalist vultures in Evian, France, French Foreign Ministry spokesperson François Rivasseau arrogantly rejected the demand. The summit was protested by thousands of anti-war and anti-globalization demonstrators. Rivasseau cited loans made to the Haitian government, while blaming alleged corruption and mismanagement by the Aristide administration for Haiti's economic problems.

At a May 23, 2003, "Flag Day" celebration attended by thousands of students and other supporters, Aristide also condemned global poverty and the Third World debt. "Two hundred years after the victorious revolution," he said, "the bull that turns the mill doesn't get to drink the sugar syrup. We refuse to be slaves to sub-human misery." (Inter Press Service, May 23, 2003).

Why is Haiti so poor?

Historians reflecting the views of racist white colonizers and imperialists have argued that Haiti is wrenchingly poor because the enslaved Africans killed all their white masters to gain independence and liberty. They assert, consequently, Haiti has remained poor and dependent and in need of resources and technology from the United States and Europe because it had no "educated" class. Government corruption is also a fundamental part of the problem, they say.

But this grossly distorts reality. Haiti's poverty lies mainly in the centuries-long crime of slavery, which produced enormous wealth for France, followed by 200 years of economic, political and military aggression waged by the European and U.S. bourgeoisies against the first free Black republic. The only country in the world where enslaved people had liberated themselves by overthrowing their masters, Haiti was a powerful symbol of resistance and had to be punished.

The country's liberation was a beacon of hope for an end to slavery everywhere. It sent shock waves through the Americas and European capitals growing fabulously rich from the brutal trade in human Black cargo. Fearing the implications for their own slave-based economies, France joined forces with the U.S. and other European powers.

In fact, after the first rebellion in Haiti, U.S. President George Washington—a slave owner himself—directed his secretary of state, Thomas Jefferson—another slave owner—to give the white planters in Haiti $400,000 for arms and food to resist the uprising. The U.S. did not recognize Haitian independence until its own Civil War that ended slavery some 60 years later.

On Jan. 1, 1804, Haitian revolutionary hero General Jean-Jacques Dessalines declared the country's independence. His proclamation was the culmination of years of a national liberation struggle enacted by enslaved Africans, who had freed themselves in a upsurge that started at a Voodoo ceremony in 1791. The revolutionary spark provided by that ceremony is one of the reasons Voodoo has been turned into a pejorative term.

The twisted, sadistic form of colonial logic—where the white oppressors get compensated for their loss of the ability to cruelly exploit, while the Black victims are condemned to punishing poverty—was also applied in Jamaica under the British colonialists, and in the U.S. after slavery ended.

The foreign imperialists and their collaborators among Haiti's bourgeoisie have a daunting task ahead. It is one that will surely fail as the people—supported by a solidarity movement abroad—continue to draw on their long history of struggle and resistance against racist demonization, neo-liberal capitalist exploitation and imperialist plunder.

Workers World July 17, 2003

Haiti's Impact on the United States
—what 'voodoo economics' and high school textbooks reveal

July-September 2003

Greg Dunkel

Inspired by the 200th anniversary of Haiti's independence, all sorts of articles on Haiti are popping up, most bemoaning its current fiscal crisis. Some examine the role the United States has played there, mostly presenting its aid programs as benevolent attempts to install democracy and alleviate poverty. Others, more accurately, analyze U.S. efforts in Haiti as stifling democracy and the people's will along with extracting every possible dollar.

But while it is important to describe the impact that the United States, the world's only superpower, has and has had on Haiti, we must note that Haiti, although poor and isolated, has also had a major impact on the United States, stemming from its place in world history as the only state ever founded through a successful slave revolution.

The successful revolution against the French slave owners is a singular event. It is the only time that slaves managed to rise up, smash their oppressors, and set up a new state and social order that reflected some of their hopes and aspirations.

There are aspects of U.S. culture, ranging from marching bands and music to dance and literature, where the impact of Haiti can be seen. But the political impact of Haiti's successful revolution is the clearest in some words and phrases commonly used in North American English and also in how the history and significance of Haiti are hidden in high school history textbooks.

When Martin Bernal wanted to uncover the Afro-Asiatic roots of Greek civilization and culture in his book *Black Athena* (1987), he looked at the words the Greeks borrowed or absorbed from Egypt or Phoenicia, among other evidence. The same kind of evidence of

Haiti's impact on the United States shows up in the mainstream U.S. press.

In the United States "voodoo" (the North American formulation of the Creole "vodou") is associated with Haiti.

Major newspapers used the phrase "voodoo economics" over 1,000 times in the last ten years. The New York Times used it at least 450 times since 1980. "Voodoo politics" shows up much less frequently—only 25 times in the last 10 years. "Voodoo Linux," a variant of a popular computer operating system, also popped up as well as the "Voodoo" graphics card for games running on PCs. There were too many descriptions of voodoo rituals to easily count.

The *American Heritage Dictionary of the English Language* even has a definition for "voodoo economics": "Based on unrealistic or delusive assumptions." But this definition hides the way the phrase is used. When Warren Buffett, the billionaire head of Berkshire Hathaway, one of the major players in the U.S. stock market, calls President George W. Bush's tax cuts "voodoo economics" (Washington Post, May 20, 2003), he was not only calling them "unrealistic." He was also predicting that they would mobilize his class, U.S. capitalists, by stirring their great greed, to support these cuts even if they were not in their long-term interests.

When George H. Bush, the father of the current president, was running against Ronald Reagan for the Republican presidential nomination in 1980, he called Reagan's supply-side economic policies, with their plutocratic catering to the rich, "voodoo economics." Reagan's appeal to the ruling class was more successful than Bush's since he got the nomination, but Reagan did feel compelled to choose Bush as his vice-president.

There are other examples. Jimmy Carter made the "voodoo economics" charge in his debates with Ronald Reagan in the '80s. Sen. Carl Levin (D-MI) in a 1992 press conference accused then President George H. Bush of conducting a "voodoo" trade policy with Japan. John B. Oakes, a former editor of the New York Times, which is considered in American politics to be "liberal," said in 1989: "George Bush, who not so many years ago was justly critical of Ronald Reagan's 'voodoo economics,' has become past master of an even more illusory art form: voodoo politics."

It is interesting to see how these white bourgeois politicians, some of whom personally have vast wealth and all of whom represent vast wealth, use this epithet, which in the context they use it has racist connotations, primarily against other white bourgeois politicians.

In my Internet searches, I came across Kòmbò Mason Braide, a Nigerian economist and political analyst. He called the recommendation that Nigeria follow the economic policies of the Chairman of the U.S. Federal Reserve Board, Alan Greenspan, "voodoo economics" and then went on to analyze its effects on the politics of the states along the Gulf of Guinea (Ghana, Nigeria, Benin and so on). Coming from an economist who lives in a part of Africa where voodoo developed, this epithet applied to Greenspan has a special sarcastic edge and Braide tries to make a strong connection to Haiti. (www.kwenu.com/publications/braide/voodoo_politics.htm)

While it is indisputable that "voodoo" is a widely used term in the United States, the historical context of its introduction into U.S. society was the uprising that began in August in the French colony of St. Domingue, 15 years after the United States declared its independence.

The U.S. bourgeoisie, which was in large part a slavocracy, was completely shocked that the enslaved Africans of Haiti could organize themselves, rise up, smash the old order, kill their masters, and set up a new state that was able to maintain its independence. This rebellion was such a threat to the existence of the slavocracy if its example spread, and so inconceivable in a political framework totally saturated with racism and the denigration of people whose ancestors came from Africa, that the only explanation that they could see for enslaved people participating in it was that they were "deluded."

They failed to consider that a majority of the enslaved people in St. Domingue had been born in Africa in freedom and remembered what it was. They did not have to be "deluded" into rebelling against their oppression. They participated willingly.

Which doesn't mean that voodoo did not play an inspirational and unifying role. It gave them the solidarity they needed to organize a mass uprising of enslaved people under the noses of the slave owners.

The slaves in the north of St. Domingue, the greatest wealth producing slave colony the world has ever known, organized for weeks beginning in early July, using the cover of the voodoo ceremonies that were held every weekend. Finally, 200 delegates, two from each major plantation in the North, gathered on August 14 at Bois Caïman, a wooded area on the Lenormand de Mezy plantation, and set the date for the uprising for one week later, the night of August 21, 1791.

Boukman Dutty, a voodoo priest, was one of the people who led the ceremony and was selected to lead the uprising. According to well-founded but oral sources (see Caroline Fick, *The Making of Haiti*, p. 93, and C.L.R. James, *The Black Jacobins*, p. 87), Boukman made both a prayer and a call to arms with the following speech:

> The god who created the sun which gives us light, who rouses the waves and rules the storm, though hidden in the clouds, he watches us. He sees all that the white man does. The god of the white man inspires him with crime, but our god calls upon us to do good works. Our god who is good to us orders us to revenge our wrongs. He will direct our arms and aid us. Throw away the symbol of the god of the whites who has so often caused us to weep, and listen to the voice of liberty, which speaks in the hearts of us all.

The uprising did not succeed completely. The plan was for the slaves in le Cap Français (now Cap Haïtien) to desert their masters and the city on the night of August 21, and the slaves on the plantations to rise up and burn them and kill their masters, join with the slaves from le Cap, then seize and destroy the city. A few plantations rose up early, tipping off the French slave owners, who retrenched in le Cap. The city remained in their hands, but they could not crush the uprising, which spread widely.

By the middle of September, more than 250 sugar plantations and uncounted coffee plantations had been burned. A major part of the colony that exported $130 million worth of goods a year, a vast sum for the 18th century, was destroyed. The smell of burning sugar, death and revolution filled the air. The slaves of northern Haiti had embarked on a irreversible revolutionary course. Petrified slave owners fled to Cuba, Jamaica, New Orleans, and the United States, the closest havens.

The U.S. press was filled with lurid stories about the "chaos" that gripped the island, the satanic rites that drove slaves into a rampaging frenzy of destruction, about white slave owners fighting for their lives. The United States had always had a significant trade with St. Domingue, even when such trade was technically illegal. The young republic wanted to keep from being entangled in the war between England and France, while maintaining significant trade with this French colony.

Still, the slave-owning President George Washington wanted to help the French slave owners, who had appealed for aid. His secretary of state, the slave-owner Thomas Jefferson, authorized $40,000 in emergency relief as well as 1,000 weapons. Then Washington authorized $400,000 in emergency assistance to the slave owners of St.

Domingue, on the request of the French government who wanted this treated as a repayment for the loans it granted during the Revolutionary War (see Alfred Hunt, *Haiti's Influence on Antebellum America*, p. 31).

Later the Spanish governor of Venezuela also granted $400,000 in aid to the French army Napoleon sent in a vain attempt to re-conquer Haiti.

The first substantial foreign aid the United States ever granted was designed to preserve slavery in Haiti. It didn't succeed.

The southern states followed the lead of the Spanish colonies like Cuba and Louisiana (Spanish until 1803, when it became French so Napoleon could sell it to the United States) in banning the importation of slaves from St. Domingue. The slave owners were trying to prevent their enslaved people from learning about Black emancipation and Jacobin ideas of republican government. So terrified were slave owners that some states briefly barred the importation of slaves from anywhere.

In 1803, just before Haiti declared its independence, Southern newspapers published a document supposedly of French origin discussing how U.S. factionalism and popular habits would allow France to spread sedition, especially if they controlled the mouth of the Mississippi. The document was probably a forgery, designed to impress Southern readers with the danger of French ideas and the vulnerability of slaves to foreign incitement (Hunt, p. 35).

The shadow of St. Domingue haunted the Southern press. As early as 1794, the Columbia (South Carolina) Herald ran a series of articles drawing the lessons of the slave insurrection. (Hunt, p. 111). Whether the first major U.S. slave insurrection in 1800 led by Gabriel Prosser was inspired by the events in St. Domingue is an open question, but both the abolitionists in the North and the slave-owners' press in the South analyzed it in that context.

The next insurrection organized by Denmark Vessey in 1822 in Charleston, South Carolina, definitely was inspired by Haiti. Vessey was born in the West Indies, traveled there as a slave trader's servant and wrote to Jean-Pierre Boyer, then president of Haiti, seeking aid. The reaction in the Southern states was to tighten the bonds of slavery.

Nat Turner's bloody revolt in 1831 again was seen in the Southern press as a replay of the tactics and the strategy of the Haitian insurrection. He was compared in morals and boldness to Haiti's founding father Jean-Jacques Dessalines. Whether or not he was actually inspired by the events in Haiti, Southern whites viewed his revolt as coming from the same volcano of revolution. After this revolt until the Civil War, the pro-slavery Southern press always tried to cast Haiti in the worst possible light, as hell on earth, in order to fight abolition and defend the institution of slavery, which made them so much money.

One of the famous skirmishes preceding the U.S. Civil War, John Brown's 1859 raid at Harper's Ferry, VA, was immediately interpreted as "an abolitionist conspiracy to instigate a slave uprising" (Hunt, p. 139). The Southern press resurrected the themes of "Northern Jacobinism" and the Haitian revolution, in lurid, emotionally charged articles, as if these were fresh events, not 60 to 70 years in the past. Even during the Civil War, Confederate propaganda used Haiti as an example of how the Confederacy was needed to protect white families from the evils of Jacobinism and abolition.

For over 70 years, Haiti was the example that Southern slave owners raised to defend their peculiar, and profitable, institution against abolition, even to the last days of the Civil War. The image of slaves breaking their chains was burned into their consciousness. The Northern bourgeoisie, opposed to slavery because it hindered their economic expansion, still were thoroughgoing racists and opposed to the revolutionary example of Haiti, even though it was not a direct challenge to their system of exploitation.

It is hard to know how much impact the Haiti revolution had on the slave masses in the southern United States. They knew about it for sure, despite the slave owners' attempts to insulate them from that example. Enough refugee slave owners were able to find refuge in the United States and Louisiana that the word spread about Haiti, about this beacon of hope, this model of self-emancipation. The historical record is still unclear about how deep Haiti's influence was.

Outside the South, however, Haiti was known and raised. In August 1843 in Buffalo, New York, at a National Negro Convention meeting, Henry Highland Garner, a prominent abolitionist and a former slave, after mentioning Denmark Vessey, Toussaint Louverture and Nathaniel Turner, said:

> Brethren, arise, arise! Strike for your lives and liberties. Now is the day and the hour. Let every slave throughout the land do this and the days of slavery are numbered. You cannot be more oppressed than you have been — you cannot suffer greater cruelties than you have already. Rather die freemen than live to be slaves. Remember that you are FOUR MILLIONS!

The Convention rejected Garner's revolutionary approach to abolition, which was obviously inspired by Haiti.

With the end of slavery in the United States, Haiti as a political issue began to fade. But its impact did not disappear. A singular event like the Haitian revolution, raised so often and so sharply both by reactionaries and abolitionists doesn't just vanish.

But the forum for using "voodoo" as a tool to attack and belittle Haiti changed. Guide books, travel writers and pop historians started filling their books, whose titles ranged from *Cannibal Cousins*, and *Where Black Rules White*, through *A Puritan in Voodooland*, with lurid and exaggerated tales of "voodoo" rituals. Books like these appeared as late as the 1970s.

Theodore Roosevelt, taking a brief vacation to the Caribbean when he was president in 1906, wrote a letter to his nephew, describing "the decay of most of the islands, the turning of Haiti into a land of savage negroes, who have reverted to voodooism and cannibalism" (Brenda Gayle Plummer, *Haiti and the Great Powers, 1902-1915*, p. 5). Roosevelt's charge of cannibalism had been made by another racist president, Thomas Jefferson, in 1804 and was so commonplace in the nineteenth century that Frederick Douglass felt he had to bring it up in his speech on Haiti.

The fact that "voodoo" has been used as a term of disparagement and contempt by so many bourgeois politicians and commentators for over 200 years makes it abundantly clear that Haiti still has a major impact on U.S. society. The fact that in other contexts like computer operating systems and computer graphics, "voodoo" has positive connotations just strengthens the argument for Haiti's impact on the United States.

Haitian history: What U.S. text books don't tell

Looking at how Haiti's history is presented in high-school textbooks in the United States gives an insight into why many North Americans know so little about Haiti and how this limited knowledge has been distorted, muffled, and hidden behind a veil of silence.

In Saint Domingue in 1790, 10,000 people made fabulous profits from owning almost all the land and from brutally oppressing 500,000 slaves, entirely African or of African descent, with some 40,000 people in intermediate positions, generally either enslaved people who had managed to buy their freedom or had a French father. Fifteen years later, in 1805, the slave-owning colony was gone, replaced by the Republic of Haiti, whose citizens were mostly subsistence farmers who had their own weapons.

It was the first successful national liberation struggle in modern times. When Haiti declared its independence in 1804, it was the only state in the world to have a leader of African descent. In fact, Jean-Jacques Dessalines, the governor-in-general in 1804, was an ex-slave who had survived a cruel master.

One widely-used U.S. high school text book, *World History: Perspective on the Past*, published by Houghton Mifflin Co., presents this struggle in just a few sentences: "Toussaint drove the French forces from the island. Then, in 1802, he attended a peace meeting where he was treacherously taken prisoner. He was then sent to France, where he died in prison. However, the French could not retake the island." (p. 536) About 30 pages later, when the subject of the Louisiana Purchase comes up, a little more is said about Haiti: "Toussaint's fighters and yellow fever all but wiped out a French army of 10,000 soldiers. Discouraged, Napoleon gave up the idea of an American empire and decided to sell the Louisiana Territory." (p. 562) (Actually, the 10,000 soldier figure is an error according to C.L.R. James, *The Black Jacobins*, p. 355.)

Another common high school text book *World History: Connections to Today*, published by Prentice-Hall, devotes almost a page to Haiti, but sums up the struggle against the French attempt to re-enslave Haiti in 1802 in just a few words: "In 1804, Haitian leaders declared independence. With yellow fever destroying his army, Napoleon abandoned Haiti."

James W. Loewen in *Lies My Teacher Told Me*, which examines 12 widely used U.S. high school history textbooks, makes it clear that *Perspectives* and *Connections* are not just two bad apples; in fact, it appears they might be better than most.

Here are the main points of the history they omit. On Feb. 3, 1802, Gen. Charles Victor-Emmanuel Leclerc, Napoleon's brother-in-law, arrived at le Cap Français (currently Cap Haïtien) with five thousand men and demanded entrance. Toussaint's commander, Henri Christophe, was outnumbered and outgunned. Rather than surrender, Christophe burned down the city (starting with his own house), destroyed the gunpowder plant, and retreated into the mountains. Jean-Jacques Dessalines, under orders from Toussaint Louverture, seized the French fort called Crête-à-Pierrot in the center of the country with 1,500 troops, held off the 12,000 French troops that besieged it through two attacks, and then his troops cut their way with bayonets through the French forces to escape.

By the end of April, Louverture had been seized and sent to France, and all his lieutenants had either been deported or incorporated into the French army. But the popular resistance continued and intensified. The French continued losing large numbers of soldiers to yellow fever as well as small-scale but persistent attacks. Cultivators, fearing the reintroduction of slavery, continued to flee to the mountains as maroons and to form small armed bands.

By the end of July 1802, when news spread that the French had reinstituted slavery on Guadeloupe, reopened the slave trade, and forbade any person of color from claiming the title of citizen, resistance turned to insurrection.

French reprisals were terrible but only seemed to strengthen the conviction of the masses that they would rather die fighting than be reenslaved. And they insisted on dying with dignity, no matter how cruel the French were. In one instance, when three captured Haitian soldiers were being burned to death, one started crying. Another said "Watch me. I will show you how to die." He turned around to face the pole, slid down, and burned to death without a whimper. A French general watching the execution wrote to Leclerc: "These are the men we have to fight!"

In another case, a mother consoled her weeping daughters as they were marched to their execution: "Rejoice that your wombs will not have to bear slave children" (Carolyn F. Fick, *The Making of Haiti*, p. 221).

In September, shortly before he died of yellow fever, Leclerc wrote to Napoleon that the only way France could win was to destroy all the blacks in the mountains—men, women, and children over 12—and half the blacks in the plains. "We must not leave a single colored person who has worn an epaulette." (Officers wore epaulettes.) The commander of the French expedition saw no other way to win other than genocide.

By the end of October 1802, the insurrection was so strong that Toussaint's officers who had disingenuously joined the French, deserted and began a counterattack. The struggle took a more organized military character, while the popular insurrection intensified.

By mid-1803, the French were being mopped up in the south. Jérémie was evacuated in August, and Cayes fell on October 17. Then Dessalines decided to move on the French in Cap Français.

Without the artillery or logistics needed to support a long siege, Dessalines decided to take le Cap by storm. He assigned a half-brigade, commanded by Capois La Mort, to storm the walls covered by the mutually supporting positions, Butte de la Charrier and Vertières. Meanwhile, two other brigades maneuvered to seize batteries protecting the city from an attack from the sea. While grapeshot cut swaths through the brigade led by Capois, the soldiers kept pressing forward, clambering over their dead and shouting to each other, "To the attack, soldiers!" On Nov. 18, their combined assault took Charrier, which opened the city to Haitian artillery. The French general agreed to leave immediately and was captured ten hours later by the British. On Nov. 19, 1803, the French army left Haiti for good.

This is the reason why "the French could not retake the island" and why "Napoleon abandoned Haiti"—the French were decisively defeated. The masses refused to return to slavery and their leaders organized a people's army that crushed the French.

World History: Connections and *World History: Perspective* don't treat Haiti's history from 1804 to 1860. That period came before U.S. capitalism had matured enough to expand aggressively into the Caribbean.

In 1825, France forced Haiti to begin paying huge reparations amounting to 90 million gold francs for freeing the slaves (worth about $21 billion in today's currency counting interest). This money, and the interest that Haiti had to pay on the bonds it floated to pay it, are what Haiti is presently demanding as reparations from France.

Even though the United States did not recognize Haiti until 1862, there was still a surprisingly substantial trade between Haiti and France and between Haiti and the United States.

With the end of the Civil War in the United States in 1865, the Caribbean became a cockpit of imperialist interventions and maneuvering. The two high school textbooks under examination mention Haiti from time to time as part of a laundry list of countries where the U.S. intervened.

But the United States was not the only imperialist power splashing around the Caribbean. In the years leading up to the first U.S. occupation in 1915, the warships of Spain, France, the United States, and Germany invaded Haitian territorial waters more than 20 times. Even Sweden and Norway got into the act.

Germany, an imperialist latecomer, aggressively pursued its interests in Haiti because it was restricted in other colonized parts of the world. Fleurimond Kerns in an article in Haïti-Progrès (May 18, 2003) describes one glaring incident:

Take the case of two German nationals living in Haiti (in Miragône and Cap-Haïtien). After going bankrupt during the period of instability between the governments of Sylvain Salnave and Fabre Geffrard, these two Germans called on the German government to demand an immediate indemnity of US $15,000 from the government of Nissage Saget. The Haitian government had to give in because of the presence of two German warships, the Vineta and the Gazella, under the command of Captain Batsch. After their departure, the Haitians found their warships damaged, with the national bicolor soiled with excrement. The date was June 11, 1872.

While historians and some textbooks do list foreign, i.e. imperialist, interventions in Haiti and the larger Caribbean, finding descriptions of resistance is much harder. In her 294-page book *Haiti and the United States*, Brenda Gayle Plummer has a paragraph on what happened in Port-au-Prince on July 6, 1861. The Spanish navy was threatening to bombard the city if Haiti did not offer a 21-gun salute and pay a big indemnity. The people of Port-au-Prince were so upset when their government capitulated that they came out into the streets and the government had to use martial law to control the situation. (p. 41)

The case of Haitian Admiral Hamilton Killick is another outstanding instance of Haitian resistance. At the start of the last century, both the Unites States and Germany deployed Caribbean squadrons. Germany wanted to project its military power to reinforce its commercial and financial push into Haiti. The United States was planning on building the Panama Canal to tie its Pacific coast to the Eastern Seaboard and open up Latin America to its further imperialist penetration.

In 1902 Germany was meddling in a Haitian power struggle, backing one leader while Admiral Killick backed the other. Kern in his Haïti-Progrès article describes what happened on Sept. 6 of that year:

> There was a major political struggle going on at the time between Nord Alexis and Anténor Firmin about coming to power in Port-au-Prince, after the precipitous departure of President Tirésis Simon Sam. Admiral Killick who commanded the patrol ship La Crête-à-Pierrot supported Firmin and consequently had confiscated a German ship transporting arms and munitions to the provisional Haitian government of Alexis.

Not sharing the position of Hamilton Killick, the government ordered another German warship, the Panther, to seize the Crête-à-Pierrot. But it didn't realize the determination and courage of Admiral Killick. At Gonaïves, the Germans had the surprise of their life. When the German ship appeared off the roadsted of the city, Admiral Killick, who was then ashore, hurried on board and ordered his whole crew to abandon the ship. The Germans did not understand this maneuver. Once the sailors were out of danger, Admiral Killick together with Dr. Coles, who also did not want to leave, wrapped himself in the Haitian flag, like Captain Laporte in 1803, and blew the Crête-à-Pierrot up by firing at the munitions. The German sailors did not even dream of an act so heroic.

Through his self-detonation, Killick not only denied the Germans possession of a Haitian ship and the German munitions it had seized, he also came close to blowing up the Panther, according to one German crewman who wrote a postcard home (Postal History: Germany—Haiti—United States at http://home.earthlink.net/~rlcw).

German influence in Haiti waned after the U.S. marines invaded Port-au-Prince July 28, 1915 and began their 19-year occupation. At that time, the U.S. had not officially entered World War One but it was concerned to stop any attempt by Germany to set up a base in Haiti and to protect the Panama Canal, which had opened for business the year before. The U.S. occupation also ended the close financial and commercial ties between Haiti and France, though not the cultural ones. (France was an ally of the United States at the time, but also an imperialist competitor in the Caribbean.)

The start of this occupation was made easy by the political and administrative instability of Haiti, but it then met with four years of fierce armed resistance from guerrillas known as *cacos* under Charlemagne Péralte, and then later under Benoît Batraville. It caused great controversy in the United States and deep resentment in Haiti.

The only mention that *Connections* and *Perspective* makes of the 19-year-long U.S. occupation of Haiti is to mention how Franklin D. Roosevelt was true to his word, true to the "Good Neighbor Policy" when he withdrew the U.S. Marines.

They fail to mention that Roosevelt's need to appear to have broken with the expensive military interventions of his predecessors obviously played a role in abandoning the protectorate in 1934, since the

United States was in the midst of the Great Depression. They also don't mention that there was a anti-occupation nationwide strike and series of demonstrations in 1929, one of which the Marines put down with deadly force (Nicols, *From Dessalines to Duvalier*, p. 151) . Over the next five years, agitation, outcry and bitterness over this issue continued, gained popular support and put relentless pressure on the U.S. to pull out.

These two textbooks ignore and obscure the role that the people and their resistance played in Haiti's history and the important role Haiti played in the hemisphere's history. They disguise the imperialist interests that U.S. and European interventions upheld by giving only brief and simplistic descriptions of major events. Even though the word "imperialism" does appear, these textbooks give U.S. students no real understanding of the racism, violence and greed that led the U.S. to repress and exploit the Haitian people for almost two centuries.

revised version of two articles that appeared in Haïti-Progrès
July & September 2003

Cuba, Haiti and John Brown
— To rebel is justified

*Why is the main boulevard in Port-au-Prince named
for John Brown?*

Sara Flounders

Revolutionary ideas carry across vast miles and through centuries. Those resisting brutal oppression draw inspiration both from living struggles and from historic examples.

Just as Cuba is today considered liberated territory by so many of the world's peoples, who live in societies of enormous racism and repression, Haiti in the 19th century shone as an example and a beacon of hope. It was the only liberated territory—in a region where chattel slavery was still the dominant social relation.

Today, although Cuba lacks rich natural resources or great military capability, its very existence continues to be seen as a threat to U.S. imperialism. The blockade and the threats have continued through Republican and Democratic administrations. Cuba's survival for 43 years is a challenge to total U.S. domination of Latin America and of the globe. Two hundred years ago this is how revolutionary Haiti was viewed.

The many U.S. efforts to overthrow the Cuban revolution through economic sabotage, blockade, sanctions, and encirclement, military aid for invasions, efforts to capture or assassinate Fidel Castro and other Cuban leaders are well documented.

All of these same tactics were used against the Haitian revolution in an age when Haiti had no allies and survived in extreme isolation. The slave-owning president Thomas Jefferson imposed sanctions on Haiti in 1804 that lasted until 1862. These decades of sanctions cut Haiti off from the world and even from the rest of the Caribbean. Every ship that docked from a European country or from the U.S. could be an invasion or carry new demands for onerous concessions. Without normal trade or economic relations the Haitian economy contracted and withered. But the very fact that Haiti survived was a challenge and the nightmare of every slave master—especially in the U.S. slave South.

In this epoch Cuba at great sacrifice has politically and often materially aided the struggle for liberation by giving safe haven to political prisoners and resistance fighters while providing thousands of doctors, technicians and soldiers throughout Africa and Latin America.

Haiti, although ravaged by years of war and sanctions, played a vital role in the liberation of Latin America from Spanish colonial rule. Ships, soldiers, guns and provisions from their meager supplies were provided to the Great Liberator—Simón Bolívar in the hour of his most desperate need.

Brutal class rule survives by ensuring that there is no alternative. The ruling class of every age well understands that ideas and example are enormously powerful. Nothing is more dangerous than success. It is their doom—staring at them.

A living example of how connected revolutionary Haiti was to the abolitionist movement in the U.S. and how Haitians viewed the struggle against slavery in the U.S. can be seen in how the raid at Harpers Ferry in 1859 and the execution of John Brown and his co-conspirators was viewed in Haiti.

The bold attempt of John Brown to seize the arsenal and armory at Harpers Ferry was not much different in planning or in its disastrous outcome than Fidel Castro's bold attack on the Moncada armory 50 years ago. Both leaders had hoped that their action would trigger an insurrection. Both defiantly used their trial as a public forum to put the system itself on trial.

While the slave owners branded John Brown a lunatic and a madman for the armed raid of the Federal Armory, the bold effort to end slavery through armed resistance and through Black and white participation had impassioned interest in Haiti.

The Haitian French language newspapers, *Le Progrès* and *Feuille de Commerce*, were filled with commentary on Harpers Ferry and on the trial and execution of John Brown and the other participants in the raid at Harpers Ferry, reflecting the interconnection between the struggle of enslaved people for freedom in Haiti and in the United States.[1]

The slave master of the U.S. had reason to fear the revolutionary example of Haiti. Haiti was not an isolated uprising of slaves. It was a living reality whenever there was opportunity and capacity. Constant armed slave rebellions were attempted in the slave states of the U.S. south. Gabriel Prosser (1800), Denmark Vesey (1822) and Nat Turner

(1831), led rebellions involving thousands of slaves. An entire military machine of militias, patrols, guards, slave catchers using the most brutal forms of torture was created in an effort to stop the conspiracies, uprisings and escapes.[2]

The fervor to abolish slavery before 1860 was a surging political movement. Abolitionists in New England organized huge rallies of tens of thousands and held international conferences. They built an underground network to give escaping slaves safe passage. Harriet Tubman, an escaped slave herself, led more than 300 enslaved people to freedom. Hundreds of safe houses were maintained. Black and white abolitionists broke into jails and attacked federal marshals to free escaped slaves to prevent their forced return south.

The debates that swirled through the abolitionist movement, in its meetings, in its many tabloids and in the entire literature of the day revolved around how could the Southern slavocracy be defeated. Would moral persuasion or political maneuvers in Congress even restrain its expansion westward? Could laws and treaties restricting the international trade in human beings end slavery? Would condemnation, outrage and religious resolutions be successful?

Within the national and the international movement to abolish slavery Haiti was seen and often referred to as a living example of a successful armed rebellion of slaves.

The great Black leader, orator, author and escaped slave Frederick Douglass, in his autobiography, wrote of the debate on the role of the armed struggle to end slavery in his description of his meeting with John Brown. "Captain Brown denounced slavery in look and language fierce and bitter, thought that slave holders had forfeited their right to live, that the slaves had the right to gain their liberty in any way they could, did not believe that moral suasion would ever liberate the slave, or that political action would abolish the system." This discussion had a profound impact on Douglass. He wrote, "While I continue to write and speak against slavery, I become all the same less hopeful of its peaceful abolition."[3]

This is what he had to say about Haiti, in a speech that is included in this book: "While slavery existed amongst us, her example was a sharp thorn in our side and a source of alarm and terror. She came into the sisterhood of nations through blood. She was described at the time of her advent, as a very hell of horrors. Her very name was pronounced with a shudder. She was a startling and frightful surprise and a threat to all slave-holders throughout the world, and the slave-holding world has had its questioning eye upon her career ever since."

Fifty years after the Haitian Revolution, slavery in the U.S. had not only survived but it was growing and expanding.

Two legal decisions passed in the 1850s reinforced slavery throughout the whole U.S. The Fugitive Slave Act allowed gangs and bounty hunters to pursue escaped slaves into the "free states" of the North. The Dred Scott decision declared even in the North freed Black people could not become U.S. citizens. The decision held that even free Black people had no rights that white people were bound to respect.

In 1854, as slavery grew stronger and extended its reach, there arose within the abolitionist movement the immediate issue of how to stop the slave South from becoming the majority in Congress through the expansion of slavery west into new states. Thousands of abolitionists uprooted their homes and moved to Kansas for the express purpose of preventing Kansas from entering the Union as a slave state. Powerful slave owners paid for hired guns to invade Kansas to burn these small farmers out and open the region for slave plantations. The whole antislavery effort seemed doomed. John Brown organized an armed resistance to the invasion of slave owners. Kansas erupted into civil war; it was called Bloody Kansas. It finally entered the Union a "free" state in 1861.

After the success of armed abolitionists in Kansas and the first military defeat of slave holders in the United States, Brown spent three years studying military tactics along with all that he could find regarding past slave revolts. He made maps of fugitive slave routes. He was especially interested in the history and experiences of the Haitian Revolution.[4]

The only Black survivor of the October 1859 raid at Harpers Ferry, Osborne Anderson, a freeman and a printer, wrote a small book about the reason for the failure of the military action. Anderson wrote to encourage future armed actions and to rebut the lies of the slavocracy that the action failed because slaves were unwilling to take up arms against their masters. He explained that the raid failed for tactical reasons, but that overwhelmingly the slaves joined the attack at the first possibility.[5]

For Haiti the struggle convulsing the slave-owning super power next door was of enormous importance. The existence and the continual expansion of chattel slavery just a few hundred miles from isolated Haiti meant that the survival of Haiti was a precarious gamble.

Brown was hanged on December 2, 1859, along with four co-conspirators. Two of the conspirators, Shields Green and John Copeland, were Black. Of great note was that Black and white participants went to their deaths unrepentant and defiant—just as the great heroes of the Haitian Revolution had done.

The trial of John Brown was covered in enormous detail in the newspapers of the day— in the "free" states and in the slave states, in Europe and Haiti. But only in Haiti were there days of national mourning for John Brown's execution. Haitians collected twenty thousand dollars for Brown's family. Twenty thousand dollars was an enormous sum in 1859, especially in such a poor and blockaded country.[6]

After the execution of John Brown in December 1859 flags in Port-au-Prince were flown at half mast. A solemn mass was held in the cathedral where the President Fabre Nicholas Geffard attended and spoke.[7]

The main boulevard of Port-au-Prince was named John Brown Boulevard. It survives to this day.

As Frederick Douglass said, "If John Brown did not end the war that ended slavery, he did, at least, begin the war that ended slavery. ... Until this blow was struck, the prospect for freedom was dim, shadowy, and uncertain. The irrepressible conflict was one of words, votes and compromises. ... The clash of arms was at hand."[8]

John Brown was a deeply religious man. He saw the struggle against slavery in biblical terms. But as he was led to his death a minister offered to pray with him. Brown refused, saying that no justifier of slavery could pray for him. His last words were: "It is easy to hang me, but this question—this slave question—that remains to be settled."

It was settled in blood. It took four years of a wrenching civil war and more than half a million deaths. But centuries of chattel slavery remain deeply imbedded in wage slavery. Racism permeates every aspect of life in the U.S. today.

The same class—North and South—who built their fortunes and accumulated vast capital through the slave trade remains in power in the U.S. today. Their rage at the Haitian revolution continues in the sanctions, military interventions and deportations of Haitians today.

The Cuban Revolution, although blockaded and under siege, has shown the next step. It will take a second, more thoroughgoing revolution that seeks to transform all capitalist property relations to begin to truly root out the heritage of slavery in the United States.

NOTES

1. Elizabeth Rauth Bethel, "Images of Hayti: the Construction of An Afro-American, Lieu De Memoire" *Callaloo*, Vol. 15, No 3, Haitian Literature and culture, Part 2 (summer 1992), p. 839.

2. Herbert Aptheker, *American Negro Slave Revolts*, International Publishers, NY, New Edition, 1974.

3. W.E.B. Du Bois, *John Brown*, International Publishers, NY, Fourth Printing, 1972.

4. Ibid, p. 97.

5. Osborne P. Anderson, *A Voice from Harpers Ferry*, World View Forum, NY, 2000, p. 123.

6. Ibid. Images of Hayti: p. 839.

7. David Nicholls, *From Dessalines to Duvalier: Race, Colour & National Independence In Haiti*, Rutgers University Press, 1996, p. 85.

8. Ibid, *John Brown*, W.E.B. Du Bois, p. 353.

Lecture on Haiti
at The Haitian Pavilion

Dedication Ceremonies Delivered at the World's Fair,
in Jackson Park, Chicago, Jan. 2d, 1893

By the HON. FREDERICK DOUGLASS,
Ex-Minister to Haiti

Some sections of the introduction and other front matter, as well as
an epilog are not included in this chapter for space reasons. For the
complete text, see http://www.webster.edu/~corbetre/haiti/history/
1844-1915/douglass.htm

— editors

PREFACE

The following lecture on Haiti was delivered in America for the purpose of demonstrating the fact to the United States that the Haitians are
people like ourselves; that what they have gained they will maintain;
that whatever concessions may be asked by man, woman or child, if
not conflicting with the constitution of their country, they will without
hesitation grant. The fact that their skin is dark and that what supremacy
they now have was gained by bloodshed is no reason why they should
be looked upon and treated as though they were unable to comprehend
those things, which are to their best interests. The course taken by their
progenitors to obtain freedom is in no manner different from that pursued by the original promoters of American independence. Our paths
are strewn with the bones of our victims. For whatever United States,
the good people of this country will be held responsible. We ask you to
read and judge well. The appointment of Mr. Douglass to represent
this country in Haiti was bitterly opposed by millions of Americans,
but in spite of all opposition he went, and since his return and the
success of his mission made public, his assailants and opposers have
repented of their error and their respect and administration for him and

for those who sent him is greater now than ever before. So far as he was concerned his services were rendered according to the opinion of the good people and the constitution of the United States. We hope the President will ever be successful in appointing another such minister to represent the United States in Haiti.

GEO. Washington, Manager. April, 1893

INTRODUCTORY

———————

Frederick Douglass in his hours of remembrance must look out upon an amazing group of years. He was just learning to read when Henry Clay was in full fame as an orator and when Daniel Webster was a young man in the National Senate. He was a slave-boy when those two orators were the giants of freedom; he was an African while they were Americans, and yet in intellectual power and in eloquence the slave and the two freeman were at last to meet. It was the destiny of the slave to behold a liberty far nobler than that freedom which lay around Clay and Webster when their sun of life went down. It was the still better destiny of the slave-lad to live and labor in all those years which wrought out slowly and at great cost the emancipation of our African citizens. His talents, his courage, his oratory were given to those days which exposed, assailed and destroyed a great infamy.

By the time Frederick had reached his tenth year he had learned to read. With reading, observation and reflection, came some true measurements of human rights and hopes, and when the twenty-first year had come with its reminder of an independent manhood, this slave made his secret journey toward the North and exchanged Maryland for Massachusetts. Ten years afterward, some English abolitionists paid the Baltimore master for his literary and eloquent fugitive, and thus secured for the famous orator a freedom, not only actual, but legal according to statute law.

———————

The reader of this lecture on Haiti will note at once that simplicity, that clearness, that pathos, that breadth, that sarcasm which are the characteristics of a great orator. In the power of making a statement, Mr. Douglass resembles Webster. The words all rise up as the statement advances, and the listener asks for no omission or addition of a term. If we select one sentence, from that one we may judge all.

Until Haiti spoke the slave ship, followed by hungry sharks,
greedy to devour the dead and dying slaves flung overboard
to feed them, ploughed in peace the South Atlantic, painting
the sea with the Negro's blood.

Such a style, so just, so full, so clear, was the form of utterance well fitted for the black years between 1830 and 1861.

This oration should not be for any of us a piece of eloquence only, full of present beauty and of great memories, but it may well take its place as a great open-letter full to overflowing with lessons for the present and the future. It is the paper of an old statesman read to an army of youth who are here to enjoy and to bless the land which the old orators once made and afterward saved and refashioned.

David Swing
Chicago, March 20th, 1893

Lecture on Haiti

Fifteen hundred of the best citizens of Chicago assembled January 2, 1893, in Quinn Chapel, to listen to the following lecture by Honorable Frederick Douglass, ex-United States Minister to the Republic of Haiti.

In beginning his address, Mr. Douglass said:
No man should presume to come before an intelligent American audience without a commanding object and an earnest purpose. In whatever else I may be deficient, I hope I am qualified, both in object and purpose, to speak to you this evening.

My subject is Haiti, the Black Republic; the only self-made Black Republic in the world. I am to speak to you of her character, her history, her importance and her struggle from slavery to freedom and to statehood. I am to speak to you of her progress in the line of civilization; of her relation with the United States; of her past and present; of her probable destiny; and of the bearing of her example as a free and independent Republic, upon what may be the destiny of the African race in our own country and elsewhere.

If, by a true statement of facts and a fair deduction from them, I shall in any degree promote a better understanding of what Haiti is, and create a higher appreciation of her merits and services to the world; and especially, if I can promote a more friendly feeling for her in this country and at the same time give to Haiti herself a friendly hint as to what is hopefully and justly expected of her by her friends, and by the civilized world, my object and purpose will have been accomplished.

There are many reasons why a good understanding should exist between Haiti and the United States. Her proximity; her similar government and her large and increasing commerce with us, should alone make us deeply interested in her welfare, her history, her progress and her possible destiny.

Haiti is a rich country. She has many things which we need and we have many things which she needs. Intercourse between us is easy. Measuring distance by time and improved steam navigation, Haiti will one day be only three days from New York and thirty-six hours from Florida; in fact our next door neighbor. On this account, as well as others equally important, friendly and helpful relations should subsist between the two countries. Though we have a thousand years of civilization behind us, and Haiti only a century behind her; though we are large and Haiti is small; though we are strong and Haiti is weak; though we are a continent and Haiti is bounded on all sides by the sea, there may come a time when even in the weakness of Haiti there may be strength to the United States.

Now, notwithstanding this plain possibility, it is a remarkable and lamentable fact, that while Haiti is so near us and so capable of being so serviceable to us; while, like us, she is trying to be a sister republic and anxious to have a government of the people, by the people and for the people; while she is one of our very best customers, selling her coffee and her other valuable products to Europe for gold, and sending us her gold to buy our flour, our fish, our oil, our beef and our pork; while she is thus enriching our merchants and our farmers and our country generally, she is the one country to which we turn the cold shoulder.

We charge her with being more friendly to France and to other European countries than to ourselves. This charge, if true, has a natural explanation, and the fault is more with us than with Haiti. No man can point to any act of ours to win the respect and friendship of this black republic. If, as is alleged, Haiti is more cordial to France than to the United States, it is partly because Haiti is herself French. Her language is French; her literature is French, her manners and fashions are French; her ambitions and aspirations are French; her laws and methods of government are French; her priesthood and her education are French; her children are sent to school in France and their minds are filled with French ideas and French glory.

But a deeper reason for coolness between the countries is this: Haiti is black, and we have not yet forgiven Haiti for being black [applause] or forgiven the Almighty for making her black. [Applause.] In this enlightened act of repentance and forgiveness, our boasted civilization is far behind all other nations. [Applause.] In every other country on the globe a citizen of Haiti is sure of civil treatment. [Applause.] In every other nation his manhood is recognized and respected. [Applause.] Wherever any man can go, he can go. [Applause.] He is not repulsed, excluded or insulted because of his color. [Applause.] All places of amusement and instruction are open to him. [Applause.] Vastly different is the case with him when he ventures within the border of the United States. [Applause.] Besides, after Haiti had shaken off the fetters of bondage, and long after her freedom and independence had been recognized by all other civilized nations, we continued to refuse to acknowledge the fact and treated her as outside the sisterhood of nations.

No people would be likely soon to forget such treatment and fail to resent it in one form or another. [Applause.] Not to do so would justly invite contempt.

In the nature of the country itself there is much to inspire its people with manliness, courage and self-respect. In its typography it is wonderfully beautiful, grand and impressive. Clothed in its blue and balmy atmosphere, it rises from the surrounding sea in surpassing splendor. In describing the grandeur and sublimity of this country, the Haitian may well enough adopt the poetic description of our own proud country: [Applause.]

> A land of forests and of rock,
> Of deep blue sea and mighty river,
> Of mountains reared aloft to mock,
> The thunder shock, the lightning's quiver;
> My own green land forever.

It is a land strikingly beautiful, diversified by mountains, valleys, lakes, rivers and plains, and contains in itself all the elements of great and enduring wealth. Its limestone formation and foundation are a guarantee of perpetual fertility. Its tropical heat and insular moisture keep its vegetation fresh, green and vigorous all the year round. At an altitude of eight thousand feet, its mountains are still covered with woods of great variety and of great value. Its climate, varying with altitude like that of California, is adapted to all constitutions and productions.

Fortunate in its climate and soil, it is equally fortunate in its adaptation to commerce. Its shore line is marked with numerous indentations of inlets, rivers, bays and harbors, where every grade of vessel may anchor in safety. Bulwarked on either side by lofty mountains rich with tropical verdure from base to summit, its blue waters dotted here and there with the white wings of commerce from every land and sea, the Bay of Port au Prince almost rivals the far-famed Bay of Naples, the most beautiful in the world.

One of these bays has attracted the eyes of American statesmanship. The Mole St. Nicolas of which we have heard much and may hear much more, is a splendid harbor. It is properly styled the Gibraltar of that country. It commands the Windward Passage, the natural gateway of the commerce both of the new and old world. Important now, our statesmanship sees that it will be still more important when the Nicaragua Canal shall be completed. Hence we want this harbor for a naval station. It is seen that the nation that can get it and hold it will be master of the land and sea in its neighborhood. Some rash things have been said by Americans about getting possession of this harbor. [Applause.] We are to have it peaceably, if we can, forcibly, if we must. I hardly think we shall get it by either process, [Applause.] for the reason that Haiti will not surrender peacefully, and it would cost altogether too much to wrest it from her by force. [Applause.] I thought in my simplicity when Minister and Consul General to Haiti, that she might as an act of comity, make this concession to the United States, but I soon found that the judgment of the American Minister was not the judgment of Haiti. Until I made the effort to obtain it I did not know the strength and vigor of the sentiment by which it would be withheld. [Applause.] Haiti has no repugnance to losing control over a single inch of her territory. [Applause.] No statesman in Haiti would dare to disregard this sentiment. It could not be done by any government without costing the country revolution and bloodshed. [Applause.] I did not believe that President Harrison wished me to press the matter to any such issue. [Applause.] On the contrary, I believe as a friend to the colored race he desired peace in that country. [Applause.]

The attempt to create angry feeling in the United States against Haiti because she thought proper to refuse us the Mole St. Nicolas, is neither reasonable nor creditable. There was no insult or broken faith in the case. Haiti has the same right to refuse that we had to ask, and there was insult neither in the asking nor in the refusal. [Applause.]

Neither the commercial, geographical or numerical importance of

Haiti is to be despised. [Applause.] If she wants much from the world, the world wants much that she possesses. [Applause.] She produces coffee, cotton, log-wood, mahogany and lignum-vitae. The revenue realized by the government from these products is between nine and ten millions of dollars. With such an income, if Haiti could be kept free from revolutions, she might easily become, in proportion to her territory and population, the richest country in the world. [Applause] And yet she is comparatively poor, not because she is revolutionary.

The population of Haiti is estimated to be nearly one million. I think the actual number exceeds this estimate. In the towns and cities of the country the people are largely of mixed blood and range all the way from black to white. But the people of the interior are of pure Negro blood. The prevailing color among them is a dark brown with a dash of chocolate in it. They are in many respects a fine looking people. There is about them a sort of majesty. They carry themselves proudly erect as if conscious of their freedom and independence. [Applause.] I thought the women quite superior to the men. They are elastic, vigorous and comely. They move with the step of a blooded horse. The industry, wealth and prosperity of the country depends largely upon them. [Applause.] They supply the towns and cities of Haiti with provisions, bringing them from distances of fifteen and twenty miles, and they often bear an additional burden in the shape of a baby. This baby burden is curiously tied to the sides of the mother. They seem to think nothing of their burden, the length of the journey or the added weight of the baby. Thousands of these country women in their plain blue gowns and many colored turbans, every morning line the roads leading into Port au Prince. The spectacle is decidedly striking and picturesque. Much of the marketing is also brought down from the mountains on donkeys, mules, small horses and horned cattle. In the management of these animals we see in Haiti a cruelty inherited from the old slave system. They often beat them unmercifully.

I HAVE SAID THAT THE MEN did not strike me as equal to the women, and I think that this is largely due to the fact that most of the men are compelled to spend much of their lives as soldiers in the service of their country, and this is a life often fatal to the growth of all manly qualities. Every third man you meet within the streets of Port au Prince is a soldier. His vocation is unnatural. He is separated from home and industry. He is tempted to spend much of his time in gambling, drinking and other destructive vices; vices which never fail to show themselves repulsively in the manners and forms of those addicted to them. As I walked through the streets of Port au Prince and saw these marred, shattered and unmanly men, I found myself taking up over Haiti the lament of Jesus over Jerusalem, and saying to myself, "Haiti! Poor Haiti! When will she learn and practice the things that make for her peace and happiness?"

NO OTHER LAND HAS BRIGHTER SKIES. No other land has purer water, richer soil, or a more happily diversified climate. She has all the natural conditions essential to a noble, prosperous and happy country. [Applause.] Yet, there she is, torn and rent by revolutions, by clamorous factions and anarchies; floundering her life away from year to year in a labyrinth of social misery. Every little while we find her convulsed by civil war, engaged in the terrible work of death; frantically shedding her own blood and driving her best mental material into hopeless exile. Port au Prince, a city of sixty thousand souls, and capable of being made one of the healthiest, happiest and one of the most beautiful cities of the West Indies, has been destroyed by fire once in each twenty-five years of its history. The explanation is this: Haiti is a country of revolutions. They break forth without warning and without excuse. The town may stand at sunset and vanish in the morning. Splendid ruins, once the homes of the rich, meet us on every street. Great warehouses, once the property of successful merchants, confront us with their marred and shattered walls in different parts of the city. When we ask: "Whence these mournful ruins?" and "Why are they not rebuilt?" we are answered by one word—a word of agony and dismal terror, a word which goes to the core of all this people's woes; It is, "revolution!" Such are the uncertainties and insecurities caused by this revolutionary madness of a part of her people, that no insurance company will insure property at a rate which the holder can afford to pay. Under such a condition of things a tranquil mind is impossible. There is ever a chronic, feverish looking forward to possible disasters. Incendiary fires; fires set on foot as a proof of dissatisfaction with the government; fires for personal revenge, and fires to promote revolution are of startling frequency. This is sometimes thought to be due to the character of the race. Far from it. [Applause.] The common people of Haiti are peaceful enough. They have no taste for revolutions. The fault is not with the ignorant many, but with the educated and ambitious few. Too proud to work, and not disposed to go into commerce, they make politics a business of their country. Governed neither by love nor mercy for their country, they care not into what depths she may be plunged. No president, how-

ever virtuous, wise and patriotic, ever suits them when they themselves happen to be out of power.

I wish I could say that these are the only conspirators against the
peace of Haiti, but I cannot. They have allies in the United States.
Recent developments have shown that even a former United States
Minister, resident and Consul General to that country has conspired
against the present government of Haiti. It so happens that we have
men in this country who, to accomplish their personal and selfish ends,
will fan the flame of passion between the factions in Haiti and will
otherwise assist in setting revolutions afoot. To their shame be it spoken, men in high American quarters have boasted to me of their ability
to start a revolution in Haiti at pleasure. They have only to raise sufficient money, they say, with which to arm and otherwise equip the mal-
contents, of either faction, to effect their object. Men who have old
munitions of war or old ships to sell; ships that will go down in the first
storm, have an interest in stirring up strife in Haiti. It gives them a
market for their worthless wares. Others of a speculative turn of mind
and who have money to lend at high rates of interest are glad to con-
spire with revolutionary chiefs of either faction, to enable them to start
a bloody insurrection. To them, the welfare of Haiti is nothing; the
shedding of human blood is nothing; the success of free institutions is
nothing, and the ruin of neighboring country is nothing. There are sharks,
pirates and Shylocks, greedy for money, no matter at what cost of life
and misery to mankind.

It is the opinion of many, and it is mine as well, that these revolutions would be less frequent if there were less impunity afforded the
leaders of them. The so-called right of asylum is extended to them.
This right is merciful to the few, but cruel to the many. While these
crafty plotters of mischief fail in their revolutionary attempts, they can
escape the consequences of their treason and rebellion by running into
the foreign legations and consulates. Once within the walls of these,
the right of asylum prevails and they know that they are safe from
pursuit and will be permitted to leave the country without bodily harm.
If I were a citizen of Haiti, I would do all I could to abolish this right of
Asylum. During the late trouble at Port au Prince, I had under the protection of the American flag twenty of the insurgents who, after doing
their mischief, were all safely embarked to Kingston without punishment, and since then have again plotted against the peace of their country. The strange thing is, that neither the government nor the rebels are
in favor of the abolition of this so-called right of asylum, because the

fortunes of war may at some time make it convenient to the one or the other of them to find such shelter.

Manifestly, this revolutionary spirit of Haiti is her curse, her crime, her greatest calamity and the explanation of the limited condition of her civilization. It makes her an object of distress to her friends at home and abroad. It reflects upon the colored race everywhere. Many who would have gladly believed in her ability to govern herself wisely and successfully are compelled at times to bow their heads in doubt and despair. Certain it is that while this evil spirit shall prevail, Haiti cannot rise very high in the scale of civilization. While this shall prevail, ignorance and superstition will flourish and no good thing can grow and prosper within her borders. While this shall prevail, she will resemble the man cutting himself among the tombs. While this shall prevail, her rich and fruitful soil will bring forth briers, thorns and noxious weeds. While this evil spirit shall prevail, her great natural wealth will be wasted and her splendid possibilities will be blasted. While this spirit shall prevail, she will sadden the hearts of her friends and rejoice the hearts of her enemies. While this spirit of turbulence shall prevail, confidence in her public men will be weakened, and her well-won independence will be threatened. Schemes of aggression and foreign protectorates will be invented. While this evil spirit shall prevail, faith in the value and stability of her institutions, so essential to the happiness and well-being of her people, will vanish. While it shall prevail, the arm of her industry will be paralyzed, the spirit of enterprise will languish, national opportunities will be neglected, the means of education will be limited, the ardor of patriotism will be quenched, her national glory will be tarnished, and her hopes and the hopes of her friends will be blighted.

In its presence, commerce is interrupted, progress halts, streams go unbridged, highways go unrepaired, streets go unpaved, cities go unlighted, filth accumulates in her market places, evil smells affront the air, and disease and pestilence are invited to their work of sorrow, pain and death.

Port au Prince should be one of the finest cities in the world. There is no natural cause for its present condition. No city in the world is by nature more easily drained of impurities and kept clean. The land slopes to the water's edge, and pure sparkling mountain streams flow through its streets on their way to the sea. With peace firmly established within her borders, this city might be as healthy as New York, and Haiti might easily lead all the other islands of the Caribbean Sea in the race of civilization.

You will ask me about the President of Haiti. I will tell you. Whatever may be said or thought of him to the contrary, I affirm that there is
no man in Haiti who more fully understands or more deeply feels the
need of peace in his country than does President Hyppolite. No purer
patriot ever ruled the country. His administration, from the first to the
last, has had the welfare of his country in view. It is against the fierce
revolutionary spirit of a part of his countrymen that he has had to con-
stantly watch and contend. It has met him more fiercely at the seat of
his government than elsewhere.

Unhappily, his countrymen are not his only detractors. Though a
friend and benefactor of his country, and though bravely battling against
conspiracy, treason and rebellion, instead of receiving the sympathy
and support of the American Press and people, this man has been denounced as a cruel monster. I declare to you, than this, no judgment of
President Hyppolite could be more unjust and more undeserved.

I know him well and have studied his character with care, and no
man can look into his thoughtful face and hear his friendly voice without feeling that he is in the presence of a kind hearted man. The picture
of him in the New York papers, which some of you have doubtless
seen, does him no manner of justice, and, in fact, does him startling
injustice. It makes him appear like a brute, while he is in truth a fine
looking man, "black, but comely." His features are regular, his bearing
dignified, his manner polished, and he makes for himself the impression of a gentleman and a scholar. His conduct during the recent troubles
in Haiti was indeed, prompt, stern and severe, but, in the judgment of
the most thoughtful and patriotic citizens of that country, it was not
more stringent than the nature of the case required. Here, as elsewhere,
desperate cases require desperate remedies. Governments must be a
terror to evildoers if they would be praised to those who do well. It will
not do for a government with the knife of treason at its throat, to bear
the sword in vain. [Applause.]

I invoke for the President of Haiti the charity and justice we once
demanded for our President. Like Abraham Lincoln, President Hyppolite
was duly elected President of Haiti and took the oath of office pre-
scribed by his country, and when treason and rebellion raised their destructive heads, he like Mr. Lincoln, struck them down; otherwise he
would have been struck down by them. [Applause.] Hyppolite did the
same. If one should be commended for his patriotism, so should the
other. While representing the United States in Haiti, I was repeatedly
charged in certain quarters, with being a friend to Haiti. I am not ashamed

of that charge. I own at once, that the charge is true, and I would be ashamed to have it otherwise than true. I am indeed a friend to Haiti, but not in the sense my accusers would have you believe. They would have it that I preferred the interest of Haiti, to the just claims of my own country, and this charge I utterly deny and defy any man to prove it. I am a friend of Haiti and a friend of every other people upon whom the yoke of slavery had been imposed. In this I only stand with philanthropic men and women everywhere. I am the friend of Haiti in the same sense in which General Harrison, the President of the United States, himself is a friend of Haiti. I am glad to be able to say here and now of him, that I found in President Harrison no trace of the vulgar prejudice which is just now so malignant in some parts of our southern country towards the Negro. He sent me not to represent in Haiti our race prejudice, but the best sentiments of our loyal, liberty-loving American people. No mean or mercenary mission was set before me. His advice to me was worthy of his lofty character. He authorized me in substance to do all that I could consistently with my duty to the United States, for the welfare of Haiti and, as far as I could, to persuade her to value and preserve her free institutions, and to remove all ground for the reproaches now hurled at her and at the colored race through her example.

The language of the President was worthy of the chief magistrate of the American people—a people who should be too generous to profit by the misfortune of others; too proud to stoop to meanness; too honest to practice duplicity; too strong to menace the weak, and every way too great to be small. I went to Haiti, imbued with the noble sentiments of General Harrison. For this reason, with others, I named him as worthy to be his own successor, and I could have named no other more worthy of the honor.

From the beginning of our century until now, Haiti and its inhabitants under one aspect or another, have, for various reasons, been very much in the thoughts of the American people. While slavery existed amongst us, her example was a sharp thorn in our side and a source of alarm and terror. She came into the sisterhood of nations through blood. She was described at the time of her advent, as a very hell of horrors. Her very name was pronounced with a shudder. She was a startling and frightful surprise and a threat to all slave-holders throughout the world, and the slave-holding world has had its questioning eye upon her career ever since.

By reason of recent events and the abolition of slavery, the enfranchisement of the Negro in our country, and the probable completion of the Nicaragua canal, Haiti has under another aspect, become, of late, interesting to American statesmen. More thought, more ink and paper have been devoted to her than to all the other West India Islands put together. This interest is both political and commercial, for Haiti is increasingly important in both respects. But aside from politics and aside from commerce, there is, perhaps, no equal number of people anywhere on the globe, in whose history, character and destiny there is more to awaken sentiment, thought and inquiry, than is found in the history of her people.

The country itself, apart from its people, has special attractions. First things have ever had a peculiar and romantic interest, simply because they are first things. In this, Haiti is fortunate. She has in many things been first. She has been made the theater of great events. She was the first of all the trans-Atlantic world, upon which the firm foot of the progressive, aggressive and all-conquering white man was permanently set. Her grand old tropical forests, fields and mountains, were among the first of the New World to have their silence broken by trans-Atlantic song and speech. She was the first to be invaded by the Christian religion and to witness its forms and ordinances. She was the first to see a Christian church and to behold the cross of Christ. She was also the first to witness the bitter agonies of the Negro bending under the blood-stained lash of Christian slave-holders. Happily too, for her, she was the first of the New World in which the black man asserted his right to be free and was brave enough to fight for his freedom and fortunate enough to gain it.

In thinking of Haiti, a painful, perplexing and contradictory fact meets us at the outset. It is: that Negro slavery was brought to the New World by the same people from whom Haiti received her religion and her civilization. No people have ever shown greater religious zeal or have given more attention to the ordinances of the Christian church than have the Spaniards; yet no people were ever guilty of more injustice and blood-chilling cruelty to their fellowmen than these same religious Spaniards. Men more learned in the theory of religion than I am, may be able to explain and reconcile these two facts; but to me they seem to prove that men may be very pious, and yet very pitiless; very religious and yet practice the foulest crimes. These Spanish Christians found in Haiti a million of harmless men and women, and in less than sixty years they had murdered nearly all of them. With religion on their lips, the tiger in their hearts and the slave whip in their hands, they lashed these innocent natives to toil, death and extinction. When these pious souls had destroyed the natives, they opened the slave trade with Africa as a merciful device. Such, at least, is the testimony of history.

Interesting as Haiti is in being the cradle in which American religion and civilization were first rocked, its present inhabitants are still more interesting as having been actors in great moral and social events. These have been scarcely less portentous and startling than the terrible earthquakes which have some times moved their mountains and shaken down their towns and cities. The conditions in which the Republican Government of Haiti originated, were peculiar. The great fact concerning its people, is, that they were Negro slaves and by force conquered their masters and made themselves free and independent. As a people thus made free and having remained so for eighty-seven years, they are now asked to justify their assumption of statehood at the bar of the civilized world by conduct becoming a civilized nation.

The ethnologist observes them with curious eyes, and questions them on the ground of race. The statesman questions their ability to govern themselves; while the scholar and philanthropist are interested in their progress, their improvement and the question of their destiny.

But, interesting as they are to all these and to others, the people of Haiti, by reason of ancestral identity, are more interesting to the colored people of the United States than to all others, for the Negro, like the Jew, can never part with his identity and race. Color does for the one what religion does for the other and makes both distinct from the rest of mankind. No matter where prosperity or misfortune may chance to drive the Negro, he is identified with and shares the fortune of his race. We are told to go to Haiti; to go to Africa. Neither Haiti nor Africa can save us from common doom. Whether we are here or there, we must rise or fall with the race. Hence, we can do about as much for Africa or Haiti by good conduct and success here as anywhere else in the world. The talk of the bettering ourselves by getting rid of the white race, is a great mistake. It is about as idle for the black man to think of getting rid of the white man, as it is for the white man to think of getting rid of the black. They are just the two races which cannot be excluded from any part of the globe, nor can they exclude each other; so we might as well decide to live together here as to go elsewhere. Besides, for obvious reasons, until we can make ourselves respected in the United States, we shall not be respected in Haiti, Africa, or anywhere else.

Of my regard and friendship for Haiti, I have already spoken. I have, too, already spoken somewhat of her faults, as well, for they are many and grievous. I shall, however, show before I get through, that, with all her faults, you and I and all of us have reason to respect Haiti for her services to the cause of liberty and human equality throughout the world, and for the noble qualities she exhibited in all the trying conditions of her early history.

I have, since my return to the United States, been pressed on all sides to foretell what will be the future of Haiti—whether she will ever master and subdue the turbulent elements within her borders and become an orderly Republic. Whether she will maintain her liberty and independence, or, at last, part with both and become a subject of some one or another of the powerful nations of the world by which she seems to be coveted. The question still further is, whether she will fall away into anarchy, chaos and barbarism, or rise to the dignity and happiness of a highly civilized nation and be a credit to the colored race? I am free to say that I believe she will fulfill the latter condition and destiny. By one class of writers, however, such as Mr. Froude and his echoes, men and women who write what they know the prejudice of the hour will accept and pay for, this question has been vehemently answered already against Haiti and the possibilities of the Negro race generally.

They tell us that Haiti is already doomed—that she is on the down-grade to barbarism; and, worse still, they affirm that when the Negro is left to himself there or elsewhere, he inevitably gravitates to barbarism. Alas, for poor Haiti! and alas, for the poor Negro everywhere, if this shall prove true!

The argument as stated against Haiti is that since her freedom, she has become lazy; that she is given to gross idolatry, and that these evils are on the increase. That voodooism, fetishism, serpent worship and cannibalism are prevalent there; that little children are fatted for slaughter and offered as sacrifices to their voodoo deities; that large boys and girls run naked through the streets of the towns and cities, and that things are generally going from bad to worse.

In reply to these dark and damning allegations, it will be sufficient only to make a general statement. I admit at once, that there is much ignorance and much superstition in Haiti. The common people there believe much in divinations, charms, witchcraft, putting spells on each other, and in the supernatural and miracle working power of their voodoo priests generally. Owing to this, there is a feeling of superstition and dread of each other, the destructive tendency of which cannot be exaggerated. But it is amazing how much of such darkness society has borne and can bear and is bearing without falling to pieces and without being hopelessly abandoned to barbarism.

Let it be remembered that superstition and idolatry in one form or another have not been in the past, nor are they in the present, confined to any particular place or locality, and that, even in our enlightened age, we need not travel far from our own country, from England, from Scotland, from Ireland, France, Germany or Spain to find considerable traces of gross superstition. We consult familiar spirits in America. Queen Victoria gets water from the Jordan to christen her children, as if the water of that river were any better than the water of any other river. Many go thousands of miles in this age of light to see an old seamless coat supposed to have some divine virtue. Christians at Rome kiss the great toe of a black image called St. Peter, and go up stairs on their knees, to gain divine favor. Here, we build houses and call them God's houses, and go into them to meet God, as if the Almighty dwelt in temples made with men's hands. I am not, myself, altogether free from superstition. I would rather sit at a table with twelve persons than at one with thirteen; and would rather see the new moon first over my right shoulder than over my left, though my reason tells me that it makes no manner of difference over which shoulder I see the new moon or the old. And what better is the material of one house than that of another?

Can man build a house more holy than the house which God himself has built for the children of men? If men are denied a future civilization because of superstition, there are others than the people of Haiti who must be so denied. In one form or another, superstition will be found everywhere and among all sorts of people, high or low. New England once believed in witches, and yet she has become highly civilized.

Haiti is charged with the terrible crime of sacrificing little children to her voodoo gods, and you will want to know what I have to say about this shocking allegation. My answer is: That while I lived in Haiti I made diligent inquiry about this alleged practice so full of horror. I questioned many persons concerning it, but I never met a man who could say that he ever saw an instance of the kind; nor did I ever see a man who ever met any other man who said he had seen such an act of human sacrifice. This I know is not conclusive, for strange things have sometimes been done in the name of God, and in the practice of religion. You know that our good father Abraham (not Abraham Lincoln) once thought that it would please Jehovah to have him kill his son Isaac and offer him a sacrifice on the altar. Men in all ages have thought to gain divine favor of their divinities or to escape their wrath by offering up to them something of great and special value. Sometimes it was the firstlings of the flock, and sometimes it was the fat of fed beasts, fed for the purpose of having it nice and acceptable to the divine being. As if a divine being could be greatly pleased with the taste or smell of such offerings. Men have become more sensible of late. They keep, smell and eat their fat beef and mutton themselves.

As to the little boys and girls running nude in the streets, I have to say, that while there are instances of the kind, and more of them than we, with the ideas of our latitude, would easily tolerate, they are nevertheless the exceptions to the general rule in Haiti. You will see in the streets of Port au Prince, one hundred decently dressed children to one that is nude; yet, our newspaper correspondents and six-day tourists in Haiti, would lead you to think that nudity is there the rule and decent clothing the exception. It should be remembered also, that in a warm climate like that of Haiti, the people consider more the comfort of their children in this respect than any fear of improper exposure of their little innocent bodies.

A word about snake worship. This practice is not new in the history of religion. It is as old as Egypt and is a part of our own religious system. Moses lifted up the serpent in the wilderness as a remedy for a great malady, and our Bible tells us of some wonderful things done by the serpent in the way of miraculous healing. Besides, he seems to have been on hand and performed marvelous feats in the Garden of Eden, and to have wielded a potent and mysterious influence in deciding the fate of mankind for time and eternity. Without the snake, the plan of salvation itself would not be complete. No wonder then that Haiti, having heard so much of the serpent in these respectable quarters and sublime relations, has acquired some respect for a divinity so potent and so ancient.

But the future of Haiti. What is it to be? Will it be civilization or barbarism? Will she remain an independent state, or be swallowed up by one or another of the great states? Whither is she tending? In considering these questions, we should allow no prejudice to influence us on the one hand or the other. If it be true that the Negro, left to himself, lapses into barbarism, as is alleged; the Negro above and beyond all others in the world should know it and should acknowledge it.

But it is said that the people of Haiti are lazy. Well, with the conditions of existence so easy and the performance of work so uninviting, the wonder is not that the men of Haiti are lazy, but that they work at all. But it is not true that the people of Haiti are as lazy as they are usually represented to be. There is much hard work done in Haiti, both mental and physical. This is true, not only of accessible altitudes where the air is cool and bracing, but it is so in the low lands, where the climate is hot, parching and enervating. No one can see the ships afloat in the splendid harbors of Haiti, and see the large imports and exports of the country, without seeing also that somebody there has been at work. A revenue of millions does not come to a country where no work is done.

Plainly enough; we should take no snap judgment on a question so momentous. It should not be determined by a dash of the pen and upon mere appearances of the moment. There are ebbs and flows in the tide of human affairs, and Haiti is no exception to this rule. There have been times in her history when she gave promise of great progress, and others, when she seemed to retrograde. We should view her in the broad light of her whole history, and observe well her conduct in the various vicissitudes through which she has passed. Upon such broad view I am sure Haiti will be vindicated.

It was once said by the great Daniel O'Connell, that the history of Ireland might be traced, like a wounded man through a crowd, by the blood. The same may be said of the history of Haiti as a free state. Her liberty was born in blood, cradled in misfortune, and has lived more or less in a storm of revolutionary turbulence. It is important to know how she behaved in these storms. As I view it, there is one great fundamental and soul-cheering fact concerning her. It is this: Despite all the trying vicissitudes of her history, despite all the machinations of her enemies at home, in spite of all temptations from abroad, despite all her many destructive revolutions, she has remained true to herself, true to her autonomy, and still remains a free and independent state. No power on this broad earth has yet induced or seduced her to seek a foreign protector, or has compelled her to bow her proud neck to a foreign government. We talk of assuming protectorate over Haiti. We had better not attempt it. The success of such an enterprise is repelled by her whole history. She would rather abandon her ports and harbors, retire to her mountain fastnesses, or burn her towns and shed her warm, red, tropical blood over their ashes than to submit to the degradation of any foreign yoke, however friendly. In whatever may be the sources of her shame and misfortune, she has one source of great complacency; she lives proudly in the glory of her bravely won liberty and her blood bought independence, and no hostile foreign foot has been allowed to tread her sacred soil in peace from the hour of her independence until now. Her future autonomy is at least secure. Whether civilized or savage, whatever the future may have in store for her, Haiti is the black man's country, now forever. [Applause.]

In just vindication of Haiti, I can go one step further. I can speak of her, not only words of admiration, but words of gratitude as well. She has grandly served the cause of universal human liberty. We should not forget that the freedom you and I enjoy today; that the freedom that eight hundred thousand colored people enjoy in the British West Indies; the freedom that has come to the colored race the world over, is largely due to the brave stand taken by the black sons of Haiti ninety years ago. When they struck for freedom, they built better than they knew. Their swords were not drawn and could not be drawn simply for themselves alone. They were linked and interlinked with their race, and striking for their freedom, they struck for the freedom of every black man in the world. [Prolonged applause.]

It is said of ancient nations, that each had its special mission in the world and that each taught the world some important lesson. The Jews taught the world a religion, a sublime conception of the Deity. The Greeks taught the world philosophy and beauty. The Romans taught the world jurisprudence. England is foremost among the modern nations in commerce and manufactures. Germany has taught the world to think, while the American Republic is giving the world an example of a Government by the people, of the people and for the people. [Applause.] Among these large bodies, the little community of Haiti, anchored in the Caribbean Sea, has had her mission in the world, and a mission which the world had much need to learn. She has taught the world the danger of slavery and the value of liberty. In this respect she has been the greatest of all our modern teachers.

Speaking for the Negro, I can say, we owe much to Walker for his appeal; to John Brown [applause] for the blow struck at Harper's Ferry, to Lundy and Garrison for their advocacy [applause], and to abolitionists in all the countries of the world. We owe much especially to Thomas Clarkson, [applause], to William Wilberforce, to Thomas Fowell Buxton, and to the anti-slavery societies at home and abroad; but we owe incomparably more to Haiti than to them all. [Prolonged applause.] I regard her as the original pioneer emancipator of the nineteenth century. [Applause.] It was her one brave example that first of all started the Christian world into a sense of the Negro's manhood. It was she who first awoke the Christian world to a sense of "the danger of goading too far the energy that slumbers in a black man's arm." [Applause.]

Until Haiti struck for freedom, the conscience of the Christian world slept profoundly over slavery. It was scarcely troubled even by a dream of this crime against justice and liberty. The Negro was in its estimation a sheep-like creature, having no rights which white men were bound to respect, a docile animal, a kind of ass, capable of bearing burdens, and receiving strips from a white master without resentment, and without resistance. The mission of Haiti was to dispel this degradation and dangerous delusion, and to give to the world a new and true revelation of the black man's character. This mission she has performed and performed it well. [Applause.]

Until she spoke no Christian nation had abolished Negro slavery. Until she spoke no Christian nation had given to the world an organized effort to abolish slavery. Until she spoke the slave ship, followed by hungry sharks, greedy to devour the dead and dying slaves flung overboard to feed them, plowed in peace the South Atlantic painting the sea with the Negro's blood. Until she spoke, the slave trade was sanctioned by all the Christian nations of the world, and our land of liberty and light included. Men made fortunes by this infernal traffic, and were esteemed as good Christians, and the standing types and representations of the Savior of the World. Until Haiti spoke, the church was silent, and the pulpit was dumb. Slave-traders lived and slave-traders died. Funeral sermons were preached over them, and of them it was said that they died in the triumphs of the Christian faith and went to heaven among the just.

To have any just conception or measurement of the intelligence, solidarity and manly courage of the people of Haiti when under the lead of Toussaint L'Ouverture, [prolonged applause] and the dauntless Dessalines, you must remember what the conditions were by which they were surrounded; that all the neighboring islands were slave holding, and that to no one of all these islands could she look for sympathy, support and cooperation. She trod the wine press alone. Her hand was against the Christian world, and the hand of the Christian world was against her. Hers was a forlorn hope, and she knew that she must do or die.

In Greek or Roman history nobler daring cannot be found. It will ever be a matter of wonder and astonishment to thoughtful men, that a people in abject slavery, subject to the lash, and kept in ignorance of letters, as these slaves were, should have known enough, or have had left in them enough manhood, to combine, to organize, and to select for themselves trusted leaders and with loyal hearts to follow them into the jaws of death to obtain liberty. [Applause.]

In forecasting the future of this people, then, I insist that some importance shall be given to this and to another grand initial fact: that the freedom of Haiti was not given as a boon, but conquered as a right! [Applause.] Her people fought for it. They suffered for it, and thousands of them endured the most horrible tortures, and perished for it. It is well said that a people to whom freedom is given can never wear it as grandly as can they who have fought and suffered to gain it. Here, as elsewhere, what comes easily, is liable to go easily. But what man will fight to gain, that, man will fight to maintain. To this test Haiti was early subjected, and she stood this test like pure gold. [Applause.]

To re-enslave her brave self-emancipated sons of liberty, France sent in round numbers to Haiti during the years 1802-1803, 50,000 of her veteran troops, commanded by the most experienced and skillful generals. History tells us what became of these brave and skillful warriors from France. It shows that they shared the fate of Pharaoh and his hosts. Negro manhood, Negro bravery, Negro military genius and skill, assisted by yellow fever and pestilence made short work of them. The souls of them by thousands were speedily sent into eternity, and their bones were scattered on the mountains of Haiti, there to bleach, burn and vanish under the fierce tropical sun. Since 1804 Haiti has maintained national independence. [Applause.] I fling these facts at the feet of the detractors of the Negro and of Haiti. They may help them to solve the problem of her future. They not only indicate the Negro's courage, but demonstrate his intelligence as well. [Applause.]

No better test of the intelligence of people can be had than is furnished in their laws, their institutions and their great men. To produce these in any considerable degree of perfection, a high order of ability is always required. Haiti has no cause to shrink from this test or from any other.

Human greatness is classified in three divisions: first, greatness of administration; second, greatness of organization; and the third, greatness of discovery, the latter being the highest order of human greatness. In all three of these divisions, Haiti appears to advantage. Her Toussaint L'Ouverture, her Dessalines, her Christophes, her Petions, her Reguad and others, their enemies being judges, were men of decided ability. [Applause.] They were great in all the three departments of human greatness. Let any man in our highly favored country, undertake to organize an army of raw recruits, and especially let any colored man undertake to organize men of his own color, and subject them to military discipline, and he will at once see the hard task that Haiti had on hand, in resisting France and slavery, and be held to admire the ability and character displayed by her sons in making and managing her armies and achieving her freedom. [Applause.]

But Haiti did more than raise armies and discipline troops. She organized a Government and maintained a Government during ninety years. Though she has been ever and anon swept by whirlwinds of lawless turbulence; though she has been shaken by earthquakes of anarchy at home, and has encountered the chilling blasts of prejudice and hate from the outside world, though she has been assailed by fire and sword, from without and within, she has, through all the machinations of her enemies, maintained a well defined civil government, and maintains it today. [Applause.] She is represented at all courts of Europe, by able men, and, in turn, she has representatives from all the nations of Europe in her capitol.

She has her judiciary, her executive and legislative departments. She has her house of representatives and her senate. All the functions of government have been, and are now being, regularly performed within her domain. What does all this signify? I answer. Very much to her credit. If it be true that all present, and all the future rests upon all the past, there is a solid ground to hope for Haiti. There is a fair chance that she may yet be highly progressive, prosperous and happy. [Applause.]

Those who have studied the history of civilization, with the largest range of observation and the most profound philosophical generalization, tell us that men are governed by their antecedents; that what they did under one condition of affairs they will be likely to do under similar conditions, whenever such shall arise. Haiti has in the past, raised many learned, able and patriotic men. She has made wise laws for her own government. Among her citizens she has had scholars and statesmen, learned editors, able lawyers and eminent physicians. She has now, men of education in the church and in her government, and she is now, as ever, in the trend of civilization. She may be slow and halting in the race, but her face is in the right direction. [Applause.]

THE STATEMENT THAT SHE IS ON THE DOWN GRADE TO BARBARISM is easily made, but hard to sustain. It is not at all borne out by my observation and experience while in that country. It is my good fortune to possess the means of comparison, as to "what Haiti was and what Haiti is"; what she was twenty years ago, and what she is now. I visited that country twenty years ago and have spent much time there since, and I have no hesitation in saying that, with all that I have said of her revolutions and defective civilization, I can report a marked and gratifying improvement in the condition of her people, now, compared with what it was twenty years ago. [Applause.]

IN PORT AU PRINCE, which may be taken as a fair expression of the general condition of the country, I saw more apparent domestic happiness, more wealth, more personal neatness, more attention to dress, more carriages rolling through the streets, more commercial activity, more schools, more well clothed and well cared for children, more churches, more teachers, more Sisters of Charity, more respect for marriage, more family comfort, more attention to sanitary conditions, more and better water supply, more and better Catholic clergy, more attention to religious observances, more elegant residences, and more of everything desirable than I saw there twenty years ago. [Applause.]

AT THAT TIME HAITI was isolated. She was outside of telegraphic communication with the civilized world. She now has such connection. She has paid for a cable of her own and with her own money.

THIS HAS BEEN ACCOMPLISHED under the much abused President Hyppolite. [Applause.] Then, there was no effort to light any of the streets. Now, the main streets are lighted. The streets are full of carriages at night, but none are allowed to appear without lighted lamps, and every attention is given to the peace and good order of the citizens. There is much loud talk in Haiti, but blows are seldom exchanged between Haitians.

EVEN HER REVOLUTIONS are less sanguinary and ruthless now, than formerly. They have in many cases been attended with great disregard of private rights, with destruction of property and the commission of other crimes, but nothing of the kind was permitted to occur in the revolution by which President Hyppolite was raised to power. He was inaugurated in a manner as orderly as that inducting into office any President of the United States. [Applause.]

BEFORE WE DECIDE AGAINST THE probability of progress in Haiti, we should look into the history of the progress of other nations. Some of the most enlightened and highly civilized states of the world of today, were, a few centuries ago, as deeply depraved in morals, manners and customs, as Haiti is alleged to be now. Prussia, which is today the arbiter of peace and war in Europe and holds in her borders the profoundest thinkers of the nineteenth century, was, only three centuries ago, like Haiti, the theater of warring factions, and the scene of flagrant immoralities. France, England, Italy and Spain have all gone through the strife and turmoil of factional war, the like of which now makes Haiti a byword, and a hissing to a mocking earth. As they have passed through the period of violence, why may not Haiti do the same? [Applause.]

IT SHOULD ALSO BE REMEMBERED THAT HAITI IS STILL IN HER CHILDHOOD. Give her time! Give her time!! While eighty years may be a good old age for a man, it can only be as a year in the life of a nation. With a people beginning a national life as Haiti did, with such crude material within, and such antagonistic forces operating upon her from without, the marvel is, not that she is far in the rear of civilization, but that she has survived in any sense as a civilized nation.

THOUGH SHE IS STILL AN INFANT, she is out of the arms of her mother. Though she creeps, rather than walks; stumbles often and sometimes falls, her head is not broken, and she still lives and grows, and I predict, will yet be tall and strong. Her wealth is greater, her population is larger, her credit is higher, her currency is sounder, her progress is surer, her statesmen are abler, her patriotism is nobler, and her government is steadier and firmer than twenty years ago. I predict that out of civil strife, revolution and war, there will come a desire for peace. Out of division will come a desire for union; out of weakness a desire for strength, out of ignorance a desire for knowledge, and out of stagnation will come a desire for progress. [Applause.] Already I find in her a longing for peace. Already she feels that she has had enough and more than enough of war. Already she perceives the need of education, and is providing means to obtain it on a large scale. Already she has added five hundred schools to her forces of education, within the two years of Hyppolite's administration. [Applause.] In the face of such facts; in the face of the fact that Haiti still lives, after being boycotted by all the Christian world; in the face of the fact of her known progress within the last twenty years in the face of the fact that she has attached herself to the car of the world's civilization, I will not, I cannot believe that her star is to go out in darkness, but I will rather believe that whatever may happen of peace or war Haiti will remain in the firmament of nations, and, like the star of the north, will shine on and shine on forever. [Prolonged applause.]

DEDICATION CEREMONIES of the Haitian Pavilion
The dedication of the Haitian Pavilion, located in the World's Fair Grounds, delivered Jan. 2, 1893, in the presence of a few of Chicago's best citizens. The short notice given to Director General Davis and the Public, is a startling occurrence and the cause of this will probably

never be made public; and still another incident which occurred during the ceremonies, is that the ground was coated with snow, and there was every sign possible to indicate that a heavy rain would soon follow. The sun had not smiled upon us all that forenoon, but just two minutes before the speaker had concluded his remarks, the sun shone forth its brilliancy directly in the eyes of the speaker who stood in a Northwest position. The sun only showed forth one minute and a half, when the clouds crept over it and darkened it from us, the rest of the day. Addressing the audience Mr. Douglass said:

Ladies and Gentlemen:— ... The first part of my mission here today is to speak a few words of this pavilion. In taking possession of it and dedicating it to the important purposes for which it has been erected within the grounds of the World's Columbian Exposition, Mr. Charles A. Preston and myself, as the Commissioners, appointed by the government of Haiti, to represent that government in all that belongs to such a mission in connection with the Exposition, wish to express our satisfaction with the work thus far completed. There have been times during the construction of this pavilion, when we were very apprehensive that its completion might be delayed to an inconvenient date. Solicitude on that point is now happily ended. The building which was once a thought is now a fact and speaks for itself. The vigor and punctuality of its builders are entitled to high praise. They were ready to give us possession before we were ready to accept it.

That some pains have been taken to have this pavilion in keeping with the place it occupies and to have it consistent with the character of the young nation it represents, is manifest. It is also equally manifest that it has been placed here at a considerable cost. The theory that the world was made out of nothing does not apply here. Material itself, it has required material aid to bring it into existence and to give it the character and completeness it possesses. It could not have been begun or finished without having behind it, the motive power of money, as well as the influence of an enlightened mind and a liberal spirit. It is no disparagement to other patriotic citizens of Haiti who have taken an interest in the subject of the World's Columbian Exposition, when I say, that we have found these valuable and necessary qualities preeminently embodied in the President of the Republic of Haiti. His Excellency General Hyppolite, has been the supreme motive power and the mainspring by which this pavilion has found a place in these magnificent grounds. The moment when his attention was called to the importance of having his country well represented in this Exposition, he comprehended the significance of the fact and has faithfully and with all diligence endeavored to forward such measures as were necessary to attain this grand result. It is an evidence not only of the high intelligence of President Hyppolite, but also of the confidence reposed in his judgment by his countrymen that this building has taken its place here, amid the splendors and architectural wonders which have sprung up here as if by magic to dazzle and astonish the world. Whatever else may be said of President Hyppolite by his detractors he has thoroughly vindicated his sagacity and his patriotism by endeavoring to lead his country in the paths of peace, prosperity and glory. And as for herself, we may well say, that from the beginning of her national career until now, she has been true to herself and has been wisely sensible of her surroundings. No act of hers is more creditable than her presence here. She has never flinched when called by her right name. She has never been ashamed of her cause or of her color. Honored by an invitation from the government of the United States to take her place here, and be represented among the foremost civilized nations of the earth, she did not quail or hesitate. Her presence here today is a proof that she has the courage and ability to stand up and be counted in the great procession of our nineteenth century's civilization. [Applause]

Though this pavilion is modest in its dimensions and unpretentious in its architectural style and proportions, though it may not bear favorable comparison with the buildings of the powerful nations by which it is surrounded, I dare say, that it will not be counted in any sense unworthy of the high place which it occupies or of the people whose interests it represents. The nations of the Old World can count their years by thousands, their populations by millions and their wealth by mountains of gold. It was not to be expected that Haiti with its limited territory, its slender population and wealth could rival, or would try to rival here the splendors created by those older nations, and yet I will be allowed to say for her, that it was in her power to have erected a building much larger and finer than the one we now occupy. She has however, wisely chosen to put no strain upon her resources and has been perfectly satisfied to erect an edifice, admirably adapted to its uses and entirely respectable in its appearance. In this she has shown her good taste not less than her good sense. [Applause.]

For ourselves as Commissioners under whose supervision and direction this pavilion has been erected, I may say, that we feel sure that Haiti will heartily approve our work and that no citizen of that country shall visit the World's Columbian Exposition will be ashamed of its appearance, or will fail to look upon it and contemplate it with satisfied complacency. Its internal appointments are consistent with its external appearance. They bear the evidence of proper and thoughtful consideration for the taste, comfort and convenience of visitors, as well as for the appropriate display of the productions of the country which shall be here exhibited. Happy in these respects it is equally happy in another, Its location and situation are desirable. It is not a candle put under a bushel, but a city set upon a hill. [Applause.] For this we cannot too much commend the liberality of the honorable commissioners and managers of these grounds. They might have easily consulted the customs and prejudices unhappily existing in certain parts of our country, and relegated our little pavilion to an obscure and undesirable corner, but they have acted in the spirit of human brotherhood, and in harmony with the grand idea underlying this Exposition.

They have given us one of the very best sites which could have been selected. We cannot complain either of obscurity or isolation. We are situated upon one of the finest avenues of these grounds, standing upon our verandah we may view one of the largest of our inland seas, we may inhale its pure and refreshing breezes, we can contemplate its tranquil beauty in its calm and its awful sublimity and power when its crested billows are swept by the storm. The neighboring pavilions which surround us are the works and exponents of the wealth and genius of the greatest nations on the earth. Here upon this grand highway thus located, thus elevated and thus surrounded, our unpretentious pavilion will be sure to attract the attention of multitudes from all the civilized countries on the globe, and no one of all of them who shall know the remarkable and thrilling events in the history of the brave people here represented, will view it with other than sympathy, respect and esteem. [Applause.]

Finally, Haiti, will be happy to meet and welcome her friends here. While the gates of the World's Columbian Exposition shall be open, the doors of this pavilion shall be open and a warm welcome shall be given to all who shall see fit to honor us with their presence. Our emblems of welcome will be neither brandy nor wine. No intoxicants will be served here, but we shall give all comers a generous taste of our Haitian coffee, made in the best manner by Haitian hands. They shall find it pleasant in flavor and delightful in aroma. Here, as in the sunny climes of Haiti, we shall do honor to that country's hospitality which permits no weary traveler to set foot upon her rich soil and go away hungry or thirsty. [Applause.] Whether upon her fertile plains or on the verdant sides of her incomparable mountains, whether in the mansions of the rich or in the cottages of the poor, the stranger is ever made welcome there to taste her wholesome bread, her fragrant fruits and her delicious coffee. [Applause.] It is proposed that this generous spirit of Haiti shall pervade and characterize this pavilion during all the day that Haiti shall be represented upon these ample grounds.

But gentlemen, I am reminded that on this occasion we have another important topic which should not be passed over in silence. We meet today on the anniversary of the independence of Haiti and it would be an unpardonable omission not to remember it with all honor, at this time and in this place [Applause.]

Considering what the environments of Haiti were ninety years ago; considering the antecedents of her people, both at home and in Africa; considering their ignorance, their weakness, their want of military training; considering their destitution of the munitions of war, and measuring the tremendous moral and material forces that confronted and opposed them, the achievement of their independence is one of the most remarkable and one of the most wonderful events in the history of this eventful century, and I may almost say, in the history of mankind. Our American Independence was a task of tremendous proportions. In contemplation of it the boldest held their breath and many brave men shrank from it appalled. But as herculean as was that task, and dreadful as were the hardships and sufferings it imposed, it was nothing in its terribleness when compared with the appalling nature of the war which Haiti dared to wage for her freedom and her independence. Her success was a surprise and a startling astonishment to the world. [Applause.] Our war of the Revolution had a thousand years of civilization behind it. The men who led it were descended from statesmen and heroes. Their ancestry, were the men who had defied the powers of royalty and wrested from an armed and reluctant king the grandest declaration of human rights ever given to the world. [Applause.] They had the knowledge and character naturally inherited from long years of personal and political freedom. They belonged to the ruling race of this world and the sympathy of the world was with them. But far different was it with the men of Haiti. The world was all against them. They were slaves accustomed to stand and tremble in the presence of haughty masters. Their education was obedience to the will of others, and their religion was patience and resignation to the rule of pride and cruelty. As a race they stood before the world as the most abject, helpless and degraded of mankind. Yet from these men of the Negro race, came brave men,

men who loved liberty more than life [Applause]; wisemen, statesmen, warriors and heroes, men whose deeds stamp them as worthy to rank with the greatest and noblest of mankind; men who have gained their freedom and independence against odds as formidable as ever confronted a righteous cause or its advocates. Aye, and they not only gained their liberty and independence, but they have never surrendered what they gained to any power on earth. [Applause.] This precious inheritance they hold today, and I venture to say here in the ear of all the world that they never will surrender that inheritance. [Prolonged Applause.]

Much has been said of the savage and sanguinary character of the warfare waged by the Haitians against their masters and against the invaders sent from France by Bonaparte with the purpose to enslave them; but impartial history records the fact that every act of blood and torture committed by the Haitians during that war was more than duplicated by the French. The revolutionists did only what was essential to success in gaining their freedom and independence and what any other people assailed by such an enemy for such a purpose would have done. [Applause.]

They met deception with deception, arms with arms, harassing warfare with harassing warfare, fire with fire, blood with blood, and they never would have gained their freedom and independence if they had not thus matched the French at all points.

History will be searched in vain for a warrior, more humane, more free from the spirit of revenge, more disposed to protect his enemies, and less disposed to practice retaliation for acts of cruelty than General Toussaint L'Ouverture. [Prolonged Applause.] His motto from the beginning of war to the end of his participation in it, was protection to the white colonists and no retaliation of injuries. [Applause.] No man in the island had been more loyal to France, to the French Republic. As Bonaparte was fitting out a large fleet and was about to send a large army to Haiti to conquer and reduce his people to slavery, Toussaint, like a true patriot and a true man, determined to defeat his infernal intention by preparing for defense. [Applause.]

Standing on the heights of Cape Samana he with his trusted generals watched and waited for the arrival of one of the best equipped and most formidable armies ever sent against a foe so comparatively weak and helpless as Haiti then appeared to be. It was composed of veteran troops, troops that had seen service on the Rhine, troops that had carried French arms in glory to Egypt and under the shadow of the eternal pyramids. He had at last seen the ships of this powerful army one after another to the number of fifty-four vessels come within the waters of his beloved country.

Who will ever be able to measure the mental agony of this man, as he stood on those heights and watched and waited for this enemy to arrive, coming with fetters and chains for the limbs and slave whips for the backs of his people. What heart does not ache even in the contemplation of his misery. It is not for me here to trace the course and particulars of the then impending conflict and tell of the various features of this terrible war, a conflict that must ever be contemplated with a shudder. That must be left to history, left to the quiet and patience of the study.

Like all such prolonged conflicts, the tide of battle did not always set in the favor of the right. Crushing disaster, bitter disappointment, intense suffering, grievous defections and blasted hopes were often the lot of the defenders of liberty and independence. The patience, courage and fortitude with which these were borne, fully equals the same qualities exhibited by the armies of William the Silent, when contending for religious liberty against the superior armies of the Spanish Inquisition under Philip of Spain. It was more heroic in the brave Dutch people to defend themselves by the water of their dykes, than for the dusky sons of Haiti to defend their liberties by famine on their plains and fire on their mountains. The difference was simply the difference in color. True heroism is the same whether under one color or another, though men are not always sufficiently impartial to admit it. [Applause.]

The world will never cease to wonder at the failure of the French and the success of the blacks. Never did there appear a more unequal contest. The greatest military captain of the age backed by the most warlike nation in the world, had set his heart upon the subjugation of the despised sons of Haiti; he spared no pains and hesitated to employ no means however revolting to compass this purpose. Though he availed himself of bloodhounds from Cuba to hunt down and devour women and children; though he practiced fraud, duplicity and murder; though he scorned to observe the rules of civilized warfare; though he sent against poor Haiti his well-equipped and skillfully commanded army of fifty thousand men; though the people against whom his army came were unskilled in the arts of war; though by a treachery the most dishonorable and revolting the invaders captured and sent Toussaint L' Ouverture in chains to France to perish in an icy prison; though his swords were met with barrel hoops; though wasting war defaced and desolated the country for a dozen years—Haiti was still free! Her spirit was unbroken and her brave sons were still at large in her mountains ready to continue the war, if need be, for a century. [Applause.]

When Bonaparte had done his worst and the bones of his unfortunate soldiers whitened upon a soil made rich with patriot blood, and the shattered remnant of his army was glad to escape with its life, the heroic chiefs of Haiti in the year 1803 declared her INDEPENDENCE and she has made good that declaration down to 1893. [Prolonged applause] Her presence here today in the grounds of this World's Columbian Exposition at the end of the four hundredth anniversary of the discovery of the American Continent, it is our reaffirmation of her existence and independence as a nation, and of her place among the sisterhood of nations. [Applause.]

The Haitian Flag — Birth of a Symbol

May 18, 2003

Fleurimond W. Kerns
translated by Greg Dunkel

This chapter describes an historic event in the Haitian revolution—the Congress of Arcahaie where the leaders from the South, almost all drawn from the freedmen, known as anciens libres *or* affranchis,*who owned plantations and slaves before the revolution started, put themselves under the command and leadership of the most oppressed. The unity that this Congress achieved was an essential step in completing the Haitian revolution.*

— editors

At the beginning of the 1800s Toussaint Louverture, then at the peak of his glory and his political-military power, expected to rule Saint Domingue, the richest French colony in the Americas. He would govern with the precepts—liberty, equality and fraternity—guiding France itself. Yet for upholding the ideals of the French revolution, the former slave, who had become Governor General in Chief, would be beaten, arrested and then expelled from Saint Domingue to end his days as a common criminal in a French prison, where he died April 7, 1803.

The commemorations unfolding in 2003 on the occasion of the bicentennial should call what happened to Louverture by its name: a political assassination. The history of Haiti, which is still the most vivid and extraordinary of any colonized or enslaved people, has some aspects which make it unique. ... [T]he events that unfolded in Saint Domingue during this period were neither improvisations or chance—they were calculated, planned and carried out by men whose objective was to free themselves from slavery. When Toussaint Louverture was arrested by Napoleon's men in 1802, a shock wave passed through the whole colony. The former lieutenants of the man who had become First Among Blacks took this arrest as a knife in the back, plunged in by

France; it was a blow which meant that, however free a Black person was, they never would be considered a human being.

The Haitian people finally decided to have no further confidence in this France whose only language was total war. In this moment of history, some officers who had fought in the ranks of the colonial army were about to play an important and fundamental role in the war for Haitian independence. They also were about to go over to the insurgent camp, that of the abolitionists and those struggling for independence. The idea of definitively splitting from France had only become popular inside the indigenous army in the days after Toussaint's arrest; he had always been politically ambiguous as to the purpose of the whole struggle, which is certainly why he ended up condemned to prison in Fort-de-Joux. [Fort-de-Joux is the French military outpost in the Jura mountains where Louverture died. *trans.*] Even before Toussaint's deportation, the war restarted in the whole colony on the orders of Jean-Jacques Dessalines, whose strategy for confronting the colonial army sharply differed from that of his former commander.

Like in any struggle for power, however, the authority of Toussaint's successor was contested by some officers, both the formerly freed [freedmen] and those recently freed [the ex-slaves]. Dessalines used two methods to win over these officers: meet the most flexible and propose a warriors' peace; threaten the recalcitrants with harsh punishment. The latter quickly understood the dangers in remaining outside Dessalines' plan and for the most part rallied to him. Once his forces were united, the big battles for the liberation of Saint Domingue could begin.

But, curiously enough, during the long military and political conflict these men had led, from Toussaint up to the assumption of overall command by Jean-Jacques Dessalines, no one had ever thought to give the indigenous army a standard different from that of the colonial army. Toussaint had led his whole war with the French tricolor—blue, white, red. Dessalines himself had taken up the torch in 1802 with the same colors but a slight difference: the general had simply removed the *coq gallois* [the French rooster, *trans.*] and the initials RF [République de France, *trans.*], which at that time were found on the white band of the flag of the French Republic.

But the generals who had fought in the French army, one of whom was Alexandre Pétion, knew the symbolic value of a standard and knew that a national flag would represent a sign of independence. From the time they rallied to the war for liberation, Pétion nourished the idea of giving the indigenous army its own flag. The happenstance of war gave him the opportunity to submit the idea to Dessalines. During the famous battle in the Cul-du-Sac, a plain not far from Port-au-Prince, on December 1, 1802, Pétion confronted the colonial troops of Gilbert Gérard. Things were not going well and he had to conduct a fighting retreat. In the course of this retreat, he lost his tricolor flag which was quickly seized by the enemy as a prize of war.

Either through a misunderstanding or a ruse of war this piece of fabric was to become the origin of the Haitian flag. The fact that the rebel army was carrying a French flag was presented by the press of the time under the title of "Proclamation." The headquarters of the French army in Saint Domingue pretended that this tricolor flag, carried as a rallying sign by the indigenous army, was proof that the insurgents were not fighting for the independence of Saint Domingue but only to keep their liberty, just like the French of the home land, a liberty that the First Consul, the dictator Napoleon Bonaparte wanted to take from them. Was this bizarre article a fabrication, a sort of intoxication spread by the French army with the aim of sowing confusion, even discouragement among the independence fighters? In any case, trap or not, this affair served to reinforce the determination of Pétion about the necessity for the rebels to have their own standard.

In February 1803, when Pétion happened upon this newspaper which contained the story of his flag lost during the battle of December 1, he raced to get the newspaper in question to the headquarters of Dessalines, the commander in chief, in Petite-Rivière in the Artibonite; he carefully explained the affair in detail and took the opportunity to advise the commander-in-chief that the revolutionary army urgently needed to adopt a different flag.

Dessalines, faithful to his reputation of not neglecting any detail and leaving nothing without a response, reacted with his characteristic spirit when he got Pétion's package. He grabbed a red, white and blue flag, and with a sharp jerk, ripped the white stripe to pieces and joined the blue and red together, making the first Haitian flag, symbolizing the union against the colonialist, pro-slavery France. That is how the famous national bicolor was born between the end of February and the beginning of March 1803. Dessalines ordered all his commanders to make their troops carry it.

But if this emblem was used to continue the war in the North and the West, the South, principally the cities of Cayes and Jérémie, were still in the hands of the French. At this time, it was impossible to get all the troops to carry this new flag, especially since certain generals in the South obstinately refused to recognize Dessalines' authority. Pétion, yet again, offered his services to Dessalines to bring these holdouts to their senses, perhaps even to save their lives.

As a former officer of the French army, he was well known among his compatriots, who like himself had been free before the revolution. He wanted to hold a big meeting with all the high ranking officers where this new flag would be adopted after debate. This would consolidate this symbol of symbols for which the people had been ready to die. Pétion finished by convincing Dessalines and his principal lieutenants, in particular his private secretary and confidant Boisrond Tonnerre, to hold a major meeting during May in Arcahaie.

This meeting, known as the Congress of Arcahaie, was set for May 14 to 18, 1803; the agenda had two essential points: the establishment of a united command of the revolutionary army under the supreme authority of Jean-Jacques Dessalines, and the adoption of a flag by the indigenous army. The two principal leaders at this time, Dessalines and Pétion, jointly drew up this agenda. On May 14, 1803, military delegations flocked to Arcahaie; only a few of them were from the South. The principal heads of the insurgency did answer the call.

The Congress was opened by Dessalines and Pétion May 15, 1803, on the Mérotte plantation. The two men focused on the military situation, insisting on the need for all forces rebelling against the enemy to unite so that victory would be more rapid and decisive. Curiously, there was not a word about the flag; priority was put on new strategies and tactics to thwart the colonial army and also to confirm Dessalines as Commander General of the army and Saint Domingue. The question of the new emblem came up on the last day, May 18. The new Commander General suggested the old slogan "Live Free or Die" be replaced by "Liberty or Death." The debate over the proclamation of the creation of a new flag lasted a whole day. It was only in the evening that the Congress of Arcahaie definitively adopted the blue and red bicolor, which is the flag of the Republic of Haiti.

Catherine Flon, a national hero, sewed the national standard at the Congress. Under these circumstances, the generals solemnly swore an oath of fealty to "Liberty or Death" on this flag which was to lead the slaves to victory and freedom. This oath, which history has named the Oath of the Ancestors, is the equivalent of the one that the deputies of the Third Estate swore at Versailles June 20, 1789, whose aim was to give a constitution to France.

Since May 18, 1803, the Haitian flag has known many changes in position or of color. These two pieces of fabric have not stopped marking the legendary side of Haitian history all the same. Obviously, the controversies between historians on the origin of this flag are far from being settled, but all agree on two points: the date and the place of its birth.

Insults to the flag

On three particular dates the Haitian flag was subjected to grave insults. There was the case of two German nationals who lived in Haiti (at Miragône and Cap-Haïtien). After going bankrupt during the period of instability between the governments of Sylvain Salnave and Fabre Geffrard, these two Germans called on the German government to demand an immediate indemnity of US $15,000 from the government of Nissage Saget. The Haitian government had to give in because of the presence of two German warships, the Vineta and the Gazella, under the command of Captain Batsch. After their departure, the Haitians found their warships damaged, with the national bicolor soiled with excrement. The date was June 11, 1872.

The Luders Affair was similar and also involved a German national. This German business man was charged with assault and battery on a policeman. Upset about his fate, the Berlin government intervened once more with two warships, the Charlotte and the Stein, and demanded Tirésis Simon Sam's government pay $20,000 to Mr. Luders and free him immediately. This time the supreme humiliation for the Haitian people was when the president agreed to hoist the German flag on the flagpole of the National Palace December 6, 1897.

Finally, profiting from the political and administrative instability of the country, the United States of America sent an expeditionary force to Port-au-Prince July 28, 1915, with the intention of transforming Haiti into a protectorate. Very quickly, all Haitian institutions came under American administration; in 1919, four years later, the collaborationist president Sudre Dartiguenave signed what was officially called the Haitian-American Convention, placing the Republic of Haiti under the tutelage of Washington until 1934. For 19 years, the Haitian flag disappeared from view, except when it was raised by resisters like Charlemagne Péralte in the Central Plateau, whose struggle was taken up by Benoît Batraville after he fell. Despite these humiliations, the Haitian people maintained their patriotism and showed they are not unworthy of their history.

Moreover, if many misfortunes and tragedies have touched the Haitian bicolor through the years, many heroic acts connected with it have also taken place from its glorious creation to May 18, 2003, when Haitians, wherever they were, celebrated the bicentennial of their national flag. On May 19, the day after the Congress of Arcahaie, Captain Laporte was heading towards Léogane to bring new instructions to the South along with two other boats. While crossing the bay of Port-au-Prince, these Congress boats crossed paths with an enemy patrol commanded by Admiral Laoutch-Tréville. Two boats had time to escape. Laporte's boat did not, so in an act of brave patriotism, he ordered his crew to scuttle the boat so it would not fall into the hands of the French, wrapped himself in the new flag from Arcahaie, and put a bullet into his head. This gesture proved to the colonial sailors that the Blacks of Saint Domingue would never accept a return to slavery.

Another piece of evidence is the celebrated battle of Vertières Nov. 18, 1803, which highlighted the indigenous army. Considered as the mother of all battles, it was with the blue-and-red flag of Haiti that the infantry of the revolutionary army conquered their right to glory confronting the troops of Gen. Donatien Rochambeau.

The most celebrated and well known of these gestures of Haitian patriotism and grandeur was the armed struggle of Admiral Hamilton Killick, September 6 1902. There was a major political struggle going on at the time between Nord Alexis and Anténor Firmin about who would come to power in Port-au-Prince after the precipitous departure of President Tirésis Simon Sam. Admiral Killick who commanded the patrol ship La Crête-à-Pierrot supported Firmin and consequently had confiscated a German ship transporting arms and munitions to the provisional Haitian government of Alexis.

Not sharing the position of Hamilton Killick, the government ordered another German warship, the Panther, to seize the Crête-à-Pierrot. But it didn't realize the determination and courage of Admiral Killick. At Gonaïves, the Germans had the surprise of their life. When the German ship appeared off the roadsted of the city, Admiral Killick, who was then ashore, hurried on board and ordered his whole crew to abandon the ship. The Germans did not understand this maneuver. Once the sailors were out of danger, Admiral Killick together with Dr. Coles, who also did not want to leave, wrapped himself in the Haitian flag, like Captain Laporte in 1803, and blew the Crête-à-Pierrot up by firing at the munitions. The German sailors did not even dream of an act so heroic.

Haïti-Progrès, May 18, 2003

U.S. embargoes against Haiti
— from 1806 to 2003

Greg Dunkel

In 1806, Haiti was diplomatically isolated. It had audaciously declared its independence two years before, after crushing the French army sent by Napoleon to re-enslave it.

But no country in the world recognized its independence. Certainly not France, which had just suffered a major blow to its fortunes and prestige. Not Spain, which still had its slave-based colonial empire in the Caribbean and Latin America. Not Great Britain, at that time the predominant world power, worried over its plantations in Jamaica, just 75 miles from Haiti, whose profits also depended on the brutal super-exploitation of enslaved Africans.

There was substantial trade between the United States and Haiti, even after the Haitian revolution ended slavery. Haiti sold coffee, molasses, sugar, cotton, hides and so on, and bought dried cod, cloth, hardware and other bulk commodities. But Thomas Jefferson, the slave-owning, slave-selling president of the United States, was terrified by the successful slave rebellion and went so far as to call Toussaint Louverture's army "cannibals." Louverture was a leader of Haiti's liberation struggle and its army.

Jefferson gave backhanded support to the Haitian struggle when its successes led France to consider selling Louisiana. But that was just a temporary maneuver. He was implacably opposed to Haitian independence.

He tried hard to prevent any contact between the United States and Haiti. Jefferson called upon Congress, which his party controlled, to abolish trade between the two countries. France and Spain, two major colonial powers in the Caribbean at the time, were also enforcing boycotts of Haitian trade. Consequently, partially in 1805 and finally in 1806, trade between the United States and Haiti was formally shut down.

Trade still continued on an unofficial basis. U.S. ships could call at Haitian ports, but Haitian ships were excluded from U.S. ports. This decimated the Haitian economy, already weakened by 12 years of hard fighting and much destruction.

In the 1820s, South Carolina Sen. Robert V. Hayne made the U.S. position absolutely clear when he stated: "Our policy with regard to Haiti is plain. We never can acknowledge her independence." Acknowledging Haiti's independence would have thrown slavery, the foundation of the South's economy and prosperity, into question.

The embargo let U.S. merchants dictate the terms of trade between the two countries, establishing a neocolonial relationship. Jefferson, and other racist slave owners, kept the United States from recognizing Haiti until 1862. The U.S. slave owners presented the racist argument that Haiti's devastating economic decline was an example of what happens when Africans govern themselves. Before the Haitian revolution, St. Domingue—its French name—was more lucrative for France than the Thirteen Colonies ever was for Great Britain. They did not mention that Haiti's problems were caused by their own cruel and punishing neocolonial economic policies and actions.

Even in the midst of a civil war fought over the existence and expansion of slavery in the United States, outright racist actions were common in Washington. In April 1862, when Sen. Charles Sumner raised the issue of recognizing Haiti and Liberia, representatives of border states like Maryland and Kentucky objected to the presence of Black diplomats in Washington. (For more information, see "The Struggle for the Recognition of Haiti and Liberia as Independent Republics," Charles H. Wesley, *The Journal of Negro History*, Vol. 2, Oct., 1917.)

French & European recognition

In the early 1800s, Haiti's government still felt threatened by France even after it had crushed Napoleon's army in 1802. For example, in 1821 France offered internal self-rule under a French protectorate. This was essentially what Louverture thought he had won in 1801 and the Haitian government saw it as a threat.

Haiti had given asylum and essential military and material help to Simón Bolívar in his struggle to free Latin America. But Spain still possessed Cuba and Puerto Rico, had claims over the eastern portion of the island of Hispaniola, now the Dominican Republic, and still profited from slavery. Furthermore, Haiti faced the hostility of the United States, even from sectors like the Northern bourgeoisie, who weren't tied to slavery but were still thoroughly racist.

In return for conditional recognition as an independent nation in 1825, President Jean-Pierre Boyer offered France 150 million gold francs as indemnity and to lower customs duties for French products to half those of any other nation. This was a tremendous sum, estimated by the present Haitian government to be $21 billion in current dollars including interest. After a show of force by the French navy in 1825, Haiti swiftly borrowed 24 million francs to pay the first installment. Full recognition by France followed in 1838.

The money was earmarked to indemnify the slave owners and their heirs for their "losses" during Haiti's revolution. For Haitians, the freedom they had won with their blood had also to be paid in cash.

After France's conditional recognition, Great Britain and the other European powers quickly followed suit. But the United States refused.

France's financial hold on Haiti continued until the first U.S. occupation in 1915. This hold was so complete that even when Haiti set up its Banque Nationale in the 1880s, it was done with French capital and French bank officers.

During the 1800s Haiti had two neocolonial overlords: France and the United States, both of which extracted as much as they could from the country, blaming Haiti's economic problems on what Haitians were forced to do.

Current U.S. boycott

In the 19th century, the United States and the European powers used Haiti's extreme diplomatic isolation and the devastation resulting from its revolution against the French slave owners to control it. In the late 20th and early 21st centuries, the United States uses Haiti's dire poverty.

Today, Haiti is the poorest country in the Western Hemisphere by any measure, comparable to poor countries in Africa.

Haiti's debt was $302 million in 1980. In 1997 it was almost $1.1 billion, which is almost 40 percent of its Gross National Product. The value of its exports has fallen to 62 percent of 1987 levels. It should be listed as a severely indebted low-income country but the International Monetary Fund and the World Bank have refused to do so.

More than 80 percent of the people in the countryside regularly don't get enough to eat. Some 50 percent of the people are illiterate. Seventy percent are unemployed. Life expectancy is 56 years and falling. Infant mortality is more than double the Latin American and Caribbean average. (Figures from PAPDA—the Haitian Platform to Advocate for an Alternative Development)

Few people in Haiti have a reliable supply of clean water and those who do buy it by the jug.

The U.S. government put an embargo on loans to Haiti from the Inter-American Development Bank and got the European Union, formerly another large donor to Haiti, to do the same. The United States took this action because in the 2000 elections, Washington's favored candidates lost.

When U.S. Secretary of State Colin Powell spoke at the Organization of American States meeting in Santiago, Chile, in June 2003, he warned that the OAS would reevaluate its role in Haiti if the Aristide government did not conform to OAS resolutions about the organization of Haiti's elections. This was also a warning to Latin American countries to follow the U.S. policy on Haiti.

The United States wants to rig Haitian elections so that its favored candidates win. In the 19th century, it used gunboats and threats to assure victory. Now it's more convenient to hide the hand that throws the rock behind an organization like the OAS.

But Haiti is not Florida, where George W. Bush stole the last presidential election. The first election that Aristide contested in 1990 was in fact more than just an election. It was a mass movement, a Lavalas flood to elect a people's candidate—and it swept aside all the encrustations and debris left over from decades of foreign interference and U.S.-backed Duvalierist terror.

Aristide's election was a shock to U.S. reliance on rigged cosmetic elections to put in politicians who will enforce neo-liberal policies.

Despite a 1991 military coup to oust Aristide that cost over 5,000 lives and all sorts of CIA skullduggery, popular support for Aristide remained strong. He and his party won the 2000 election. The real reasons the U.S. and European governments are withholding aid from Haiti are to force concessions out of Aristide—or topple his administration should he not submit—and to punish the Haitian masses as in the 19th century for daring to make a revolution that ended slavery.

Part II

❧❧

Aristide's Election

The Only Way

to the memory of Jacques Roumain

Paul Laraque

you tell me freedom
I see cooperatives and plows
factories and union workers
running water in the fields
the streets for the people
schools for our children

I see a city reaching out to a village
an arm naked as a face
one by one
countrysides are lighting up
creating a necklace of light
in the country Jean-Jacques has given us

the Pont-Rouge* leads to Péralte's cross
the Party takes on the bloody heritage
Haiti is urging our age in the hard fight
o my old enemies
the seeds from your days are numbered
our just demands are growing like flower spikes

I salute you Mayakovsky
my song was but one cry
if a woman's heart is lightened
the spirit will shatter mystery's chains
her eyes are the color of wheat
her flesh summer's heat

I've found love again without any vertigo
it soars tall like a stem

ripping shadows that assail us
when the sun of desire shines at last
my name gushes from your depths
as happiness can keep the windows closed

I tell you freedom
and it's a word of peace
it's a word like tractor dam fertilizer
I'm taking you by the hand to the sources of life
here are the people the masses assembled
for a harvest of morning dew

---

* Pont-Rouge is a bridge in Port-au-Prince where Desssalines was killed Oct. 17, 1806.

Interview with Ray Laforest
— Haitian Trade Union Organizer

Johnnie Stevens

Ray Laforest is director of organizing for AFSCME, District Council 1707. He has been a labor organizer for the past twelve years, and is also very active with WBAI and Pacifica Radio network on the national level. Johnnie Stevens of the Peoples Video Network interviewed Ray Oct. 5, 2003, for a video that is intended to be a companion to this book.

— editors

Johnnie Stevens: Ray, could you give us the history of your involvement in the movement, both in Haiti and here in the United States?

Ray Laforest: My own personal history started in Haiti. In a comfortable background, father a doctor, solid middle class. The contradictions of the country weren't obvious to me. When Papa Doc took power, I was about 10 years old. My parents supported the candidate of the bourgeoisie, Louis Déjoie. It became clear to me as I grew older that Papa Doc was indeed the "devil incarnate" but it also became clear to me that he was reacting to preexisting conditions in Haiti. So I started questioning my conditions of privileges.

I also started questioning the contradictions inside the church. As I grew older and started studying history I learned about the role of the church in pacifying people and justifying power. So my first struggle against the system had two prongs:

    1. Against the temple of power that was the government and its policy of violence against the Haitian people;

    2. Against my religious, moral explanation from the church for why things happened, as a justification for behavior.

    I became connected to what later was called the theology of liberation and joined an organization called Haiti Progress, which had nothing to do with the newspaper of the same name, founded years later.

My family, while it did not question its privilege, did believe in a modicum of democracy and liberal justice and I guess that is where I started from. I demanded that these principles be applied. Haiti Progress was an organization that understood we were in the grip of fascism before the left itself decided so. We tried to develop a program for the participation of the Haitian people for the benefit of the masses, from a liberal point of view, I would have to concede, and that force would have to be applied to meet the force of the government. The left decided that the time was not ripe for the people to rise up and apply force.

Johnnie Stevens: Ray, so what did you do after you joined Haiti Progress?

Ray Laforest: Haiti Progress was a paramilitary organization that functioned in clandestinity. Every individual was a member of a cell, and when they rose high enough, they became the head of the cell. The work was difficult and security was primary. You could not have open meetings. As a matter of fact, we extended our education by having someone every week read a book and reporting on political economy, world history, Haitian history, and support from other Caribbean countries, like Cuba and the Dominican Republic.

We even considered guerrilla warfare. I was a member of the paramilitary section, helped train people and took actions that put my life in danger. Most of the members were young and Catholic and as we were growing up, we were evolving. We started from the base of an engaged church, a church of action. The religion we believed in was a religion tempered by reality, a religion of social action for our brothers and sisters.

As Castro's revolution unfolded, in a country just 45 miles from Haiti, we became very involved in it, supported it, and were inspired by it. He demonstrated very clearly that it could be done, and that the notion in Haiti which Duvalier had carefully cultivated, using vodou by the way, that he was all-powerful and had spies everywhere, was false. By putting our lives on the line, we could indeed change our world. There was no greater calling than to bring the Haitian people to justice and dignity.

Most of the people around me became much more radical. I rose through the ranks and actually got to the point where I could have bilateral contacts with our organization and with other organizations.

We got to the point where we had to consider overthrowing Duvalier.

Because of threats to my life, I had to leave Haiti in 1968. Before I left, PUCH — the United Communist Party of Haiti — was formed. It was a fusion of the two major communist parties of Haiti. Because of the fusion and the increasing strength of the left, the CIA moved in and helped Duvalier set up spies inside the PUCH. Actually, three months after I left, comrades from my cell and adjacent cells were arrested and savagely tortured

By 1969, comrades coming back from the Soviet Union and elsewhere were ready to bring the struggle to a different level and so was the other side. PUCH was infiltrated almost to the top. Within a year the forces of the PUCH were attacked and forced to disband, even though they put up a fight dying with weapons in hand.

The destruction of the left created a vacuum into which the forces of liberation theology could move. The next level of struggle took place behind the protection of the Catholic church, which was connected to the Church of Rome. Duvalier responded by expelling every foreign priest and prelate, including the head of the Haitian church, and installing Haitians who were connected to him. Still there were many active priests who discussed the theology of liberation.

This vacuum enabled the movement, led by Fr. Aristide and other priests like him, to lead the contestations and struggles for justice and dignity for the mass of the Haitian people.

Johnnie Stevens: What about the labor movement in Haiti?

Ray Laforest: After the U.S. invasion in 1915, sugar cane workers and peasants were dispersed to Cuba and the Dominican Republic because HASCO [the Haitian American Sugar Co.] got much of the best land in the country and moved sugar processing outside the country. The workers movement under the Duvaliers was very difficult, because as soon as it grew strong, the government moved brutally against it; they had to go underground; if they were caught, they were tortured. They were treated like the rest of the population.

Johnnie Stevens: What was your life like after you came to the United States in 1969?

Ray Laforest: When I came here in 1969, there was an emerging Haitian presence around Broadway in the 90s in Manhattan. As housing grew available, many of the new immigrants went to Brooklyn. As the Haitian community developed, it went through the same stages as other communities. With differences, obviously; unlike Jamaicans and Trinidadians, they spoke a different language. If a Dominican came here, he or she could speak to the whole Spanish speaking diaspora. Haitians were much more isolated.

Also Haitians were independent in 1804, so much earlier than all the other countries in Latin America, and were very isolated. Even as recently as 10 years ago, there were many more links between the Haitian community, and Jamaicans, and other groups, even Dominicans, in New York than there were in Haiti.

The first stage was to survive, to get a job. Since I came from a more privileged background, when I got here, I had a job waiting for me. Most Haitians at that time worked factory jobs with a huge amount of overtime, without any protection from unions, or worked two jobs. A lot of the money went back home. Slowly they would bring their wife or husband, then the children. It was a difficult life.

Because of repression and the harsh economic conditions there during the '70s, very directly connected to political struggles in Haiti, even people who came here for economic reasons considered themselves as political, more than economic, refugees. They were completely turned towards Haiti and a presidential candidate Daniel Fignolé, who started his political career as head of the Mouvement Ouvrier Paysan [Worker Peasant Movement], had lived here for a while. Many other prominent political figures in Haiti were forced out by the Duvaliers and came here to live.

Haitians were so devoted to Haiti that it took the violence of the Duvaliers to drive them out of their country. They had worked in the sugar industry in Cuba and the Dominican Republic but had always gone back until it grew too dangerous. Even Haitians who had lived in this country for years would say they were "Haitian" when they were asked. This cut them off from the reality around them, just working for many hours, not doing politics until the weekend.

Johnnie Stevens: When did you get involved with the labor movement as an organized activist?

Ray Laforest: It took me a while, actually. In Haiti the work force was always very small. Any contact between my organization and a workers organization would have been done very quietly and very discretely, otherwise severe consequences, including death, would have been immediate. So personally, I had not done work with organized labor in Haiti. The Duvaliers made it clear to business owners that they would not tolerate the presence of trade unions in Haitian factories.

When I came here, my political work was organizing to get Haitians to realize that Papa Doc could be defeated, that it was in our ability and duty to do so. There was very little time spent in improving housing and employment conditions for many years. This was not just my personal position but was widespread in the Haitian community.

Johnnie Stevens: How did you do your political work in the Haitian community?

Ray Laforest: The Haitian community here was growing, because of economic and political repression in Haiti; people in Haiti began realizing they had another option. People started becoming taxi drivers, restaurant workers, home health care providers as their English improved.

One particularity about Haiti is that education has always been free, so you could have people from a very poor background who still could get educated. Actually Papa Doc became a physician for free, though he had to work for the government in return for his education. Some educated Haitians came here, but more went to French-speaking West Africa or Quebec, where language didn't make it harder to get professional jobs.

Migration out of Haiti has always been connected to the need to make a living, to feed your family, to survive and thrive.

When it became clear that the Cuban revolution was communist as well as nationalist, the U.S. changed tactics and the Alliance for Progress was part of that change. It became clear that for the bourgeoisie to have a system of profitable exploitation, they couldn't have backward, semi-feudal conditions like you had in Haiti under the Duvaliers. For production, you needed to modernize and get people to absorb the ideology of capitalism, in particular, that if you produce, things will get better. When things don't work out, it's your own fault. If you run for office or you support a candidate, you nominally support democracy. When you have a dictatorship like the Duvaliers, you can control things more tightly but you also have resistance.

As people started organizing, guided, or perhaps it's better to say, inspired by the Cuban revolution, the U.S. response became more modulated. In Haiti, after Papa Doc died, the U.S. saw an opportunity to use his son Baby Doc as some one who grew up in wealth and privilege; Baby Doc had married a daughter of the traditional bourgeoisie, a marriage that was symbolic of what the U.S. wanted, a dark-skinned member of the agricultural bourgeoisie allying himself to a light-skinned member of the export-import bourgeoisie. It worked well for them, to a certain extent.

But the exploitation and violence that was occurring in the countryside, along with the land being washed down the mountainside, forced hundreds of thousands of peasants off their land, either into cities like Port-au-Prince or onto boats that took them here. As companies began to invest in Haiti, their labor force was being created as peasants were pushed into the cities.

But the tradition of struggle continued. It was centered around ideology and the activities of the Catholic Church, the base of the Church, the ti legliz, the little churches, where Aristide began. The left also functioned as best it could, mostly outside the country. Newspapers like Haïti-Progrès were founded and the resistance inside Haiti grew. Repression also grew but the people were fed up and the repression only made more people determined that Duvalier had to be removed. Finally Reagan plucked Baby Doc out in 1986. On a U.S. Air Force plane. Reagan wanted to save the Haitian army, the major tool that the U.S. used to control Haitian society.

Johnnie Stevens: Let's talk about repression here. We saw big marches, 20,000 people or more, after the attacks on Dorismond and Louima, about the same time as Seattle. What I'm asking is that as more people got here and worked, did repression follow?

Ray Laforest: Exactly. For a long time, when Haitians suffered harassment, say a taxi driver got slapped around and was told to stop talking with that funny accent, they accepted it, went home, licked their wounds and resolved to be more careful the next time. The community was so small it wasn't conscious of itself, didn't have the organizations to respond.

But as the community grew bigger and bigger, there was a sense of pride, of clarity in this achievement, so by the time we saw the reactions of the community to the police brutality that you talked about or to being called AIDS carriers, the strength of the movement inculcated in Haiti became useful in the American context. As their ties grew, as their kids started going to school here, they realized that they couldn't go back to Haiti because there was no job for them there, they realized that they were living in the belly of the beast here and that there was a role for them living here.

They realized that where you are is where you are, that issues here are just as important as issues in Haiti.

One of the real successes of this movement, this organizing, was when 100,000 Haitians, coming from all over on a work day, shook the Brooklyn Bridge marching on Wall Street to protest the Centers for Disease Control claiming that Haitians were AIDS carriers. What made Haitians angry was that they were the only group singled out by the CDC as a nationality, that their children were teased mercilessly in school, they were told they couldn't give blood. The police were totally surprised because this demonstration was completely organized outside the American press, yet we were able to achieve that incredible organizing just from within the Haitian community. All of the Financial District in lower Manhattan was paralyzed.

The numbers that came out against police brutality, for rights as immigrants, against abuses of our immigrant status were slightly smaller but still significant.

So like other communities, the Haitian community is maturing and realizing that they are not just Haitian, that they are Black people. Their position as an African people is a reality that they will have to attend to. This growing realization has allowed us to seek alliance with the American Black community and to appreciate the struggles that they have gone through.

Johnnie Stevens: There was a very large demonstration yesterday over attacks on immigrants. How did the Haitian community relate to that march?

Ray Laforest: Even as the community becomes adapted to the reality here, it is still impacted tremendously by what is happening in Haiti. The Haitian masses were united in getting rid of the dictatorship and the Duvaliers, a large majority supported the Lavalas movement and Aristide but they are splintered now, with people settling in and dealing with daily problems, a whole range of issues. It is much more difficult to bring out the community over specific issues.

One of the consequences . is that an organization like RADDI, *Rasanbleman ayisyen pou defann dwa imigran*, [Haitian Mobilization to Defend Immigrant Rights] which was quite a radical group, is defunct. To take me as an example, I am still active in the Haitian community but I am also involved in a media struggle with WBAI and Pacifica. While this is a tool that is very necessary for progressives and working people, and would benefit every community, including the Haitian community, it keeps me from dedicating myself to the Haitian community the way I used to.

But the Haitian community is still a very radical community with a long history of struggle and it fights very strongly for change.

Crushing Victory for Aristide
Despite Bazin's maneuvers

December 19 to 24, 1990

Haïti-Progrès Staff
translated by Greg Dunkel

> — *The struggle is just beginning because imperialism does not like the example of a people liberating themselves.*

The people did not wait for all the official results before they showed their joy. Convinced that from now on they will have Aristide as president, even though the proclamation won't come for several days, "Lavalas" poured into the streets of the capital [Port-au-Prince] by the hundreds of thousands, people of all ages, waving branches, singing, and dancing with an indescribable enthusiasm. An extraordinary mass phenomenon and one which shows to what point the people, so often presented as ragged, illiterate and backward, have the desire to live in dignity and independence, and are politically conscious.

Indeed, this wasn't drunkenness and carnival, no more than it was a simple march. It was the celebration of an immense victory, a victory which left the entire world dumb struck. Because once again Haiti had succeeded in astonishing the world by undoing all the plans, all the plots without help from the outside. An unimaginable euphoria with chants like "Nou te vote kòkman, nou genyen lavalsman" [we voted roosterly (Aristide's election symbol), we won Lavalasly] or "kòk la beke, kòk la beke Bazin, li beke makout" [The rooster pecked, the rooster pecked Bazin, it pecked the Macoutes].

There was a lot of "pawòl piman" [sharp words] against Bazin, such as "Yo volè bilten mwen, yo vote pou Bazin" [They stole my ballot, they voted for Bazin], Aristide's victory also being revenge on the lackeys of imperialism.

When the first partial results were released by the CEP (Provisional Election Council) on Dec. 17, enthusiasm and joy knew a new high point. According to these results, based on 27,227 voters in the

Northeast, South, West and Center, Aristide had 70.6% of the vote and Bazin 12.6%, with the other candidates having very minor tallies. Still according to the partial results released Dec. 18, the enormous difference between the two principal rivals, Aristide and Bazin, continued to hold. On the countrywide level, the distance between the two—according to the last partial results—is 54.35 %. If there are still some changes, they will not be enough to reverse the results—the tidal wave in favor of Aristide foretells the triumph of this electoral campaign.

Confronted with such a situation, what can the United States do?
"All the official counts of the observers indicate that Fr. Aristide is the clear winner in the first round," declared Bernard Aronson, deputy secretary of state for Inter-American Affairs. "We congratulated him on his victory and told him that the United States supported the democratic process." (New York Times, Dec. 18, 1990) Aronson was part of the official delegation sent to Haiti by the Bush government. As for Jimmy Carter, at a press conference held at the El Rancho Hotel December 17, 1990, he judged that the elections had been free and the outcome believable. "I saw much enthusiasm, joy and gaiety among the Haitian people. It is very rare that this occurs anywhere in the world." Even the UN and OAS observers echoed his sentiments. Joao de Médicis—the personal representative of the secretary general of the UN—said, "We are satisfied that the people had the chance to vote; there have been some material difficulties but in our opinion these difficulties did not at all affect the results."

According to Radio Métropole, the French parliamentarians sent as observers judged that "the election in Haiti was carried out in a correct and dignified fashion," that "the results of the election are incontestable ... clear, transparent and trustworthy" and that "it should be respected by everyone." Finally, the Caribbean Church Mission "declared itself impressed by the lucidity of men and women in rural areas, who, though often illiterate, could vote nearly without difficulty using five ballots." (Haitian Press Agency, Dec. 18, 1990)

The major U.S. press also yielded. The New York Times of December 18, 1990, pronounced that Aristide had been elected in "a crushing fashion" and benefited from "enthusiastic support." Besides the news articles, an editorial appeared recognizing the long struggle of the Haitian people. "Neither the failed elections nor the military coup d'etats have extinguished their conviction that they must also have the right to exercise democracy as others do."

These are some beautiful concessions—one could almost believe that the U.S. government itself had become a devotee of democracy when its official delegation declared: "In the name of President Bush and the American people, we congratulate the Haitian people on the success of the first round of their general elections. ... The vote was free and credible." However, one cannot be naïve and take these congratulations for ready money. The United States did not suddenly convert to true democracy, but they have been impressed and they reported that it was impossible to go against this tidal wave not only because it would be too scandalous, but because the Haitian people's response could only be suppressed by a gigantic blood bath.

That did not keep the U.S. from resorting to all sorts of underhanded maneuvers. Thanks to Antoine Izméry, a member of the group *Onè Respe pou Konstitisyon* (Honor and Respect the Constitution) who denounced them, we have proof that Carter engaged in all sorts of maneuvers to benefit Bazin. Bazin had based his whole presidential campaign for president on co-optation and the power of money. He didn't miss a chance through his henchmen to engage in manipulation and fraud.

The struggle is just beginning because imperialism does not like the example of a people liberating themselves. In the context of Latin America where it is commonplace for elections to be manipulated to look like they are democratic, the case of Haiti is even more unusual. But the people have demonstrated that they have what it takes to effectively pursue the struggle: lucidity, vigilance, determination, the desire to live free and independent and not be subjected to puppets like Bazin.

For the Caribbean and Latin American people, for people all over the world, this victory gives a magnificent example and brings great consolation. Misery, repression, illiteracy, foreign interference, millions of dollars invested to manipulate and corrupt the people, all shredded and smashed. And this result is also reason for pride and joy for all the progressive militants who harvest today the fruits of long labor in politicizing the people. With redoubled energy, confidence and joy the popular organizations and all progressives are now going to roll up their shirt sleeves to get on to the second stage of the struggle: the realization of this "civilization of love" that Fr. Aristide proposes to build with the Haitian people.

Haïti-Progrès, December 19 to 24, 1990

Carter Tries to Intimidate Aristide

December 19 to 24, 1990

Haïti-Progrès Staff
Translated by Paddy Colligan

When the U.S. pretended to applaud the Aristide victory and to congratulate the Haitian people today, didn't they give him a Judas kiss, considering all the maneuvering they had done to steal the election victory? One of the main figures orchestrating this plot was none other than Jimmy Carter, who has reinvented himself as a globetrotter going around the world wherever there are elections and guaranteeing victory to the Balaguers or the Endaras. In Haiti, he would have been quite happy to see Bazin, the protégé on the U.S. payroll for many years, carry off the victory. He did all he could to ensure this. Antoine Izméry, member of the group *Onè Respe pou Konstitisyon*, [Honor and Respect the Constitution] spells out precisely how Carter did this in an interview he gave to us on December 18, 1990.

"Sunday afternoon (Election Day)," he reported, "from 3:00 to 5:00 PM, the entire Carter delegation met with Aristide. From the way they spoke, they made it seem like Aristide was going to lose and they wanted him to promise that he would order the people not to go into the streets (. . .) Little was made of the fact that this was highly irregular." Earlier Izméry had noted that there were rumors going around, particularly in Miami, that Bazin would be the next president.

Then, according to Carter['s plan], in the middle of Election Day, with crowds of people lining up before polling places, Aristide was already supposed to admit defeat. Can you imagine such arrogance and such interference on the part of a man charged with supervising a delegation of election observers?

When Izméry became aware of this, he did not remain idle but immediately went to the El Rancho Hotel, where the delegation was staying, so he could speak with Carter in person. When Izméry arrived, all the members of the group had left. "I had Carter informed," Izméry continued, "that he would have to take responsibility for the bloodbath which might take place the day after Bazin became president in the wake of this skullduggery that he was managing. And then I had a drink and waited for Carter to return with his team." Some journalists arrived, among them one from the Washington Post, who knew Izméry and to whom he told this development. "He took some notes," Izméry relates, and then he said to me, 'Antoine, McNamara is right there. Let me talk with him. Is that a problem for you?' I said, 'Not at all.' When he told it to McNamara (former president of the World Bank and secretary of defense under Kennedy), all hell broke lose. They did not want that reported by the press. It was then 8:30 or 9:00. Then, one after another, each member of Carter's team came to see me. (. . .). They asked me why I was making such a statement, all the while saying that it was not true, that they wanted to help us, etc."

Antoine Izméry said he was interviewed by Jim Wright, former member of Congress; Andrew Young, former ambassador to the UN and former mayor of Atlanta; Robert Pastor, an academic from Atlanta, and some people whose names he did not know—at least five people—all but Carter and McNamara. He was told that he had misunderstood, that it was a question of language and other things like that to calm him down. But Izméry stuck to his position, using the examples of the Dominican Republic as well as Panama where—he said—it was only the Canal that the U.S. wanted to defend. "I gave them several examples of this and I told Andrew Young not to forget why he had been fired from his position at the UN—simply for meeting with Arafat."

Izméry refused to deny his statement to the Washington Post journalist and the only promise which he made was that he would call him and tell him the version held by the Carter delegation "but," he specified, "this would take nothing away from what I said before." Izméry, people know, has the habit of crossing his t's and dotting his i's and is not easily impressed, but you can also see how he was scandalized by Carter's attitude.

So, there it is—Carter had quite simply decided that Aristide ought to fade away and he was doing his best to intimidate him with that arrogance typical of the United States. Afterwards he realized the scale of his blunder and tried to minimize it, making excuses. But in light of the experiences with Carter in the elections in many countries, we cannot doubt that he wanted to get Bazin through. The case of the Dominican Republic, so close to home, is very much alive in the minds of the

Haitians because each of them knows that Carter approved the election of Balaguer, a disciple of Trujillo.

The frustration of the United States is understandable—after investing millions of dollars in him, constructing his image and promoting him tirelessly for years, their protégé collapsed pitifully at the finish line. Fine words are good but they also serve to sap the vigilance of the Haitian people and that is extremely important. On December 16 Haiti gave a very good example of democracy to the whole world by acting like a civilized and responsible people. In exchange, the U.S. with their flood of "observers," who said they came to give support, did not even have the patience to wait until the end of the voting before resorting to dishonorable maneuvers to block the road to democracy. Like Father Aristide said, the Haitian people wants very much to have friendly relations with the U.S., but with one extremely important condition: that there is mutual respect and complete equality between the two parties.

Haïti-Progrès, December 19 to 24, 1990

Aristide: The People's Candidate

— Operation Lavalas barricades the road against the macoutes

October 24-30, 1990

Haïti-Progrès Staff
Translated by Greg Dunkel

Even while arousing an immense enthusiasm among the people, Aristide's candidacy has raised certain questions among militants in popular organizations. In an interview with us October 22, 1990, Fr. Aristide once again clarified the reasons for his decision to run and at the same time to unleash "Operation Lavalas."

(This interview was translated from Creole by Haïti-Progrès.)

Haïti-Progrès: October 18, you announced you were a people's candidate and said you had entered this battle to advance the struggle. That is why you had decided to be a candidate. Could you clear up what this means for you?

Fr. Aristide: For me, who never had the foolish desire to be a candidate and who is now the people's candidate, this means:

1. To accept putting the people's will over mine because if mine determined what was happening, I would not be the people's candidate today. So I recognize that I have been given a lesson in democracy.

2. For someone like me who has the Christian faith and who in particular usually celebrated mass at St. Jean Bosco, who had lived the mystery of the sacrifice into which Jesus entered for the deliverance of mankind, today I confront a sacrifice not only of my faith but of my entire body. It is not me who will deliver the country, it is the entire

country which will deliver itself. But just as we have arrived at a historic rendezvous, where this sacrifice is necessary, I have consented to make it.

Besides, I've already been dead since Freycineau, since September 11[1]; since then, life has only given me a reprieve, a gift. Thus, why shouldn't I give the rest of my life?

3. I accept the reasoning of those who refuse to participate in elections; it is reasoning which is correct in essence because elections are still an arm used by the ruling classes to maintain the same class relations, consequently the same system of exploitation. This type of elections is fixed, the great majority of people are excluded from them and if the impression of change is given, it is only cosmetic change, makeup, without the essence being changed.

So, this candidacy is in a context where I say to myself: Asking for Lafontant's [2] arrest, for security, demanding the rope of justice be placed around the criminals' necks so we can participate in the elections didn't start today. But it is for this very reason that the enemy put Lafontant in play and let him hold his arrogant convention at Vertaillis[3], so that we would be still angrier and we would not participate in the elections. They want the world to believe that we, the Haitian people, participated in elections in order to have the Macoutes return. Before such unparalleled impertinence, the Haitian people must be aware that they must play their ace of trump, since the Macoutes have played theirs. Avril[4] was their previous ace and now Lafontant has replaced him.

So our strategy is not to promote their elections but to convert the elections into a flood, an "Operation Lavalas" to barricade the road against the Macoutes. Leaving from there, organization is indispensable, it is necessary that the revolutionary energy released by this social phenomenon be converted into organizational energy so that we can keep the reins of the movement in hand. So what we want—a country where people will be truly human—can emerge.

Haïti-Progrès: Some popular organizations, which are still your allies, feel that you have betrayed them by announcing your participation in the elections. Have you changed strategies or have your tactics been modified to arrive at your initial aim: a thoroughly complete change in Haiti?

Fr. Aristide: It is my tactics that have changed. If I had changed my line or camp, if I had abandoned the camp of the people, I would merit a good "Père Lebrun"[5]. I said it in Brooklyn and I say it again: The day I betray the people, give me a "Père Lebrun." If I had set up as a candidate and played the same game as those competing for the conquest of power, that would have been extremely grave. However, if beyond such an emotional reaction, we make a calm analysis, we will realize that the best way to achieve the goal we set ourselves is to employ this tactic.

This reaction is normal and besides I should say that it is not easy to take such a decision. It is only after many reflections and much analysis, after many prayers and much listening that I opted for such a tactic. I do not think that it is in contradiction with the objective I pursue.

The popular organizations have the right to criticize it, and severe and rigorous critiques are needed in the struggle. In addition, militants going in the same direction are not obliged to see things in the same way. Revolutionary tolerance must be practiced. Even when the tactic is seen as not contrary to the aim sought, we can still disapprove of certain ways of acting but no one can pretend to own the truth. In the struggle we also discover that the masses often are not necessarily at the same level of analysis. If we go too quickly, we leave them behind. Even if our analysis is correct in connection with reality, it possibly might not be the lever for mobilization that we need. We think that this tactic constitutes a lever for mobilization that makes the flood grow. Now our task is to enrich it, to complete it in a fashion so that the enemy does not benefit from it but we can harvest the fruits of our work.

Haïti-Progrès: Fr. Aristide, in the course of the press conference that you held, you said that this "flood" could be realized through elections or outside of them. Can you make what you mean by that clear to us?

Fr. Aristide: We are responsible people, we do not see a way to take power in elections while forgetting about all the rest. If we increase our resources and our capacity to augment the flood, we will be stronger in quantity and quality. And if we see at a certain time the enemy wants to create a blood bath at any price, the same authority which permits us to orient the Lavalas will permit us to remain outside the elections and to reject them entirely. *Pitou nou rejete l nèt si nou pa kapab pran l nèt* [we prefer to reject them completely if we cannot win them completely]

But if we can decisively carry the elections, then we will do it. We thus need to simply follow the evolution of things while re-enforcing our organization at the same time to be in control of the situation. It is a battle; we can't foresee exactly when we will have to stand up—a minute and a second after noon or 3 am. That depends on the fashion we control things on the ground.

Haïti-Progrès: You have said you are the candidate of the people. What do you mean by this since we know that it is the FNCD, the MOP and the PPNH which have chosen Fr. Aristide as their candidate?[6]

Fr. Aristide: By claiming their choice, these parties reflect other calls which come to me from nearly everywhere; they are conscious that the most important of these calls is not a candidate for their profit but a symbolic candidate which permits them to arrive at a united strategy in order to let loose the "flood," so that each candidate does not drag a small group behind him, so that they do not drink the soup of elections with a fork of division. Because in that case, the Macoutes will mark "twenty points" on us [that is, will win, *trans.*]

In this sense, I am conscious that it is the FNCD on a legal level which has made me a candidate, assumed the responsibility of choosing me and supplied very significant cooperation so that it wasn't just other organizations as well as parties that were in agreement. In that case, I would have had their consent but that would not have given me legal status. From then on, it was a *konbit tèt ansanm*, a united work cooperative that is in the process of forming the better to unleash the "flood." In that sense, I believe that is really a fine proof of openness, of understanding, of listening in the movement. We need to continue organizing ourselves in this fashion so gradually we recover the large united current which cut across Feb. 7.[7] We must not let it disperse if we are to get a better future for Haiti.

Haïti-Progrès: In the popular sector, some still say that the bourgeoisie collapsed Feb. 7, that they got us Namphy and Ertha Trouillot and that today, since you have been endorsed by the Convergence Démocratique and some other sectors, that now they have launched you.[8] What do you think of such an opinion?

Fr. Aristide: In the first place, I respect an opinion which is not mine. That does not mean that I share it, no more than I reject it *a* *priori*. On the basis of this respect, I adopt an attitude of dialog and I try to do it without pre-judgment, since I am perhaps not entirely correct. Each of us can have part of the truth and dialog can permit us to complete it. So I don't have a problem with people who talk like that. I would display an ideological arrogance if I were to accept rejecting an opinion without respecting those who are disposed to dialog with me. That would be the attitude of a dictator.

However, if your mother is sick and fading, before you ask yourself if you are going to give her some ginger or cinnamon, you look around to try to get her back. After that, you search for a doctor, then what medicine to give her. Things are done in stages and this is also true in the revolutionary struggle. We are currently in the first stage; Haiti, like a mother, is fading into the arms of Lafontant. This tactic has served to wake up her children to see how to deal with the question. This way of seeing things is in contradiction with certain militants for whom it is a form of demobilization. Perhaps they did not understand or hear what I said, or perhaps I did not sufficiently dialog with them, if indeed our divergences appear as total opposition. I believe that in a struggle, different approaches are necessary. From the moment when we have the same vision and are moving in the same sense, that must open into the capacity to respect certain differences which are not in essence contradictory.

At the same time, I believe in God and I cannot put my faith aside to make politics, replace politics by my faith or my faith by politics; one meets the other. When the prophet Isaiah preached in the city of Jerusalem on social corruption and he saw that the people were not paying attention to his words, he ripped off his pants, shorts and shirt, then totally nude, he marched through the city of Jerusalem. People then wondered what was happening and he said: Oh! You see me now, and he explained the causes of his act. I do not say this to neglect the political dimensions to the profit of the prophetic dimension. But I also believe that plain politics can benefit at a certain moment from prophecy, because reality is complex, dynamic, total. Reality is not just politics without other aspects. That is the dialectic of a struggle and the tactic chosen can raise diverse interpretations. I think that when each of us is conscious of only having a part of the truth but not the entire truth—even if we were to have it entirely—we would live in a very interesting country.

Haïti-Progrès: If I understand it, it is a tactical alliance which is necessary to block the Macoutes who are surging with Roger Lafontant?

Fr. Aristide: Exactly. In Nicaragua, at a certain moment, there was a tactical alliance. Before the final battle, Commandant "Zero" was in a similar position. After July '79, he found himself in another. What was the social origin of Commandant "Zero" and so many others? No matter, it is to recognize the moment when history gives us the conjuncture for a tactical alliance. Today, this alliance must be converted into an "Operation Lavalas" to block the return of Duvalierism, which would be negative for those who are very revolutionary, those who are a little less revolutionary and those who are not revolutionary but desire change. And so the tactical alliance is positive for all.

Haïti-Progrès, October 24-30, 1990

Notes

1) At Freycinau, just south of St. Marc, Father Aristide barely escaped death in a roadway ambush by Macoutes in August 1987. On Sept. 11, 1988, Macoutes attacked his church, St. Jean Bosco, in the capital's La Saline slum while he was giving mass. Twelve were killed and 77 wounded. Held at gun point, Aristide barely escaped again.

2) Roger Lafontant, former head of the Tonton Macoutes and a minister during the Duvalier dictatorship, was a candidate in the 1990 presidential elections.

3) Duvalierists of all stripes, vowing to regain political power in Haiti, held a convention in October 1990 at the Vertaillis Night Club.

4) Gen. Prosper Avril, the eminence grise of the Duvalier regime, came to power in a military coup in September 1988 but popular uprisings forced him to flee Haiti in March 1990.

5) Père Lebrun was a colorful tire salesman in the capital, whose name become synonymous with "necklacing." After the Macoutes committed some terrible act, like the Sept. 11 St. Jean Bosco massacre, angry crowds counterattacked by killing one of the perpetrators and setting his body ablaze with flaming tires.

6) Front National pour le Changement et la Démoctatie, Mouvement pour l'Organisation du Pays, Parti Populaire National Haitien were three bourgeois, populist parties.

7) Feb. 7, 1986, was the date Jean-Claude "Baby Doc" Duvalier left for France on a U.S. Air Force plane.

8) Gen. Henri Namphy was head of the military government after Duvalier; Ertha Pascal-Trouillot was provisional president from March 1990 to February 1991. The Convergence démocratique in 1990, which is not the same group as the Washington-backed opposition front with the same name founded in 2000, was a grouping of liberal bourgeois parties and groups.

Part III

After the Coup

Exile Is Stale Bread

Paul Laraque

exile is stale bread
a sour orange
it's a withered plant
a cursed fig tree

exile is bitter coffee
curdled milk
a rotten avocado
a mango full of worms

exile is washing your hands
and wiping them on the ground
trading garbage for dust
trading rain for snow
trading a snare for a trap

exile's a vulture
a little demon on a treacherous road
a werewolf in broad daylight
exile's a shark in the sea

exile is prison
Malis* gets political asylum
but Bouki's an economic refugee
exile's a concentration camp

exile without you would be hell
you pulled me from the mouth of despair
in the cold you bring fire
you're the light in the darkness

* In Haitian oral literature, Bouki represents the masses and Malis, the elite.

The Real Objectives of the Occupation

Sept. 21-27, 1994

Ben Dupuy

When Bill Clinton gave a talk on television September 15, 1994, in order to justify the invasion of Haiti by the United States, he only had one word to say: *dictator.* The "dictators of Haiti" must leave, he said, because they have committed too many terrible deeds. "The dictators have launched an intimidating terror campaign with rape, tortures and mutilation. Some people have died from hunger. Children have perished. Thousands of Haitians have left the country, headed for the United States through dangerous waters." Clinton did not stop there, describing in detail the "reign of terror" which exists in Haiti, with children being killed, women being raped and priests killed.

What can be done then to end "the nightmare of such a carnage" except to send troops to force the dictators to leave, since, according to the president of the United States, "we have tried everything, persuasion and negotiation, mediation and condemnation"? And "it is necessary to be clear, only Gen. Cédras and his accomplices are responsible for these sufferings and this terrible human tragedy. It is their actions which have isolated Haïti."

A simplistic speech for a public conditioned to interpret political reality according to a prefabricated schema, even more when it is a question of a Third World country. After Panama, where the North American intervention supposedly had as an objective to do away with Noriega, a dangerous drug trafficker, after Somalia where it was necessary to drive away the "warlords," headed by General Aidid, now it's the "troika of dictators" whom the devoted Americans want to remove from power in Haiti. Who could be against such a good deed?

Even more since Aristide himself could not be more in agreement with it. And in a symbolic fashion, he made it known directly from the White House, thanking Clinton for his "historic statement." "In understanding our suffering," he continued, addressing the North American president directly, "you nourish a grand hope, the hope for peace, the hope of reconciliation." To believe Aristide, this will occur because "the prompt and determined action by the international community through Resolution 940 will lead us rapidly toward a climate of peace with the approach of legislative elections in December."

It is the classic *happy ending*: once the gang of putschists is eliminated, the army will buckle down to reconstruct the country and in a climate of harmony among all the reconciled sectors will prepare itself for the passing of power to a new president in 1995. Indeed, Clinton said in his speech and Aristide was anxious to repeat: Democracy will only be truly installed after the second elections, another way of saying after the departure of Aristide himself.... . Such is the idyllic vision presented to us, which in particular the Lavalas bourgeoisie maintains. Its thesis is summarized as: it's not that we really want an intervention but there is no other alternative, it is the only way to make the putschists leave. In the U.S. media—particularly on television—this thesis is translated with few nuances into the propaganda that the Haitian community is practically 100 per cent in accord with the North American intervention.

As a consequence, popular support is imparted to what in reality is precisely directed **against the Haitian people,** the true target of the United States. As we have already underlined on several occasions, this is much less an intervention than a **prolonged military occupation by the United States** to definitely break the popular movement.

Haitians must not think "that they can do what they want"

This is what the journal The Nation, well-known in the United States, just showed in a striking fashion in an article called "The Eagle is landing." Its author, Allan Nairn, has specialized in covering the operations of the United States in Latin America and Asia since 1980, which says he knows a great deal about all their secret actions and other maneuvers to dominate the peoples of the Third World. Nairn put forward an analysis of the plan presented by the legitimate government to its foreign lenders in Paris last August 26 as nothing more than a new version of the "American plan" (see Haïti-Progrès, September 14-20, 1994).

The central idea of this article is the following: If the United States intends to occupy Haiti, it is because that appears to be the best, indeed the only, way to definitively smash the guts of the popular movement.

> According to documents and extensive conversations with U.S. military and intelligence planners, no matter how Lieut. Gen. Raoul Cedras is removed—through invasion, coup or deal—the United States intends to contain Haiti's popular movement, by force if necessary. The objective, in the words of one U.S. Army Psychological Operations official, is to see to it that Haitians "don't get the idea that they can do whatever they want." (Nation, 10/3/94, Vol. 259, Issue 10)

That's it, the real reason for the occupation, what has appeared to the United States as the gravest danger and has guided their action since the development of the popular movement in 1985-86: the fact that the Haitian people are threatening to escape from their control, and, to a degree, have succeeded.

We know that, if the United States favored the fall of Jean-Claude Duvalier, it was to block a radicalization of the popular movement, or, in the words of Col. Steven Butler, "who helped do it," it was "an attempt to stave off 'massive internal uprisings.'" Without that the United States would have had no problem supporting Duvalier

> even though, according to Butler, U.S. radar had detected that his ranch was being used to run cocaine into the United States. Only when it looked as if the populace might sweep the system aside did Washington decide that he had to go. (Nation, op. cit.)

Since then, the United States has attempted to control Haiti by putting some new structures in place because there has been a certain emptiness at that level after the fall of Baby Doc. That explains why Col. Butler says:

> "In that year and a half to two years after Duvalier fell, things were in such a flux. Democracy, freedom, people were suddenly publishing—writing in Creole for the first time— everybody was very enthusiastic, and really thought something was going to change, and so there were a lot of strange people coming and going, and we didn't know who they were. And nobody had a handle on it, particularly in the outback, because the Tonton Macoutes had had total control in the interior and now they were gone." (Nation, op. cit.)

The Macoutes also had a handle on the network of informers and telephone taps. The army then turned toward the United States.

> But Congress blocked the requested aid, and the CIA moved
> in, quickly filling the vacuum by creating Haiti's National
> Intelligence Service, or SIN, ostensibly an anti-narcotics
> group, which watched and attacked Haitian dissidents. (Na-
> tion, op. cit.)

That has already been denounced and we know that the SIN, re-
cruiting some notorious military Macoutes, received between $500,000
and $1 million a year to sow terror and eliminate the opposition. We
also know that people like Cédras and Michel François as well as a
number of FRAPH leaders have been directly trained by the United
States, as Allan Nairn underlines:

> The CIA, for example, ran a course for Haitian operatives,
> which, according to Haitian officials, was taught by two white
> North Americans and included instruction in surveillance,
> interrogation and weaponry. The point of training is simply
> efficiency; what matters is the mission. Today, the CIA is
> beefing up its Haiti station, bringing in more operatives and
> recruiting new Haitian assets. (Nation, op. cit.)

We see in what fashion the United States applied themselves between 1986 and 1990 to put in place new structures permitting them at
the same time to infiltrate, control and dismantle the popular movement. But in order to make this viable in the long term, they would
need a strong political authority, a Bazin who would serve as a screen
for the army and a performer for the United States. A plan which the
election of Aristide had stymied. Now that the backbone of the popular
movement had been broken after three years, it was necessary to go
further and assure long-term control of the country. They knew that the
occupation could not be as warmly applauded as they pretended.

> One U.S. Psy Ops official who specializes in Haiti predicts
> that, if there is an invasion, initially people will cheer the
> ouster of Cedras, but that "anti-U.S. sentiment"—indeed,
> popular attacks on U.S. forces—could be expected within a
> four week period. This would be less likely if Aristide were
> to come back fast, but even then, he said, the danger of up-
> rising would remain if popular expectations were not met
> soon. (Nation, op. cit.)

But these expectations can only be disappointed since the occupation has no intention of responding to them, all the while giving itself

new means to block any revolt. In the eyes of the Special Operations officer, to do that, the methods are simple:

> "You publicize that you're simply not going to tolerate that kind of stuff." With regard to mass demonstrations, an intelligence official said: "Simple. You don't let it happen. There is no such thing as a demonstration while you're there." (Nation, op. cit.)

Very simple indeed: you prohibit and you repress. That's all. This is the return of democracy under the aegis of the North American army. And that was indeed what was being planned with the putschists, because while the "last chance mission" occupied the front burner of the political scene, the occupation was actively being prepared.

> The occupation scenarios being discussed involve elements from the very Haitian armed forces and police who are today the ostensible U.S. adversary. These scenarios also include faces familiar from earlier U.S. assaults on Panama, El Salvador, Nicaragua and Guatemala, as well as such familiar tactics as suppression of demonstrations, activation of U.S. intelligence contacts within rightist paramilitary fronts, mass detention of civilians and the tapping of political data banks. (Nation, op. cit.)

That's what awaits us: a large scale repression led jointly by the North American troops, their intelligence services and their local employees from the Haitian army and police. And, as Nairn notes, the occupation troops of the first phase are designated to withdraw in the weeks or the months following the departure of Cédras.

> ... a host of U.S. military, CIA and civilian advisers are slated to stay behind, participating in Haitian affairs more deeply than they have in years. ICITAP [U.S. Department of Justice's International Criminal Investigative Training Assistance Program] for example, the U.S. agency assigned to rebuild the Haitian police, is due, according to its chief Haiti planner, to stay for three years, bringing in several hundred U.S. trainers to mold a 5,000-man Haitian force. (Nation, op. cit.)

Police designated above all to break any attempt at revolt or insurrection, as one of the Pentagon planners of the occupation said. Patrols comprised of both North American troops and Haitian police, according to him, will "probably be used to maintain order in the event that 'somebody from the hills decides to start an insurgency.'" For this control at all levels, whether a popular demonstration or a general insurrection, adequate supplies are necessary.

> A U.S. contractor who works for the State Department said that the naval task force now standing off Haiti has replaced its stocks of anti-armor weaponry with crowd-control gear including shields, gas masks and clubs. He said fears were running high in Haiti about the possibility of U.S. troops confronting organized slum dwellers, an encounter that would have "obvious consequences" for the unarmed Haitians. (Nation, op. cit.)

That's what the United States came to fight: the people who live in Cité Soleil, Raboteau and other popular neighborhoods, who can only revolt against their "saviors" when they quickly become frustrated seeing what the "return to democracy" means. And shields and gas masks are evidently very useful to struggle against the "people" in collaboration with the Macoute soldiers who have acquired a lot of experience over the past three years which they will have the pleasure of transmitting to their bosses from overseas. Besides, what could be the objective of the occupation if not to come to the aid of the Haitian army to reaffirm the power of the dominant "elite" who collaborated so well in the overthrow of Aristide.

> One veteran intelligence officer said that an early priority for occupying forces should be to establish comfort for "the people who would feel protected by us: the middle class, the U.S. educated, some of the business community"—those who live up on the hills above the privation of Port-au-Prince. (Nation, op. cit.)

Aristide charged with helping the occupiers
To put it in plain language, it is necessary to abolish everything in the Lavalas movement left over from its beginnings, which has a popular, anti-Macoute and anti-imperialist character. Only a foreign occupation will permit the authority of a ruling class tied to the United States to be installed. Such is the reasoning of the United States which only intends to reestablish President Aristide in power—at least—formally to better arrive at this objective. All things considered, it is Aristide himself who by giving the green light to foreign intervention

will have best served the designs of the United States.

In this sense, Aristide is in no way an obstacle because, on the one hand, it is thought—in particular by the intelligence officer already cited—that his "old reformist economic program had now passed into history and would probably not be permitted to be revived." On the other hand, his presence on the scene is seen by some as the best way of blocking the people from revolting.

> Although one senior Pentagon planner says that "the sooner we can get Aristide in there to give his message of reconciliation and law and order, the better off we'll all be," others are uncertain about whether he will play ball but note that, regardless, he won't really be in charge. The Psy Ops official, for one, says that, under occupation, much of the Haitian military/administrative infrastructure will transfer its loyalty to the new "gwoneg (`big man')," meaning "whoever is setting the rules." And "the new big man," he says, "would be the United States." (Nation, op. cit.)

Thus, President Aristide is used essentially in two ways: one as a pretext for foreign occupation; the other as a way to block any popular resistance. The United States got their victim, the one whose mandate they practically wasted in exile, to collaborate with this *tour de force*. Their plan for "reconciliation" is nothing more than submission to Macoutism. Aristide lends himself to this with fervor, because reconciliation is his leitmotif, reconciliation with the assassins and torturers of the army, those who rape young women and kill children to the great scandal of Clinton. This shows up in flagrant fashion in the speech Aristide gave September 16, 1994, at the White House where he justified the amnesty granted to the putschists, which will be "part of the reconciliation and of the process of reconstruction" on this basis.

Later in his speech, addressing the army directly, he opened his arms:

> Members of the military, we will create jobs for you. You will not be isolated. You are the sons of the land, the nation's citizens. Stop the violence. Do not be afraid. We say no to vengeance, we say no to retaliation. Again and again, day after day, we will continue saying no to vengeance, no to retaliation. Let us embrace peace. When? Now. Is it too late? No, the time is now. The restoration of democracy will bring peace for all, reconciliation among all, respect and justice for every single citizen.

And he repeated once again his tedious refrain, dictated by his tutors:

> Stop the violence. Do not be afraid. We say, and we will be
> saying again and again, no to vengeance, no to retaliation.
> Let us embrace peace. When? Now. Is it too late? No. The
> time is now. (New York Times, Sept. 17, 1994)

To whom is this talk directed if not to those responsible for the thousands of assassinations, which have taken placed since September 30, 1991. Without counting the disappearances, tortures, rapes and other horrors impossible to itemize. Without any equivocation, Aristide guarantees that nothing will happen to them. Provided they stop their massacres, they will be welcomed with open arms and if they can't be kept in the army, they shouldn't be afraid—jobs will be found as well as a host of other compensations. This is besides what was explicitly presented to Haiti's lenders in the plan we discussed above. In these conditions, we understand why some people prefer the rapid return of Aristide so that, using his authority, he will help the occupation troops control the people. Even if he might not be prepared for that, he could not present a danger—if it is true that he returns—because he will be totally at the mercy of the occupiers who control the entire situation.

In the case of Panama, by example and according to "the official inquiry into the occupation" of this country, it was planned from the outset that the U.S. army govern de facto through the Southern Command. At the last minute, it was decided to install Guillermo Endara as president, but

> his government was, as the Pentagon study put it, "merely a
> facade." Beyond formalities for the public, the U.S. military
> task force "found that it had no choice but [to] lead the Gov-
> ernment of Panama." A U.S. general had a desk in Endara's
> office and was patched into the President's radio communi-
> cations network. (Nation, op. cit.)

Such is the role that will be forced on President Aristide and he will be incapable of opposing it, if he would ever want to. In addition, the popular movement will be at first plunged into a certain confusion by the guarantees granted by Aristide to the occupation. This is emphasized by Major Louis Kernisan, an American of Haitian origin, who after being an attaché to the U.S. embassy in Haiti from 1989 to 1991, is now part of the Defense Intelligence Agency (DIA) and was one of the key planners of the occupation of Haiti.

"Popular uprising? Under the watchful eye of 6,000 or 7,000 international observers? I doubt it. This is only the kind of shit they've been able to get away with when there is no-body watching.... They tried that before and it brought them two years of embargo and their little guy in golden exile in the States." (Nation, op. cit.)

It must be said that in Kernisan, the United States has found an individual more royalist than the king; according to him, the occupation 1915-1934 "clearly benefited the island in a number of respects." Aristide displeases the royalist in him because his government at the beginning had a popular character. In particular, he objects to the abolition of the "section chiefs" because "Without them, 'rural populations [were] left to police themselves.'" No question of allowing such a thing, not even some rise in workers' salaries, because, according to the well-known logic, which the intelligence officer cited above also supports, "You've got to take advantage of what asset you have, and in Haiti that happens to be cheap labor."

The reign of populism is truly finished and what is being sketched out is a jolt towards an "authoritarian right" like the one in El Salvador. In Haiti, it is—as we have already said—FRAPH which will assume this role; FRAPH is a terrorist group which has been identified as a creation of the United States. Besides one of its leaders is particularly appreciated. According to a North American intelligence analyst, if "Jodel Chamblain is a cold-blooded assassin, a psychopathic killer," Emmanuel (Toto) Constant is, on the other hand, "a young pro-western intellectual ... no more to the right than a young Republican; in the United States, he would be considered as center right." In this case, does he have a promising political future? It is very possible, because while FRAPH was first utilized as an instrument of terror, now FRAPH is going to give itself a more alluring cover and the North American intelligence official who presents such a flattering image of Constant, thinks that the U.S. could very easily work with him. He has "even divulged that, contrary to Washington's public posture, U.S. intelligence 'encouraged' Constant to form what emerged as FRAPH." Thanks to which the popular movement was able to be severely weakened.

Some U.S. officials say that though they are prepared to rein in the popular movement, its capacity for frontal resistance has been hurt by the winnowing terror of the armed

forces and the FRAPH. The Psy Ops man says that through
spies and "demonstration killings," the "military has tried
to atomize society much the way that Pinochet did in
Chile.... they've largely destroyed civil society ... ." (Nation, op. cit.)

More than ever, the only thing left to do is to finish the work. That
task will be done not only by totally dismantling the popular movement but also by establishing what could be called a substitute "popular" movement, one which works hand in hand with the United States
and financially depends on it.

This project has already been put into motion with the Integrated
Project for the Reinforcement of Democracy in Haiti (PIRED) created
by U.S. Agency for International Development June 1993 in order to
fabricate a "popular" movement controlled by the United States. It's
the same for the Human Rights Fund—which we considered in an
earlier article—which specializes in the human rights sector.

So there is no need to be astonished that in the past few months
some groups pretending to be "popular" have popped up. For example,
the PLANOP, Platform of Popular Organizations, has as its leader Jean
Nazaire Tide, formerly in "Wind From the Storm," who played a major
role in the destabilization of Aristide. PLANOP appears on the list of
those groups to be financed in the framework of PIRED.

This puts a strong emphasis on "the importance of an 'organized
civil society'" through socio-professional groups, unions, diverse as-
sociations, that being considered as "the key for any program for 'the
control of the populace.'" For this control, the United States already
has at its disposal a number of intelligence sources: the USAID possesses some of them "from its programs for financing and guiding
Haitian popular groups"; the Immigration and Naturalization Service
has computerized files on 58,000 Haitians who have requested political asylum. Finally, the intelligence branch of the U.S. army equally
has some "via the S-2 section of the 96th Civil Affairs Battalion, which
has been assigned to monitor the refugees at the Guantanamo Bay detention camp."

It has been confirmed that these refugees are closely watched by
spies and Macoutes in the service of the United States.

According to a report by Capt. James Vick of the 96th, who
also served in Panama and in Desert Storm, the unit devel-

ops "networks of informants" among the Haitian detainees and works with Marine Corps Counterintelligence in "identifying ringleaders of unrest and in weeding out troublemakers." According to Captain Vick, the Creole-speaking interpreters at the camps submit to daily debriefings which "yield ... an information harvest" on possible "destabilizing influences." (Nation, op. cit.)

A "close cooperation" between the U.S. army and the Haitian military

We say once again: everything has been used to assure the control and planned dismantlement of the popular movement. There have been: physical eliminations by the FRAPH under the orders of the United States; co-optation and recovery which are actively pursued, going hand in hand with infiltration and espionage, because it is certain that these "popular" groups born in the wake of the coup d'etat are manipulated by the CIA. Finally, those who tried to escape the repression, either by fleeing by boat or attempting to make an asylum request in Haiti, just wound up in their great majority in a U.S. file. Now, according to a memorandum by the North American ambassador, they are going to encourage and finance "responsible elements within the popular movement" as well as "moderate Duvalierist factions." All this is aimed at destroying what remains of combativity inside the country, the ultimate target of the occupation.

Major Kernisan says it as well with compelling logic:

> Who are we going to go back to save? You're going to end up dealing with the same folks as before, the five families that run the country, the military and the bourgeoisie. They're the same folks that are supposed to be the bad guys now, but the bottom line is you know that you're going to always end up dealing with them because they speak your language, they understand your system, they've been educated in your country. It's not going to be the slum guy from Cité Soleil. The best thing he can hope for is probably 'Oh, I'll help you offload your cargo truck.' Because that's all he has the capacity to do. It'll be the same elites, the bourgeoisie and the five families that run the country. (Nation, op. cit.)

Is it for this that the popular movement has struggled so hard since 1986? Is it for this that the Haitian people elected Father Aristide? Is it for this they have suffered so much for the past three years? What was presented as its deliverance was in fact the last knot to seal its definitive submission. How then can one dare to say that despite all it is the least bad solution and it will at least let the Haitian people be delivered from their principal oppressors?

What do a Cédras, a Biamby or a Michel François represent, when others who are exactly the same take up the baton, but this time directly under the supervision of the North American military having already proved themselves in Panama or Iraq? This collaboration has just been noted in black-and-white because in ex-president Jimmy Carter's infamous accord with the putschists it says that "to put this accord into effect, the police and Haitian military will work closely with the Military Mission of the United States." And further on, it makes reference to the coordination of activities of this Mission with "the Haitian military's high command," the same putschists whose so-called departure Aristide had demanded.

So in short, this occupation, so desired by the official sector of Lavalas and quasi-openly demanded by Aristide, is turning against him because it is with the putschists that the occupiers officially collaborate. And it is there where we see also how criminal—and we weigh our words—it was to let the community in the 10th Department (Haitians living outside of Haiti) and the Haitian people living inside Haiti believe that the occupation by the United States would permit the departure of the putschists and the return of President Aristide. It is in vain that the latter has debased himself until he turned into an Endara, the putschists are harvesting the fruits and the people are going to be the principal victims. It is also the logical conclusion of the coup d'etat, in which, as Allan Nairn says, the American eagle has just landed on its prey and is trying to annihilate all the gains won by the Haitian people through the hard struggle of these last years.

Haïti-Progrès, Sept. 21-27, 1994

Behind the U.S. Rhetoric on Haiti

Oct. 17, 1991

Sam Marcy

Whatever the imperialists do in Haiti, they do for themselves. Whenever they appear to do something progressive, it is either a sham or a concession wrested by the pressure of the masses.

The diplomatic corps of U.S. imperialism seem to be up to their necks in complex maneuvers to aid the restoration of Jean-Bertrand Aristide to his elected post as president of Haiti.

All this has been accompanied by florid rhetoric about the need to broaden "democracy" in the Western Hemisphere. In Bush's words, this would be possible because, "with the exception of Cuba," democracies have been gaining full control of their destinies in the Western Hemisphere.

It was only a week ago, on Oct. 1, that Bernard Aronson, U.S. assistant secretary of state for Inter-American Affairs, said the elections that brought Aristide to power "were held under unprecedented international supervision. The OAS and the UN both oversaw them. Therefore, they have a legitimacy not just in Haiti but internationally. So it is very important, in our point of view, that they be defended."

Why now the sudden shift in U.S. policy toward Haiti? The Bush administration is now concerned over Aristide's "human rights record." It has suddenly found out that Aristide was weak on defending the "human rights" of the Duvalierists. A great deal of prominence is being given to a move in the Haitian National Assembly to elect an interim president—not Aristide, of course, who was elected by the Haitian people last December with 67% of the votes.

The change can be seen in this quote from the San Francisco Chronicle (Oct. 5):

> Business leaders yesterday expressed fear that Aristide's return to power might mean the start of a blood bath against the army and other groups, including better-off members of Haiti's bourgeoisie. Several businessmen referred to a speech

Aristide made Sept. 27, in which he appeared to extol the
recent practice by some of his supporters of using a tire necklace known as a 'Père Lebrun' to burn people alive.

Policy shifts during Vietnam War

This shift in U.S. policy is reminiscent of the Vietnam War. The
State Department and Pentagon occasionally drove the media up the
wall with contradictions that forced the newspeople to lie and later
have to retract their stories.

The journalistic team of brothers Marvin and Bernard Kalb, who
worked first for CBS and then for NBC, were quite prominent in exposing contradictory public statements of the State Department. Finally in 1984 the department co-opted Bernard Kalb, making him their
spokesperson.

In October 1986, however, after a briefing by Kalb on the bombing
of Libya, a high State Department official completely demolished what
he had said, giving a totally different version of the same event. Kalb
quit his job in protest. Thereafter, the State Department went back to
its regular procedure. Whenever an important shift in policy was contemplated, they would call in the chief executives of the networks and
the publishers of the print media for a long discussion. Then the journalistic corps would do their job in accordance with the bosses' instructions.

That is how it is today. The media is an instrument of imperialist
finance capital and must perform its duties accordingly.

Shift in tactics

It doesn't take a von Clausewitz to know that this current shift by
the Bush administration toward the military coup in Haiti is a tactical
one and does not involve a change in strategic objectives.

Let us take the statement by the head of the military camarilla, Briga-
dier General Raoul Cédras, whose hands are stained with the blood of
the Haitian people. He is reported to have said: "Today the armed forces
find themselves obligated to assume the heavy responsibility to keep the
ship of state afloat.... After seven months of democratic experience, the
country once again finds itself a prey to the horrors of uncertainty."

In a formal sense, Cédras' statement seems to be in direct contradiction with the pronounced policy of the U.S. and the other Western
imperialist powers to support a democratic government in Haiti headed
by its elected president, Aristide. Cédras appears as the avowed enemy

of democracy while the imperialist powers are its fervent, unwavering supporters. But let us look a little closer.

Cédras is not condemning democracy in general. He is condemning the proletarian democracy that the Haitian masses have been engaged in since Aristide's election last December.

They have been taking destiny in their own hands. They were also practicing democracy when they meted out proletarian justice to their tormentors, the murderous Tonton Macoutes.

When proletarian democracy and proletarian justice begin to take hold, democracy becomes a danger to the imperialist bourgeoisie. Then it becomes clear they are just as concerned with getting rid of that democracy as Cédras is.

Thus, the line of Cédras and that of the imperialist bourgeoisie are not at all antithetical, even though Cédras himself may be forced out of his military position. It is just that he says it so brutally and frankly. What the imperialists have in mind, as they have shown on so many occasions throughout their history, is to establish a pro-colonialist democracy.

The imperialist masters want to see the democratic facade function in an orderly manner, so that it sustains capitalist exploitation and imperialist oppression. When that fails, then the military, the trained cadres of imperialism, step in to establish "order."

Any kind of democracy where the masses have a real say in running their own economic affairs is considered political interference in the affairs of the bourgeoisie.

Went overboard at first

The Bush administration has drunk some very heady wine while pledging its partnership, so-called, with the Gorbachev bourgeois restorationists and the new East European governments. It spoke about democracy in such lyrical terms that usually skeptical progressive people were beginning to take the demagogy for good coin. Even some of their own administrators have gotten carried away with it.

At first, this "democracy" demagogy seemed so appropriate for Haiti. Didn't it prove that Bush's New World Order meant opposing military dictatorship and allowing the people uninhibited rights to organize, freedom of the press, freedom to criticize? But all this turned out to be mere froth.

What changed everything was the turn of events among the Haitian masses themselves. They have directed their wrath not only against the military and the paramilitary Macoutes but also against the compliant bourgeoisie in Haiti, against the merchants and the entrepreneurs who, while often speaking out loudly against the military and also bemoaning the ever-present hand of foreign finance capital—U.S. and French, as well as others—will always prefer them to the rule of the masses.

So now there has been a swift change in tone by the Bush administration. They realize that, even with the masses being subdued by naked terror, a full-scale revolutionary convulsion has been provoked by the coup, a virtual second phase of the Haitian Revolution that began with the overthrow of Duvalier.

While the U.S. and its collaborators may have thought they could ingratiate themselves with the masses by intervening under the cover of restoring Aristide, they now realize they can't fool the people that way. Nor can they change the collective mind of the masses by cooking up a deal whereby Aristide is permitted back under conditions that would make him a mere front for imperialist intrigue and brutal military rule.

U.S. imperialism has hopelessly discredited itself with the masses. Only the Haitian bourgeoisie are willing to compromise with imperialism, but they fear for their necks. That's how vigorous the revolution is. It's a genuine attempt at a social revolution, not just a change in the political scenery. The realization of this has caused the abrupt about-face in the tactical approach by the State Department.

Nature of the state

An understanding of the situation in Haiti requires a clear Marxist understanding of the nature of the bourgeois state.

The state is not just a collection of political and social institutions. It is not just the National Assembly, important as that may seem at some periods. In times of acute crisis the parliament is revealed as nothing but a talking machine. Nor is the judiciary in any better shape.

Who rules in Haiti? The state — that is, the military. As Friedrich Engels long ago explained in his monumental work, *The Origin of the Family, Private Property and the State,* the state when stripped down to its skeletal essence is the bodies of armed men. All else is subordinate.

Without the bodies of armed men and women, no state, whether bourgeois or proletarian, can long exist as long as there are still class antagonisms that rend society apart. The state is an instrument of class domination. In times of acute crisis, when one class challenges another, this domination can only be exercised by the armed terror of the state.

What is Aristide's biggest sin? He realized the importance of establishing the embryo of another state, a state based upon the poor and the oppressed. Suddenly all the bourgeois papers have pointed to 300 palace guards trained by the Swiss as the beginning of an independent paramilitary force, which could become the possible basis for a people's army.

For a while the imperialist bourgeoisie winked at this development as nothing more than a palace guard. But the sudden rising of the masses has made the imperialist bourgeoisie more circumspect. They are now putting a spotlight on some of the changes that Aristide made earlier: the retirement of several officers out of line and the promotion of others; the failure to submit the names of new officers to the National Assembly, where they might not have been confirmed; and stirring insubordination among the poorer rank-and-file soldiers.

Aristide's attempt to reshuffle the military staff in and of itself did not arouse the State Department or the Pentagon. Suddenly, however, all this has become important. It is because it hints at the development of a workers' militia, the only true alternative to the military camarilla trained, fed, clothed and housed by the imperialist bourgeoisie. A workers' militia is the only answer to the vicious terror squads, to the trained thugs nurtured, cultivated and trained by the U.S. But it also must be armed and trained.

In the final analysis, to overthrow the yoke of imperialist domination one must look to victorious revolutions like in China, Cuba and Vietnam. Of course, a social revolution and the withdrawal of U.S. imperialism through peaceful means is more desirable. But where has that ever happened? Where has true independence been achieved that way?

The military establishment of the bourgeoisie in a colonial country cannot be dissolved by edict. History shows that Marx was right. The old machinery of state cannot be taken over, let alone permit itself to be dissolved. It must be broken, and it can only be broken by the self-effort of the masses themselves in shaping their own state.

The body of armed men and women in modern times can only be dissolved when class antagonisms have been dissolved. Only then will there be peace and no necessity for coercion, repression, or domination of one group of the population against another. And class antagonisms will disappear only when social equality has been attained.

That may be a considerable distance in the future, but there is no other road, as history has shown.

Workers World, Oct. 17, 1991.

Tenth Department Haitians Massively Mobilize

Greg Dunkel

Most immigrant communities, preoccupied with making a living, fitting in and solving their daily problems, do not organize themselves as a community to take on big political issues. The Haitian community in the '70s and '80s fit this model. They were quiet, hardworking and isolated from the wider communities by their language and traditions; their political focus was Haiti.

But beginning in 1990, the Haitian community in New York started to make a major impact on the political scene in New York.

AIDS March

Many demonstrations have been called historic. Some have stood the time test, others have faded. The April 20, 1990, march from Grand Army Plaza in Brooklyn, across the Brooklyn Bridge to Wall Street still resonates.

April 20, 1990, was a Friday, a work day, but still 100,000 or so Haitians assembled and marched, to the surprise and consternation of the cops and to the shock of the financiers on Wall Street. This was nearly one-third of all the Haitians living in the New York Metropolitan area. The financial moguls had their neighborhood clogged with tens of thousands of orderly but insistent Black people who were protesting a decision by the Centers for Disease Control that Haitians (and West Africans) carried AIDS. That's why the CDC had issued a ruling forbidding Haitians to donate their blood to blood banks.

Haitian children in U.S. schools were subjected to unmerciful teasing about being "dangerous and infected"; Haitian doctors, nurses and medical workers were afraid for their jobs. But most importantly, the national pride of Haitians was deeply impugned — their blood, their life essence, was so unclean, according to the CDC, that they had to be officially shunned. They were the fourth "H" after homosexuals, hemophiliacs and hypodermic drug users. And they were the only nationality singled out by the CDC.

Even after this massive march in the streets, it still took a month or so of dawdling, advisory committee meetings, reports, studies and whatnots before the government felt that enough time had passed that it wouldn't appear to be bowing to pressure from the community. It did finally revise the ban.

The Aristide campaign

The Haitian community had other issues on its agenda during 1990. In New York and other cities with large Haitian communities, massive support rallies that filled stadiums were organized on short notice after Father Jean-Bertrand Aristide's late decision in October to run for president. The communities' focus shifted to Haiti and the huge political events happening there.

The diaspora, Haitians living abroad in what Aristide called the Tenth Department (Haiti is made up of nine geographic departments), responded with hundreds of small meetings, parties, all sorts of appeals to help Aristide counter the millions his main opponent Marc Bazin was receiving from Washington.

His victory Dec. 16, 1990, (see the chapter in this book on "Aristide's crushing victory") produced an outburst of joy both in Haiti and in the diaspora.

The coup against Aristide Sept. 30, 1991, was followed by immediate protests in Washington, Miami, Boston, Montreal and New York, with a major protest in New York announced for Friday, Oct. 11. In the words of the New York Times, "... the police had not expected such a large turnout — even though the 300,000 members of the Haitian community in New York have shown a readiness to voice their political concerns." (NY Times, October 12, 1991)

"After all," one cop explained to me on that day, "it's a work day. Who'd think so many people would show up?" Not many cops showed up at Grand Army Plaza in Brooklyn, even after it was clear that tens of thousands of protesters were going to come out.

The march down Flatbush Avenue to the Brooklyn Bridge filled that wide street. When it got to the bridge, it was clear that the pedestrian walkway was too narrow so the marchers took and filled the entire Manhattan-bound side of the roadway. They started pouring into Manhattan's financial district around 11 a.m. and a large contingent headed toward Battery Park at the tip of Manhattan, where an official rally with speakers and a stage was scheduled. The most common chant was "Democracy or death" and there were a profusion of signs supporting President Aristide and denouncing the coup in English, French and Creole.

Another large contingent decided to go to the Stock Exchange. When they got there, the crowd grew silent, when Wilson Désir, Haiti's Consul-General in New York, mounted the steps of Federal Hall and said: "Not only in New York, but all over the world, Haitian people are demonstrating to tell the world community that Aristide is our leader and we want him back to power. I am asking you here today to continue demonstrating until we have what we want."

Ben Dupuy, then Haiti's ambassador at large, drew large cheers when he announced that the United Nations General Assembly had just passed a resolution condemning the coup.

When he came to speak at the United Nations Sept. 29, 1992, almost a year later, tens of thousands from the Haitian community along with progressive supporters came out. The Haitian communities in New York and elsewhere did keep up the pressure until the United States returned President Aristide on Oct. 15, 1994, not so much to stop the coup but to prevent a revolution.

The AIDS issue also resurfaced after the coup against President Aristide. Over 1,000 people were killed in the first few weeks of the coup and wave after wave of boat people began fleeing the vicious repression afflicting Haiti. Soon thousands of refugees, intercepted by the U.S. Coast Guard at sea, were being held and "processed" in unfair hearings at the U.S. Naval Base at Guantanamo Bay, Cuba. The vast majority were sent back to Haiti. Less than ten percent got political asylum in the U.S.

The United States Immigration Service stacked up about 300 Haitian refugees in Guantanamo, even though their asylum claims had been approved, because they had AIDS. Unable to legally return them to Haiti, the U.S. government kept these HIV-positive Haitians behind barbed-wire in a dusty, scorpion and rat-infested compound at Guantanamo.

The Haitian community and the Haiti solidarity movement didn't let the issue of the treatment of HIV-positive Haitians drop, even though they were concentrating on developments in Haiti. The demonstrations were small, generally a few hundred, but frequent and militant. About four to five thousand demonstrators did come out on Feb. 7, 1993, for a march through Manhattan on the United Nations. Finally, a federal judge ruled in June of 1993 that it was illegal to keep HIV-positive Haitians in Guantanamo.

A couple of the smaller demonstrations stand out. Under the Rockefeller Center Christmas tree wishing the detainees a Merry Christmas. Another small, mainly Haitian demonstration in the Greenwich Village area, a march from the INS office in Lower Manhattan to Washington Square in late fall 1992—on the sidewalks. I was talking to a contingent of ACT UP, a predominantly North American gay and lesbian group working militantly around the AIDS issue, that had just joined the demonstration when the march stopped. The sidewalk had run out and the cops had blocked the demonstrators who had taken the street.

A group of older Haitian women were sitting in the street, chanting, when I got to the front of the march. A cop came up and asked: "What are they saying?" A young Haitian man with the ACT UP contingent answered: "The street or death. They grew up under Duvalier." "Oh," was the response. The cop went back to the police commander, who shrugged and let the march proceed.

Struggles around Abner Louima & Patrick Dorismond

August 9, 1997, there was a disturbance outside Club Rendez-vous, a Haitian nightclub on Flatbush Avenue in Brooklyn, and the cops grabbed a young Haitian man named Abner Louima. They beat him as they took him to the station house, beat him in the station house and then one of them, Charles Schwartz, held him down while another cop, Justin Volpe, shoved a toilet plunger into his rectum.

Police brutality is not new in the Haitian community, but this depraved infliction of human suffering sparked a wave of anger in the Haitian community and a strong response in the African American and Afro-Caribbean communities. August 16 saw some 20,000 people, mostly Haitians, march from the nightclub where the incident started to the 70th Precinct, where Schwartz and Volpe were assigned.

Chanting "Seven-oh, KKK, got to go," waving Haitian flags and beating drums, dancing in 90-degree heat, the crowd marched on the 70th precinct, where it stayed for nearly four hours, making clear its disgust with the actions of the cops. A number of signs also raised the fact that the United States was using cops from this very precinct, the 70th, in Haiti to train the new Haitian National Police to "respect" civil rights. There was another major march on Friday, August 29, 1997, which drew seven to ten thousand people and at least 2,500 cops, according to press reports.

March 16, 2000, two cops tried to entrap Patrick Dorismond in front of a Manhattan nightclub, called the Wakamba Lounge, a few blocks south of Times Square. They asked him if he had marijuana to sell them. Witnesses reported that Dorismond angrily rejected their request. Moments later, a third back-up cop shot and killed the young man who was scuffling with the first cops.

Mayor Rudolph Giuliani further inflamed the crisis in the days after Dorismond's death. At news conferences, Giuliani tried to demonize Dorismond as having been "no altar boy." (Actually, he had been one.) The mayor illegally produced juvenile arrest records that had merely resulted in two disorderly conduct pleas and a sealed juvenile arrest made when Dorismond was 13 years old.

Dorismond was a 26-year-old worker and came from a well-known Haitian family. On March 18, two days after he was killed, a thousand people marched from the Wakamba Lounge through midtown Manhattan and blocked traffic to protest the killing. The people who marched—Dorismond's family, neighbors, fellow workers, members of the Haitian community, African Americans, progressive whites—expressed their grief and anger, as well as their determination to stop police brutality in New York. Phannon, a neighbor of the Dorismonds who had watched Patrick grow up, told me: "I am one angry Haitian woman. This is the last one. We don't need another. There won't be another."

Close to 20,000 angry Haitians and their allies joined Dorismond's funeral procession March 25, 2000. People sang, danced, drummed and shouted slogans against the police, Mayor Rudolph Giuliani and Police Commissioner Howard Safir. Some carried placards recalling the many victims of police violence. Others denounced the mayor as a "lougarou," a demon in Haitian folklore that sucks the blood of babies. The Haitian flag was seen everywhere.

In front of the Holy Cross Church where the funeral rites were held, a rebellion erupted as the body was carried out. Four demonstrators and 23 cops were injured and 27 people were arrested—including an 80-year-old man and a pregnant woman who police brutally dragged by her hair.

There was another demonstration April 20, 2000, the tenth anniversary of the 1990 AIDS march, that was fueled by Mayor Rudolph Giuliani's continued defamation of Dorismond. Over 10,000 people, mostly Haitian, marched from Grand Army Plaza in Brooklyn across the Brooklyn Bridge to rally in front of City Hall in lower Manhattan. "Uproot Giuliani"—in Creole, "Giuliani, rache manyòk ou"—was the sentiment expressed by most who marched.

Daniel Simidor, who chaired the rallies at both ends of the march, said, "Giuliani killed Patrick Dorismond twice: once with a bullet and the other with his mouth." At the opening of the first rally, he said, "This is a protest against police brutality inflicted on any person of color"—Haitian, Jamaican, Latino or African-American.

Because of the revolutionary history of Haiti, both in the struggle against the French and the struggle against the U.S.-backed Duvalier dictatorships, Haitians in the Tenth Department, especially in New York City, came out in massive numbers against issues that affected them. They had an influence on the wider progressive community in New York, from the AIDS movement and the Afro-American, African and Caribbean-American communities that also have to confront police brutality and racism.

What stands out about these protests is that the most significant ones took place on workdays, which meant that their participants were engaging in a one-day strike and lost a day's pay to express their political views. This is not common in U.S. protests. In addition Haitian demonstrations have drawn a significant proportion of that community out into the streets, even though it is an immigrant community subject to pressures from the INS.

The 29 years Haitians spent protesting the Duvalier dictatorships has instilled in the fabric of that community a militancy and a spirit of struggle which have inspired progressives of all nationalities in New York and indeed, throughout the U.S.

Part IV

❧❧

After 2nd U.S. Occupation

Reign of a Human Race

Paul Laraque
Translation from French by Rosemary Manno

you say democracy
and we know that it's tin from Bolivia
copper from Chile
petroleum from Venezuela
sugar from Cuba
raw materials and profits

you say democracy
and it's the annexation of Texas
the hold-up of the Panama Canal
the occupation of Haiti
the colonization of Puerto Rico
the bombing of Guatemala

you say democracy
and it's America to the Yankee
it's the rape of nations
it's Sandino's blood
and Péralte's* crucifixion

you say democracy
and it's the plunder of our wealth
from Hiroshima to Indochina
you spread the slaughter everywhere
and everywhere ruin

you say democracy
and it's the Ku Klux Klan
o hidden people
inside your own cities
an ogre is devouring your children

Ubu** from the empire of robots
you let your ravens fly
from Harlem to Jerusalem
from Wounded Knee to Haiti
from Santo Domingo to Soweto
the people will be waving
the torch of revolution

Night is a tunnel opening on the dawn
Viet-Nam stands like a tree in the storm
the frontier which marks the place of your defeat
history's lessons have no recourse
a footbridge stretches from Asia to Africa
the reign of the white race is ending on earth
and the reign of the peoples in the universe is beginning.

---

* Charlemagne Péralte, leader of the *caco* guerrilla resistance, was assassinated by U.S. Marines in 1918. The Marines photographed Péralte's body strapped to a door, a pose which bore striking resemblance to artistic interpretations of Christ's crucifixion.
** A character with supernatural powers in works by Alfred Jarry (1873-1907), a French avant-garde playwright.

No Greater Shame

May, 2003

Edwidge Danticat

From the outside, it looks like any other South Florida hotel. There is a pool, green grass, tall palms bordering the parking lot. "We make old fashioned comfort a brand new experience," the brochure at the front desk of the bright, spotless lobby reads. The elegant rug that leads from the front entrance to the elevators is decorated with yellow and orange fan designs that reminds me of the Shell company logo, but what they are meant to recall is the imprint of the Comfort Suites hotel chain.

An ordinary guest may not even be aware that their stopover for the night, or their vacation home for a few days is indeed a prison, a holding facility for women and children who have fled their homes, their countries, in haste, in desperation, in pain, hoping for a better life.

In late February of 2003, I visited, along with radio journalists Michele Montas and J.J. Dominique, filmmaker Jonathan Demme, activist Marlène Bastien from Haitian Women of Miami and attorney Cheryl Little of the Florida Immigration Advocacy Center, among others, the Comfort Suites at 3901 SW 117th Street in Miami, where several Haitian women and children are jailed. Our visit began with a warning from the hotel manager that we were not allowed to enter the lobby with film or video cameras. However, pen and paper were not banned, so I was able to jot down some notes.

Once we passed the manager's scrutiny, we were turned over to an immigration official, who met us at the elevator. We were told that the visiting rules for the hotel were the same as The Krome Detention Center, which we had visited earlier that day. (More on that later.) The film and video ban was reiterated. This time we were also told that audio recording devices were forbidden. We were informed that we wouldn't be allowed to go up to the rooms with the coloring books and crayons we had brought for the children. We needed special permission from a higher official at Krome, who had to inspect and approve them first. We were not to give anything, anything at all, to the detainees without prior approval, which made me wonder if we would be permitted to touch them, hug them, or hand them a napkin, should they start to cry.

Finally our IDs were checked, our bags and purses searched and we were escorted into the elevator. Nervously, a few of us commented that it was ironic that a place called "Comfort Suites" was also a jail. I had a flashback to several conversations with my friend, the filmmaker Patricia Benoit, who had been a volunteer English teacher for Haitian refugees at the Brooklyn Navy Yard detention center in the early 1980s. Later she would write in an essay about her experiences there: How she was haunted for years by the voices of guards who after inspecting her bag, would flash a smile and reprise "with perfect timing, the refrain of a television commercial: 'Welcome to Roach Motel.'" The point was that you could check in, but couldn't check out.

I had that same uneasy feeling in the elevator, that we were on the threshold of a kind of experience that you could enter into but never leave. As the elevator neared our floor, we all grew quiet, those of us on our first visits to the prison/hotel, extremely fearful of what we might actually find.

It was an ordinary hallway, except that it seemed rather narrow. Maybe it was the way I was feeling, crammed, afraid, judging the space by the fact that it might be the only open area that a large number of people might tread for months on end. We thought we would take turns visiting the people we had come to see in their own rooms, but they'd been gathered for us in a "neutral" room. While we walked to that room, we caught glimpses of other detainees, other women and children, Eastern European and Latin American women, we were told, lying in bed, watching television, the only view of the outside world they were allowed, while waiting for their eventual release.

At the end of the hallway, in a small room were the people we had come to see. I will not name them or describe them in too much detail, not because they are nameless or faceless, but because I don't want what I write here to put them in danger, both small and large dangers. I don't want a guard to give them an extra push. I don't want them to be denied a rare change of clothing. I don't want their cases prejudiced.

In that room, we meet a mother and her three-year-old daughter. The little girl's eyes are ashen, her face as gray as the mandatory sweat suit all the detainees wear. The mother tells us that her little girl has been asking her for a single thing for weeks. The little girl wants to go for a walk. Just a walk outside in the fresh air. The little girl wants her feet to touch the green grass. She wants to sit under one of those tall palm trees downstairs. She wants to feel the sun on her face. The little girl's request seems small in the larger scheme of the world, the world of people who come and go as they please. But tearfully, the mother says, she can not grant her that. Nor can she even dream of it now for herself.

We also meet a little boy. He is wearing a gray adult-sized T-shirt. There is not a uniform small enough for him, so he doesn't have pants. We are told that many requests have been made by the lawyers for the little boy to be allowed a pair of pants. So far, the requests have been ignored.

We meet a pretty young woman, who tells us that she's lost a lot of weight, not only because of the sadness and chagrin that plagues her constrained life, a life where she is forbidden to even stand in the hallway we have just walked, but because she can't bring herself to eat the food that's brought to her from The Krome Detention Center. She's not choosy or picky about food, but the food "just won't stay down," she says. It's bland, tasteless and it gives her diarrhea. Another woman quietly nods her agreement. The food just won't stay down.

If their bodies are not being fed, in this room or others like it, their spirits are even more starved. They are not allowed visits here at this hotel. Family members must visit them at The Krome Detention Center, which is about fifteen minutes away. The guards must accompany them on these visits, which must be announced as much as a week in advance. And sometimes, most times, they are not even taken to Krome for their visits. Or sometimes they are brought there late and they miss their loved ones. Family members, on rare occasions when they do get to speak to them on the telephone—for they need phone cards and money for these phone cards to make calls—tell them that they came to Krome to visit them and waited for them in vain.

Many of the women and children at the hotel have brothers, fathers, husbands at Krome, whom they rarely see or don't see at all. Earlier on the visit to Krome, we met a family. The mother and children were being held in the hotel, and the father and eldest son at Krome. That family only saw each other during their hearings at Krome. They were only allowed to wave, the mother told us, not touch. She had not touched her husband, and the children had not kissed or hugged their father in months. It took the presence of U.S. Representative Kendrick Meek, his mother, the former congresswoman, Carrie Meek, and a handful of prominent visitors to make a reunion possible, for a father to hold his children, for a wife to kiss her husband shyly, in front of all of us, on the cheek.

The women in that hotel room were feeling sick, they told us. At times they spoke fast, as if fearing they might forget something and at other times, just moaned, unable to utter another word. They did not easily have access to doctors. And in the rare urgent cases when they saw a doctor, they did not feel thoroughly examined. They felt as though they were simply being given pills, the purposes of which they did not fully understand.

In early April, a few weeks after our visit, a two-year-old boy living in the hotel was rushed to the hospital. I can write his name here because his case was reported in an April 12th [2003] article in The Miami Herald. Jordan Guillaume's case echoes many of the pleas we heard that day. "Jordan, like other children under the age of 6 at the hotel," Jacqueline Charles reported in the Herald, "isn't allowed out of his room in the Comfort Suites Hotel in West Miami-Dade to either play or interact with other kids....The only time detainees are allowed to breathe fresh air is when they are being transported by guards to an appointment. ..."

Jordan had been sick for weeks, reported Charles "unable to properly eat and sleep, sometimes banging his head against the wall at night... His breathing was loud and labored, and he was barely able to open his eyes. ..."

What crime did Jordan and these other children commit that they should be treated like this? How many others are banging their heads against these same walls at night?

One of the people on the visit that day asks the guard sitting in a corner of the hotel room if she has any children. She, a slim African-American women with curly hair, says yes she has a teenage son. Doesn't it hurt her to imprison children? we ask.

"I'm just doing my job," she says. "If you have questions or concerns, speak to my boss."

It is hard for me to tell who her boss is. Is it the tall woman we met earlier at Krome, the one we were told would ultimately decide whether the crayons we brought for the children in the hotel would reach them? Is it U.S. Attorney General John Ashcroft? Tom Ridge, head of Homeland Security? President George W. Bush himself? Or is it ultimately me, the taxpayer? Are my hard-earned dollars contributing to this, the detention of my own?

Sensing the end of our visit growing near, the women tell us how often six of them must live together in one small hotel room. They are lucky if the others crammed in with them are friends or family members, but sometimes they are placed with strangers, which can lead to some tension. Some of them must sleep on the floor when there is not enough space on the beds or couches. They miss their own clothes, some small marker of individuality. They miss food they recognize, food that stays down. They miss religious rituals, church services and Mass on special occasions. They miss seeing their children go off to school.

We leave for we must, each of us, making silent promises that later we would timidly divulge. A press conference is held outside the hotel. We are told by the hotel manager that it can not take place on hotel premises. So there, on the side of the highway, with cars noisily speeding by, some honking so that they might be noticed by the television cameras, the visitors take turns speaking. Michele Montas. Then Jonathan Demme. Then Marlène and Cheryl and others. I fear that the spot by the highway is way too noisy for such an important moment of testimony. The microphones might not catch every word of what the speakers all have to say. It's so important that they are heard. They are bearing witness.

That day, I made a silent promise to write this piece. I made a promise to personally boycott Comfort Suites and whatever other companies associate with them and encourage as many people as possible to do the same.

Now out by the highway, as the press conference proceeds, my mind returns to Krome, which we had visited earlier that morning. Even before setting foot on its premises, Krome had always seemed like a strange myth to me, a cross between Mount Olympus and hell. I imagined it was something like the Brooklyn Navy Yard, where my parents had taken me on Sunday afternoons when I was a girl, to visit with people we did not know but feared we might, people who always wanted us to call someone on the outside for them, "pass a message" on the radio, to let loved ones know that they were still alive, people who as my father used to say, "could have very well been us." Krome was like my memory of the Brooklyn Navy yard and worse. Endless security checks. Hearing rooms. Isolation. There was a gloom over the buildings, a gloom you could see, but also feel. Krome's silent despair became visible when group after group of men in identical dark blue uniforms walked into a covered stretch of the courtyard, a space surrounded by barbed wire and vending machines, which seemed to be a painful taunt to someone who couldn't afford to purchase anything there.

The men walked in two straight lines and sat on long cafeteria tables with seats on either side. But they all sat on one side of the table, the side closest to the outside and waited to tell their stories.

"My name is…" they say. "I came on the July boat." Or I came on the December boat. Or the most famous one of all, the October 29th 2002 boat, the landing of which was broadcast on national television. Part of their identity now, like our slave forebears is the ship on which they arrived, the vessel on which they made it to American shores. They listen patiently to words of encouragement, first from Representative Meek, then his mother. Then when it is their turn to speak, they speak in clear, loud voices, as if suddenly empowered by this brief opportunity to break their silence. Some invent parables to explain their circumstances. One man tells the story of a mad dog who threatens a person and forces that person to seek shelter at a neighbor's house. "If a mad dog is chasing you, shouldn't your neighbor shelter you?" he asks. The others moan, nod, whisper "Amen," "Se vre." They understand. We understand. Another sings a song about a mud slide that's washed away everything he owns. Another reminds the group how Haiti helped the United States gain its independence. The American revolution's battles of Savannah, Georgia, are recalled. One man shouts in English, "We were the first black republic."

In private conferences, they point out the irony that Haitian refugees were once held at a military camp in Guantanamo, Cuba, where now, so-called terrorists from Al-Qaeda and the Taliban are being jailed. One man asks us to tell the world that the detainees are hit sometimes. He tells of a friend who had his back broken by a guard and was deported before he could get medical attention. They tell of how the other detainees from other countries spit and rub dirty mops on their faces. They tell of guards who tell them that they smell, who always remind them that they will never get asylum, that they will be deported in the end. They say the large rooms where they sleep in rows and rows of bunk beds are often cold, so they shiver all night, can't sleep, catch colds, and suffer from "fredi" all over their bodies. They tell of the food that rather than nourishing them, punishes them. They tell of how "white" prisoners, prisoners from every other country, are fed before they are. They tell of arbitrary curfews, how they are woken up at 6 AM and forced to go back to that cold room by 6 PM. They tell how even the toothpaste they are given to brush their teeth makes their gums bleed and gives them mouth sores. I see some men who look too young to be the mandatory eighteen years old for detention at Krome. A few of them look fourteen or even twelve. How can we be sure that they're not younger, I ask one of the lawyers, if they come with no birth certificates, no papers. The lawyer answers that those who are in charge of such things determine these young men's ages by examining their teeth. I can't escape this reminder of the auction blocks of our ancestral past, where mouths were pried open for cursory analyses of the teeth. One man who has received asylum, but has not yet been released, shows us the burn marks all over his arms and chest and belly. His flesh is seared white, rows and rows of keloid scars. It seems like such a violation, to look at his belly, the space where the scars dip further down his body. But he is used to showing his scars, he says. He had to show them to the judge to make his case.

I come across a man who, liked a few others, looked vaguely familiar. Someone I might have seen somewhere else. It is possible that I know him, I tell myself. Haiti is small. He, like a few others, says he wants to go back. Perhaps this is what is hoped for. That the Krome experience will be so demoralizing that many more will ask, plead, beg to return home. One man says, "If I had a bullet, I'd have shot myself already. I'm not a criminal. I'm not used to prison." The shame of being a prisoner looms large. A stigma some can't shake. To have been handcuffed, many say, rubbing that spot on their wrists where the soft manacles were placed on them soon after they made it to shore, "I have known no greater shame in my life."

I meet an older man who comes from Bel Air, the same area in Port-au-Prince where I spent the first twelve years of my life. His eyes are reddened. He can't stop crying. His mother died last week, he says and he can't even attend her funeral. He tells me his mother's name and when he describes her house, the house where he used to live in Bel-Air, I can see it, having just been back there, in the old neighborhood, for the funeral of my Aunt Denise. I offer him my condolences then tell him about my aunt. He knew her. Perhaps she knew him too, having run a small grocery shop in the neighborhood for years. For a few minutes, his attention shifts from his loss to mine. He offers me his condolences. He tells me to offer his condolences to my uncle.

In late April, I am appalled, but not totally surprised—for US Immigration policy against Haitians is often mind boggling—when Attorney General Ashcroft justified his decision to veto a judge's decision to release eighteen-year-old David Joseph on a $2,500 bond, by arguing that Haiti harbors potential terrorists. I had met David Joseph during that visit at Krome. He is a quiet and somber young man, reed thin and sad and he is not a terrorist. (And how can we trust these people when they call anyone a terrorist if they mistake a young man like David as one?) David fled Haiti with his younger brother after he was burned and stoned. His father had been severely beaten. He was granted bond by the highest immigration court in the land until Mr. Ashcroft personally blocked his release. In his decision, Ashcroft suggests that David Joseph and the others are a threat to national security. How come someone like David is considered a threat to national security, when Emmanuel Constant, the former head of FRAPH, a militia group that's suspected of having killed more than 5000 Haitians in the early 1980s, is not?

The other reason given for these unfair "indefinite" detentions — you can imagine that indefinite might sound like eternity to someone who's in jail, be it a gilded one like the Comfort Suites or a more obvious one like Krome — is fear of a mass exodus from Haiti. Is there no fear of a mass exodus from Cuba, which is actually (unfairly or not) on the list of so called terrorist states?

Soon after Mr. Ashcroft's absurd declarations, U.S. State Department and Coast Guard officials were said to be scratching their heads over Mr. Ashcroft's claim that Pakistanis, Palestinians and others are using Haiti as a staging point to get into the United States. I was scratching my head too. But I was also pained. Pained for David Joseph and the others I met, who now have no idea when they will emerge from this most horrifying distortion of their American dream, which is now only made up of prison nightmares.

First published in The Haitian Boston Reporter in May, 2003

The Longest Day

Stan Goff

Stan Goff was the Master Sergeant or "top" of a U.S. Special Forces team during the 1994 U.S. military occupation of Haiti. He was almost court-martialed for the zeal with which he pursued coup henchmen. This account, slightly edited, of his team establishing their base in the northeastern town of Fort Liberté is taken from the book he wrote about his experiences in Haiti, Hideous Dream.

This was it. At 0300, I went to each team member's bunk and woke him up.

I was tired enough and stretched thin enough to obsess, and that is what I did. My obsession was Pascal Blaise, the head of a gang of *macoutes* in Fort Liberté, who did most of the dirty work for the local FRAPH. His capture and arrest would be a defining act, one that would send all the right messages to all the players in one fell swoop.

I was growing comfortable with acid smell of me, mixed with layer upon layer of insect repellent, applied through the night. I smoked until my tongue was bitter and cracking.

My commanding officer, Captain Mike Gallante, was ready within five minutes. In the 3:00 AM darkness, the boys muddled around, brushing teeth, boiling coffee, pissing outside the vehicle arch, folding cots, stuffing their sleeping gear into their rucks, and jamming the rucks into the potential spaces of the top heavy Toyota flatbed, parked in the courtyard. I woke the reporters at 3:30. Tony Marcelli, the Reuters man, asked if I'd like a cup of brewed coffee from his Thermos. Gratefully, I freed my canteen cup from my "load carrying equipment" harness (LCE) and accepted.

Captain Joseph, an English speaker from the Armed Forces of Haiti (FAd'H) on Colonel Simone's staff, was designated to guide us, but he had not shown up, and in my obsessive sleepless state that tardiness became a source of intense pressure.

I finished my coffee and started warming up for my Tasmanian devil role. I could feel it coming. Control, the ultimate burden and the ultimate necessity at this juncture. I started snapping like the Alpha hyena; Why isn't the truck strapped in yet, get everyone over here by quarter til, wherethefuck is that fuckin' FAd'H captain, we're getting on the road by four or else, eat that cold goddammit and get moving-- you can eat on the road.

Operational Detachment Alpha (ODA) 356 was up, and I believe I took a moment to hint at browbeating their captain if they weren't ready on time. Are the radios checked? Well, where the hell is mine. Fuck me with a jackhammer, we've only been waitin' a thousand years to do this, this is it, this is our mission, are we gonna be late for it too. Oh, I was in fine form. Click. Click. Click.

At quarter to four we sat the team down. We reviewed our actions, who goes where, who does what. The key thing was the sub-element designated to get Pascal Blaise. When I saw the reporters focused elsewhere, I would discretely signal the boys to move on Blaise. The problem we anticipated was using the locals. Communications Sergeant Ali Tehrani could talk to them in French, but Tony spoke French and Creole. I could use Spanish, but Claudia spoke Spanish better than I did. I would have to be pretty cagey to elicit the location of the house, without the reporters figuring it out.

356's job was just to establish a loose perimeter around the front of the garrison to hold back crowds as they developed, and to guard our gear until we could find a place to unload it.

It was already hot, and my acrid damp fatigues were already being resoaked with sweat.

Captain Joseph did not show. So at ten after four, with me in a near rabid condition, we departed. I felt myself calm down, the minute we passed through the town arch on the road out of Ouanaminthe. We moved at a snail's pace over a dreadfully pitted road through as black a night as one can imagine with a clear sky. The sounds of the engines, the Toyota, the Hummer, the three reporters' 4x4s, cut a wake in the unmechanized silence of the Haitian night. The headlights played over huts, *raket* hedges, slipshod fences, roaming livestock, and an occasional timid and fearful eye peering out of a slumbering domicile.

We encountered a confusing fork in the road about thirty minutes out, and that's when Captain Joseph's jeep slid into the convoy out of nowhere. Joseph got out smiling and told us to follow him.

An hour out of Ouanaminthe, we entered an area almost devoid of structures, nothing but rolling grassy fields beyond the *raket* that lined the roadside. Suddenly we were in a town, and no sooner were we in the town, than we passed under the yellow concrete arch, announcing FORT LIBERTE. Under the name of the town was inscribed, LA DULCE DANS L'EFFORT. The sweetness is in the effort. I don't know why, but *Arbeit machen frei* jumped into my head.

The first hint of dawn was sneaking into the east as we pulled up in front of the garrison, and the soldiers began streaming out onto the porch of the caserne to get an anxious look at their new reality. The streets were otherwise empty.

356 deployed at both ends of the street. I sent everyone else inside. Each man had something to look at, construction of the garrison, weapons, sleeping quarters, latrine facilities. Mike was escorted by Fad'H Lt. Percy and Joseph to talk again with Captain Pierre Ulrick, commander of the Fad'H casernes in Fort Liberté. Ali had all the soldiers turn in all their weapons to the arms room, a filthy, spider-ridden room, heaped with old mildewed uniforms, forgotten documents, hundreds of weapons in various states of serviceability.

I slipped down the street to the corner, where people were singing at 5:00 AM. It was the big round pavilion we had seen on the satellite imagery that Vincent and Freddy, our local civilian contacts, had identified as a big Baptist Church. I motioned a somewhat surprised master of ceremonies to the door. The preacher said something to the two dozen or so worshippers, then came outside and offered his hand. He spoke English. I was in luck.

I asked him if he knew of a Pascal Blaise. He assented and asked what it was we wanted with that man. I said we needed to contact him. Did he know where Blaise lived? Down that way somewhere, he pointed, to the North. He was sure it was nearby. I thanked him, afraid I may have already tipped Blaise off. I was beginning to have supernatural expectations of the Haitian grapevine.

I rejoined our group at the garrison. The reporters were having a field day, shooting pictures of the disoriented Haitian soldiers, popping flashes at the stacks of accumulating weapons. They're attracted to the same stuff as adolescent boys. Guns, gore, cheap drama.

Dawn was lancing further and further into the sky with brilliant yellow and salmon rays. A small crowd was beginning to amass on the street. It was not yet a demonstrative crowd, just curious. I approached them and asked who spoke Spanish. A very dark-skinned man stepped forward and began conversing in perfect Dominican Spanish. He told me he was a fisherman from Fort Saint Joseph, the neighborhood at the North of town, across the "causeway." His name was Dumas. He said he did a great deal of business in the Dominican Republic, and that he had lived several years in Santo Domingo with members of his family. I asked him if he would interpret. He agreed gladly.

The members of the crowd eyed us suspiciously. The reporters they glared at with open hostility. I briefly wondered what the problem was. I decided to give a short speech.

"I am the operations chief for the team of Special Forces soldiers you see here. My name is Stan," I began. "We ask that you not interfere with the operations of the American soldiers. There are so few of us. We are obligated to protect everyone in the city. That includes you and the Haitian military." This brought some grumbles. "Do not worry about any more abuse from these people. We will supervise their every activity, until the central government of Jean-Bertrand Aristide decides what to do with them." Aristide's name brought a little cheer. The crowd was beginning to swell as people entered from every corner. "We understand that you not only fear the soldiers, but that there are *macoutes*, FRAPH and *attachés*." Demonstrated understanding of this fact met with much nodding and murmuring. "They will not threaten or harm you any longer." The excitement grew in the gathering. "We are here to restore the rightful government. We are going to ask your help in this task. There will be only eight of us staying in Fort Liberté. We need you to act as our eyes and ears. We need your leaders to exercise restraint, and to prevent violence or revenge.

"You have not been allowed to demonstrate your happiness at the return of Father Aristide. That is now permitted. You may fill the streets with celebration if you like. The only thing we ask is that you do not attempt to enter the garrison or make contact with the soldiers. I am a soldier under orders to protect all people from any form of violence, and I ask your cooperation, so that I may stay firmly on the side of the people.

"Most importantly right now I need for you to keep your distance from the entrance to the caserne, so we can finish our business here and get established. Within the next few days, my captain and I will attempt to meet with all the leaders in Fort Liberté. Especially with the leaders of Lavalas, with whom we have had good relations in Gonaïves and Ouanaminthe.

"Lavalas has exercised discipline in preventing retribution and counter-violence against collaborators with the tie facto government. We desperately need the cooperation of the people of Fort Liberté in taking this first critical step toward democracy."

The speech met with strong, general approval, and the original climate of suspicion seemed to have evaporated. I then called my Spanish speaking fisherman friend over to the side. I explained that I needed his help locating some people, but that we would have to be discrete. He was very keen to help.

Did he know where Pascal Blaise lived? Yes, of course he did. Would he guide us there when I gave the signal? Yes, he would, but what did we want Blaise for? To arrest him, I said. He became so animated I had to tell him to calm down, lest the cat get out of the bag. Was there anyone else I wanted to arrest? I wanted Blaise's inner circle. I wanted the leaders and members of FRAPH. I wanted to question Neal Calixte, the former ambassador of François Duvalier to France and treasurer of the local FRAPH chapter. All this met with profound approval and an excitement he seemed barely able to contain. I told him to wait on the corner, until the big man who spoke French came to get him.

I pulled out Ali, our medic Gonzo, and senior weapons man Rod and pointed out the guide. I told them to mill around until the reporters seemed to be distracted, then grab him and go get Blaise. Then I told Mike that we were about to execute the move against Blaise. Mike asked if they had commo. I assured him that they did. Ali had the radio on his LCE. Mike called for a commo check. Ali acknowledged.

Suddenly, the guys took off. They weren't waiting for the reporters to be out of the way.

Holy Shit! I told Mike. Look at that.

The three were walking purposefully down the middle of the street, with the guide in tow, and the reporters were dashing off behind them like sharks on a chum trail. Mike and I were frantically calling on the radio, telling them abort, abort, abort, but no one acknowledged. Mike and I started skipping off behind them, preparing to stop the detention face to face.

We didn't catch them. Blaise's house was so close they arrived even before the reporters caught up. Behind us, the crowd was trailing. We caught up with the reporters, and rounded the corner to the left, to see Ali already pointing a weapon in the space between two houses, shouting orders in French.

Fuck it, I said. I dove into the middle of it. A man was face down on the ground, and Ali told me that Blaise was in the house. I told him and Gonzo to go through the back door, while the reporters were busy snapping pictures of the prone man, so they wouldn't see our guys make the entry.

Ali and Gonzo emerged in less than a minute, with Blaise, half dressed and sleepy-eyed. Is that Blaise, I asked the fisherman. He nodded. Show me the rest, then.

Mike asked what was going on. Ali explained that the man on the ground was Blaise's chauffeur, and pointed to Blaise. I explained that we were going ahead with a general roundup, now that the shit was on. Mike concurred, and gave me the go ahead.

I told the fisherman to show us the people we wanted. Crazily, he pointed out three people who were in the street by now, watching all the commotion around Blaise's house. They were dumbfounded as we pushed them to the side and flex cuffed them. The crowd now joined in. They understood what we were doing. More people were pointed out, some now as they slipped away from the crowd, seeing the danger of detention. Within two minutes we had rounded up ten detainees. The reporters were confused and excited, snapping pictures and rolling tape, and jockeying for position. Some were rapidly changing to faster film to accommodate the not quite light, predawn conditions. Miraculously, no one had witnessed the actual entry into Blaise's house through the back door. Not that it mattered. The reporters were less interested in rules of engagement and shades of gray therein, than in getting the best pics.

We ordered the crowd to stay back, and members of the crowd echoed the commands, eager to help their liberators. We decided we had enough. I told them to move the detainees back to the caserne.

In front of the caserne, a couple of FAd'H stepped out to talk to Blaise and the others, and I snapped at them to move back and shut up. One of the Creole translations of "shut up" is *shut up*, a holdover from the Marine occupation. All but one of the prisoners had assumed his place in single file, and were kneeling as instructed. I stormed over to him and told him to get down. He gave me a look between defiance and fright, so in English I barked "Get down, Goddamn it!," pushing down on his shoulder and foot-sweeping the back of his knee. He dropped down with finality, then lowered his head in surrender.

I looked up and saw Claudia, the freelance reporter who had declared her admiration for my humanity to her companion two days before, and she was crestfallen. The reality of force had replaced her admiration with disillusion. She came over to me, the chill in her attitude visible, keeping her distance from the smell I was exuding, and asked if we were applying any "rules of evidence or due process" to this roundup. Where would I present that evidence? I asked. In the local court? Maybe I should run the "evidence" over to the local Haitian forensics lab! I was ordered to detain anyone associated with FRAPH. The people who gave me that order would decide what to do with them. As far as I was concerned, Fort Liberté was under martial law. She scribbled officially and stalked away, secure in her comfortable, bipolar, petit-bourgeois morality.

356 was heavily occupied maintaining the standard crowd line around the front of the garrison. Fort Liberté was waking up, and they wanted to know what was going on.

The caserne was near condemnation. There was no way we would be able to live there. I sent Kyle and Ali to recon for a house. They came back in twenty or so minutes, telling us they had found a first class hotel, something none of us would have hoped for. It was the hotel owned by Calixte, the former ambassador to France under Papa Doc. Kyle was excited by the prospect. He was keen to move into comfortable quarters, and Calixte had offered to put us up for the nominal fee, provided we keep the unwashed mobs from ransacking him. Ali insisted that we provide security for him, too.

Ali was a sucker for anyone who spoke pretty French, himself despising the plosive cadences and simplified conjugation of Creole. Kyle's problem was different. Kyle epitomized many of the criticisms I had of Special Forces. He was ignorant of doctrine and pretended he was superior to it, a case of buying into the SF mystique. He was more concerned with how he looked than how he performed. He assumed because he understood the engineering part of his job that he was exempt from other "soldier" skills and tasks. He felt he was entitled to higher levels of comfort than conventionals and Rangers--that the austerity they endured was for the simple minded and not for "special" people like Green Berets. From my first days on the job, he had resented my opposition to that sense of entitlement, and my insistence on mastery of basic military doctrine as the foundation for conducting "special" operations. I hated the mystique. So our antagonism, while never loud and open, was early and consistent. He would take the refusal to use the Hotel Bayara as our quarters as some kind of personal affront.

I told them to send two FAd'H to the hotel to guard it, with instructions to merely prevent entrance with minimal force, and to bring Calixte to me.

Were we going to make a deal for the hotel, they asked, seeming very much in favor of the idea. I doubt it, I said. I'm going to arrest him. Both men looked taken aback, but both knew I was sleep deprived, single-minded and cross, so they went back to the hotel to detain Neal

Calixte. Could we just take the hotel over, like appropriate it? they queried. Just bring me Calixte, I said.

When they came back with Calixte, he was stiff-backed and indignant, demanding to see someone in charge, with an absolutely outraged French wife in tow. Both were in their early sixties, well kept, accustomed to command, her more than him. We told her that she was not under arrest, but she refused to leave his side, and we decided not to wrestle an obstinate sixty year-old woman. She stayed. We sat them both down in the courtyard of the prison with the rest of the detainees, where they immediately wanted to talk with Blaise. All were told not to utter a sound.

Ali and Calixte were engaged in an animated conversation, and I asked Ali to translate the gist of it to me. Calixte was a former ambassador, he said, and claimed to have diplomatic immunity. This claim caused some hesitation on Ali and Rod's part. Mike was there by then, and seemed curious but disinclined to intervene. As far as he was concerned, the operation was going grandly, and there was no reason to fuck with success. He was going to let me have my head. So I overruled the hesitancy of Rod and Ali. Fuck him, I said. Tell him he is the local chief financier for FRAPH, that we know it, and that he is going by helicopter to Port-au-Prince tomorrow. Ali translated.

The question of food came up. How do the prisoners eat? We decided to give each detainee an MRE and to allow them to eat it. We had to remove all the flex cuffs. Mrs Calixte did not have cuffs on, since she had not been detained. She was detaining herself.

Calixte never lost his *hauteur*.

Interview pursuant to Article 15-6 investigation of the action of Master Sergeant Stanley A. Goff, 500-58-5666, ODA 354, Company B, 2nd Battalion, 3rd Special Forces Group (Airborne) for actions taken during Operation Restore Democracy, September-December, 1994, in the Republic of Haiti. Investigating Officer: Major Robert McCoart. Interviewee: Master Sergeant Goff.

Are you anti-FRAPH?
Yes.
Why?
They're a death squad network.
According to the task force command, they are to be treated as the legitimate political opposition.

They're still death squads. Were we ordered to work with them, too?
No, you weren't ordered to work with them. But it sounds like you harassed them.
I arrested them when I had permission.
You arrested a man with diplomatic immunity too.
How can someone have diplomatic immunity in his own country when he's not an ambassador any more?
Didn't your own team warn you that you shouldn't arrest Nyll Calixte?
My team also wanted to move into his hotel. I ran the team.

At around 8:30 AM, Vincent, Ronnie and Freddy, another civilian contact, showed up. They cruised through the caserne and assessed what was going on. Vincent told us we had done marvelously and had detained exactly the right people. He asked if we needed anything. Yes, I told him. A house. We still needed to unload our truck full of supplies and establish communications with higher headquarters. And we may need a little help with the ever swelling, now dancing-and-singing mass of spectators outside the caserne.

In front of the caserne, Vincent gave a short speech to the crowd. They cheered him, then broke up and dissipated into a handful of people. 356, who was growing impatient, relaxed a bit, and collapsed their perimeter onto the caserne porch, in the shade, protected from the sun which was growing more viciously hot by the minute. Time was passing more quickly than we had imagined. Before we knew it, it was 10:00 AM. I began to stress about getting a house, and clearing 356 out of there.

During one respite in the frenetic activity, the reporters got to me, and asked why we had arrested all those people. I explained what I had learned before we left Ouanaminthe, and they all exchanged knowing glances. That was why everyone was so hostile, they concluded, when they had been in town the day before we arrived. The people they had interviewed, thinking they were speaking with the leaders of Fort Liberté, had been Neal Calixte and Pascal Blaise. They had hobnobbed around with these guys in public, slavishly writing down everything they had said, and reported to us how unfriendly Fort Liberté was -- how people peeked suspiciously out their doors at them. They had been interviewing the two most feared and hated citizens in town. I decided then and there that I needed to get out of the military and become a journalist. I, at least, did some of my homework.

Then Vincent showed up with a young Frenchman, who could only be described as blonde headed, blue eyed and pretty. He seemed so pretty, in fact, that it was hard to imagine him here in Haiti, in Fort Liberté, the land that time forgot, where beauty was not manifest in prettiness, but in the stark business of survival. He was introduced as the administrator for Doctors Without Borders, and he had a handful of keys that, Vincent explained, were to our new house.

Doctors Without Borders had left Fort Liberté during the "troubles" with the Cédras regime, and this administrator had remained behind, in his own words, as a witness. We were here, now, and his job was done. He would be leaving, but the house had a current lease, and he wanted to let us use it. We walked two blocks South from the caserne, and he led me up the porch of a block house, painted yellow, with a small carport on the left as you faced it. It was a concrete porch, half wrap-around, with houses on both sides within four feet. We went in, and the place was covered in grime and cobwebs. The bathroom had a sink and a toilet, but no running water in either. The shower had a head, but the tile shower floor below it had been built with one small oversight ... there was no drain. Obviously, the shower had never been used. The Frenchman told me that there was a 1500-gallon cistern atop the house that had to be pumped full from the underground cistern, which he showed me on the East side of the house. There was a comparatively large living room, on the wall of which was perched a huge black spider, and an adjacent hallway, leading to two small bedrooms on the West, two large bedrooms on the East, and one more large room in the North or back of the house. There was no kitchen. There was no electricity. But there was space, space enough to move in and store our gear. I thanked him enthusiastically.

Kyle, Ali and Gonzo started bitching as soon as we began to unload our cargo into the house. They wanted to move into the hotel, and they felt that I was fucking over the team, making then live in the "shithole." It was better than anything they had lived in since we got to Haiti, but Special Forces—as I pointed out—suffers frequently from brattishness.

I told them shortly and sharply that I didn't want to hear their whining, and that there was no way we were going to move into that hotel, giving the appearance that we (1) were going to simply appropriate anything we needed, and (2) that we were in bed with the bad guys. Our comfort was still secondary to the mission. This was a concept that was lost on them and would remain lost on them. It never really occurred to them that we shouldn't simply impose our will on Haitians, and that it was more important to win their loyalty than it was salve our own pride. These attitudes were serious indicators, and I slapped them like mosquitoes. Click.

The spider on the wall had left me with an uneasy feeling.

We posted two men on the garrison, then brought everyone to the house to quickly download all the equipment. The hot bull labor reminded us that we were frazzled, exhausted. When we were established, albeit by a mere figurative toehold, in the house, I let 356 go back to Ouanaminthe. It was noon.

Vincent, Ronnie and Freddy came by to say they would be returning as well. I thanked them all from the bottom of my heart for their help.

Mike, the reporter from the Los Angeles Times, and I went over to talk with Doctor Max Mondestin, the regional surgeon, head of the regional hospital in Fort Liberté, and cousin of Adele Mondestin, the mayor whom we had not yet met.

Max asked that we refrain in the future from bringing rifles into the hospital. We apologized and agreed to comply with his wishes. We assured him that we wished to be as non-disruptive as possible, and asked his assistance with explaining our mission in Fort Liberté, since he probably came in contact with more people than anyone in town, and because he had the reputation as a public benefactor who was apolitical. He said he would do what he could, but that he wished to remain outside politics and military operations. We assured him that we understood and promised to stay in touch. Our objective was to educate the local population about our mission and to provide stability as quickly as possible. We were not there to solve Haitian problems. We had neither the understanding nor the resources to do that. He seemed plea sandy surprised by our low-key approach we expressed our intention to follow. We talked casually for a while, and learned that he had done his residency at Boston College and that he had returned to Haiti to do what he could for his people.

A year later, when I would return, Max would be packing up to take a job with the World Bank. So much for first impressions.

The rest of the day proceeded with the cleanup of the FAd'H headquarters, inventory and confiscation of weapons, and ordering the house. We hung a canvas field shower in the bathroom, but had to root through the liberated American Airlines tools to find a large punch, which we used to knock a hole in the tile for a drain. We started rotating members of the team into the shower, and people started dropping their fatigues into buckets of water to soak.

Percy stayed with Skye and Rod at the caserne, where he translated in his halting way, occasionally taking time to explain that we had to watch out for the people, because they were planning to storm the garrison and kill everyone.

By mid-afternoon, we started vehicular and dismounted patrols, partly to provide a security presence and partly to familiarize ourselves with the layout of the town. The reporters had described the place correctly as a town that died during the day. The streets remained nearly deserted, and I began to fear we had inherited a ghost town, that the mornings crowd was some kind of crazy hallucination brought on by fatigue and dehydration.

I made a decision to eliminate any patrols that night, except for emergency, and to drop down to a one-man radio watch, rotated hourly. I wanted everyone to get a solid good nights sleep. I detected an attitude on the part of the guys that the mission was over, and everything else was a denouement. I attributed this to exhaustion. I would find that this was one of the worst miscalculations I would make during this mission.

Just before dark, we got the call that the helicopter was inbound to pick up our detainees. Rod had recorded their names, date of birth, ostensible employment, and anything else he found out that seemed pertinent. Kyle, Rod and Gonzo went out to the landing zone (LZ) we had identified in a field about a mile out of town (chosen to prevent helicopters from blowing the roofs off of houses, a problem that had cost considerable sums to repair in Ouanaminthe).

When they returned, we were reviewing what had to be done and what needed to be done, and what the goals were for the immediate future in Fort Liberté. Emphasis was on maintaining stability with patrols and ready reaction to monitor demonstrations, making contact with community leaders, and a systematic expansion of our influence to outlying communities. October 15th was our milestone, because Mike and I agreed that once Aristide was back, the excitement level that anticipated his return should drop off.

While we were meeting, the drums started, somewhere off in the South end of town. It was dark, and the beat pierced through the darkness over the broken rooftops, with the syncopated chanting. *Manifestation*. And it was coming our way, to the garrison. Everyone automatically started donning his web gear. We knew the drill well. We delegated. You and you, on the vehicle, follow the demonstration, watch for any troublemakers, and watch the buildings around the demonstration to make sure no one attacks the demonstrators. Be obvious about the protective mission. It'll keep the crowd friendly. You and you, to the front of the garrison. When the demonstration halts there, the vehicle guys will dismount and assist in holding the line. You and you, maintain security and radio watch here at the house. Get us a quick commo check all round. Make sure the aid bag is in the vehicle.

Within five minutes, we were posting. We followed the demonstration, and as we predicted, they ended up in front of the garrison. The FAd'H soldiers stood on the front porch of the caserne, blustering and terrified. There were only about ten of them left for the evening. We had sent the others home.

What we were treated to was interpretive dance. As the demonstrators settled into their static rhythm, several members of the crowd, children and adults, leapt into a clearing that the crowd made to provide a stage. There, to the beat of the drums and the cyclic crests of the converted African melodies, scenes of choreographed violence were dramatically rendered; police batoning the people, people being dragged away and beaten and shot, women being raped; the performance was amazing, not just for content, but for its production values. I regret that I did not have a video camera.

The production seemed to satisfy the crowd. They began moving off to the South, directly toward our new team house. Which is exactly where they went. We moved with them. We sat on the porch blocking their way in, so a wave of enthusiasm didn't crest them directly into the house. We had gained a lot of experience. We guarded covertly, sitting and smiling, not standing with weapons at the ready, providing a line, which we enforced by gently guiding people back into the crowd, especially youngsters, who were the point persons for crowd advances. We sat on the steps and the wide concrete porch rail, and the crowd sang to us in welcome. The ubiquitous tree branches, symbols of solidarity with Father Aristide, were used by young girls, to fan our sweaty faces, while hands young and old reached out to touch us, to seize our hands, by children to feel our white skin. We left the Hummer headlights on the crowd, to aid surveillance, and so we could see each other in the non-electrical Haitian night. We were surrounded by a sea of smiles, by the sour smell of a throng, by the ever more familiar music of the street, by tears of gratitude.

Behind my confident smile, I wondered, as I had since we arrived, if we weren't about to betray them all. Fraud, a voice kept saying. Judas. Tool.

Mike made his last journal entry for that day, when the host of people had gone to bed, and we were left with snoring and the steady hiss of the SATCOM radio and the gentle Caribbean breeze whistling over the roof. "GREAT DAY!"

[Calixte was released within days by U.S. presidential order, and Blaise a short time thereafter–*Ed.*]

First printed in "Hideous Dream: A Soldier's Memoir of the US Invasion of Haiti"

Class Analysis of a Crisis

November 19, 2002

Kim Ives

This past week saw dueling demonstrations between thousands of pro- and anti-government marchers in Haiti. Political tension, violence and lawlessness are growing. Telephone calls and Internet chat rooms are filled with rumors and speculation about how events will unfold.

To understand the nature of the crisis shaking Haiti today, it is essential to understand the class forces at play.

The destabilization campaign against the Haitian government is being led by the Bush faction of the U.S. bourgeoisie, which is arch-reactionary and hostile to regimes which even pay lip-service to a progressive agenda, as Aristide once did. Two conservative retreads from the previous Bush administration, Undersecretary of State for the Americas Otto Reich and Ambassador to the Organization of American States (OAS) Roger Noriega, are spearheading the campaign to uproot Aristide, whom they charge is becoming an "illegitimate president" of a "pariah state," even as other OAS states stand by wringing their hands at the plight of the besieged president.

Meanwhile, the majority of the Haitian bourgeoisie, as represented by the Association of Industries of Haiti (ADIH), the Chamber of Commerce and of Industry of Haiti (CCIH) and, more globally, the Civil Society Initiative (ISC), has allied itself with the forces of its age-old rival, the landed oligarchy or *grandons*, whose purest recent political manifestation was the Duvalier dictatorship (1957-1986). The armed expression of the *grandons* under the Duvaliers was the Tonton Macoutes, who were the eyes, ears, and fists of this class. The remnants and descendants of this brutal corps live on in Haiti. Neo-Duvalierist political representatives are often referred to, in Haitian political parlance, as the Macoute sector.

This "Macoute-Bourgeois" alliance is embodied in the Democratic Convergence opposition front, which is funded by Washington's National Endowment for Democracy (NED). Social democratic groups like the Struggling People's Organization (OPL) of Gérard Pierre-

Charles, the National Progressive Revolutionary Party (PANPRA) of Serge Gilles, and the National Congress of Democratic Movements (KONAKOM) of Micha Gaillard and Victor Benoit represent the bourgeois current, which favors taking power through political wrangling facilitated by the OAS and Washington's diplomatic muscle.

The Macoute current favors the "zero option," code for the violent overthrow of Aristide. The Mobilization for National Development (MDN) of Hubert DeRonceray, the Christian Movement for a New Haiti (MOCHRENA) of Pastor Luc Mesadieu and, increasingly, the Democratic Unity Confederation (KID) of Evans Paul are the foremost representatives of this tendency.

Despite Washington's backing, the Convergence has very little support among the masses across Haiti. But two weeks ago, it got collaboration from former soldiers, as represented by former putschist Colonel Himmler Rébu. Aided by intense media coverage and increasingly desperate living conditions, the Convergence/Rébu alliance was able to pull several thousand people in its train during a November 17, 2002, march in Cap Haïtien (see Haïti Progrès, 11/20/02).

Since his emergence as a firebrand priest from Port-au-Prince's La Saline slum, Aristide has had as his principal base Haiti's growing strata of unemployed urban poor. The ranks of this dispossessed, desperate class have swelled as falling prices for coffee, cocoa and sugar, cheap food dumping from the U.S., and neo-liberal reforms have driven peasants off the land and into Haiti's miserable slums. Aristide's populist sway over this volatile class is the essence of his power, and it is precisely what the Haitian ruling class fears and U.S. officials distrust.

Aristide has attempted to sell himself to Washington as the intermediary who can control and reign in this explosive underclass in exchange for a few crumbs from the ruling class table. Hence he periodically whips up the unemployed masses, and then soothes them, as a demonstration of his power.

On the other hand, he has also sought to reassure the U.S. and Haitian ruling classes by integrating businessmen and Duvalierists into leading positions in his government and party, pushing it even more to the right. The Lavalas Family party has sold off state industries, begun the sale of Haitian territory for free-trade zones, cracked down on union organizers, and acquiesced to treaties allowing unilateral U.S. penetration of Haitian territory.

While the Clinton administration was willing to gamble on using Aristide to control Haiti, the Bush administration is not. On the contrary, they have counterattacked. Washington has pushed through the OAS two resolutions which compel Aristide to arrest the popular organization leaders which effectively coordinate the slum masses into a political force. Aristide is being forced to saw off the branch on which he sits.

By blocking some $500 million in international aid and loans to Haiti, Bush has worked to discredit and trap Aristide, who made rosy campaign promises to the masses now suffering and hungry as never before. Disillusionment with Aristide is growing as he fails to deliver.

Meanwhile, other political forces have begun to emerge. For years, the National Popular Party (PPN) has focused its organizing in the Haitian peasantry, which is still Haiti's majority. In May and October 2002, the PPN organized two mass marches in Port-au-Prince and Cap Haïtien to propose a "popular alternative" to the Convergence and Lavalas Family (see Haïti Progrès, 5/8/02 and 10/23/02).

The peasantry, as in many Third World countries, comprises most of Haiti's working class, although they labor under feudal relations of production, paying landowners with a portion of their crops. Haiti's wage-earning proletariat works primarily in the assembly industries ringing the Port-au-Prince airport. This work force has shrunk by about two-thirds from its peak of about 60,000 in the early 1980s because foreign investors have fled from the political struggle that has rocked Haiti since 1986, when the Duvalier dictatorship fell.

The Convergence may rend into rival factions as the crisis matures. Already, one hard-liner, Leslie Manigat of the Assembly of Progressive National Democrats (RNDP), broke away from the Convergence in 2002 because of its continuing negotiations with the Lavalas Family. Tensions are likely to grow as Washington, ultimately, decides whether to try OAS-controlled elections in 2003 or the "zero option" sooner to remove Aristide and his party from power.

It is ironic, but historically predictable, that the bourgeoisie is collaborating with former soldiers and Macoutes. In 1987, the neo-Duvalierist sector, working through and with the Haitian Army, massacred Haitian voters to block the election dreams of the bourgeoisie, united at that time in the Group of 57. The bourgeoisie may come to rue today's alliance. "The Macoutes never share power with anybody," the PPN's Secretary General Ben Dupuy warned in a Nov. 21, 2002, press conference.

Similarly, Aristide's decline has resulted from his notion that he could somehow appease Washington through concessions. He cannot, a lesson Nicaragua's Sandanistas learned during the 1980s.

Aristide's party will likely provide little support or defense as the crisis grows, and it may also fracture. Many of the Lavalas Family's elected officials are archetypal petty bourgeois opportunists, intent only on snagging a government post with which to enrich themselves through corruption or personal projects like radio stations, bus lines, or supermarkets.

Unfortunately for Washington, it has no viable alternative to Aristide in Haiti and no Haitian Army (disbanded by Aristide in 1994) through which to make a coup, as was done in 1991. The only standing military force on the island is the 24,500-man Dominican Army, to which the U.S. is now sending 20,000 M-16s as part of a multi-million dollar military aid package (see Haïti Progrès, 11/20/02). Some 1000 U.S. soldiers will also be stationed in the Dominican Republic, supposedly for training purposes. Most certainly, both U.S. and Dominican forces will be poised for a military intervention into Haiti if and when the moment comes. Ironically, this scenario looms as Haiti prepares to celebrate the bicentennial anniversary of its January 1, 1804, independence.

Despite this ominous outlook, the Haitian people have managed to foil Washington's best laid plans repeatedly over the past 16 years since the fall of the Duvalier regime. Whatever unfolds in the weeks ahead, the Bush administration and its Haitian allies can expect fierce resistance from a nation and a generation which has learned many lessons and shed many illusions on its march toward democracy and independence.

Haïti-Progrès, Nov. 19, 2002

Postscript: In the year between the time this article was first published in Haïti Progrès and when this book was edited, there have been several developments.

The offensive of the Bush administration and its local acolytes against the Lavalas government has intensified. At the time of this writing, even the bourgeois current of the Democratic Convergence, emboldened by anti-government guerrilla actions, shrill media attacks, and Washington's highly aggressive actions worldwide, seems to have opted for Aristide's overthrow and shunned the bargaining table. Meanwhile, to counter Washington's destabilization campaign, the PPN has fiercely defended the Haitian government against unconstitutional removal. While still presenting itself as the "people's alternative," the PPN organized two more mass demonstrations in the capital in March and September to urge Aristide to act more decisively to counteract U.S.-sponsored subversion.

Although allied with the Lavalas Family, the PPN has remained critical of its timidity and backpedaling, as well as its embrace of "free trade zones," one of which was completed in Haiti's northeast and began operating in the fall of 2003, while another is planned to be constructed near Cité Soleil.

Also, several pro-government popular organization leaders in Haiti's slums have died under mysterious circumstances, in particular Amiot "Cuban" Métayer in September 2003 in Gonaïves. These killings have injected confusion into Haiti's volatile slums, provoking violence that has been fanned and fed by the opposition with rumors, money, and guns.

HAITI:

A political and class-conscious people

Dec. 24, 1998

Maude LeBlanc

Excerpts from a talk given by Maude LeBlanc, co-director of Haïti Progrès newspaper, at a conference Dec. 5, 1998

U.S. imperialism is very upset with how things have been going in Haiti. Despite sending troops and investing close to $3 billion to overhaul the country along neoliberal lines, they have not achieved their goal. Thus the title of a New York Times piece a couple of weeks ago: "Political Feuds Rack Haiti: So Much for Its High Hopes."

The article complains that the "hopes for an era of prosperity and stability have evaporated" because of a "16-month political squabble between [former president] Aristide and other leaders of the fracturing Lavalas coalition." According to the Times, this "squabble" is leaving "Haiti's foreign allies disillusioned and exasperated."

Of course they are disillusioned and exasperated. The Haitian people are not going along with their plans. They are resisting the dictates of Washington and the under-the-table deals of the Haitian ruling class. This has people like U.S. Secretary of State Madeleine Albright addressing the Haitian government of President René Préval quite undiplomatically. "The Haitian people deserve a democratic form of government and they deserve the ability to have the fruits that the international community is trying to give them," she said.

Isn't that nice? They are trying to give us democracy. They are trying to gives us fruits. What is the matter with us?

Well, the fact of the matter is that we, the Haitian people, are very political and class conscious, and understand that the only democracy they respect is the one they control and the only fruits they are interested in are the ones they can steal from us. As you all know, Haiti is home to the only successful slave revolution in history, so we don't take kindly to being enslaved. Aristide, who at one time may have been going along with or pretending to go along with the American plan, is now one of its fiercest opponents. And if the imperialists hate anyone, it is someone who they thought they had bought as their lackey who then double-crosses them.

Aristide thinks he can reconcile with the Haitian bourgeoisie and imperialism and come to power through elections. The National Popular Assembly (APN) feels such a program is based on illusions. Furthermore, the APN aims to go beyond a mere redistribution of wealth; it calls for the redistribution of property—land to the peasants and factories to the workers. But at this time, the APN doesn't have the strength and full trust of the masses to carry such a program forward. This is where Marxism is so critical. It allows a working-class party to identify class allies on the road to liberation. In Haiti today, our principal ally is Aristide and the Lavalas Family.

This alliance is very disturbing to the Haitian ruling class and to Washington. Most recently, the APN and Lavalas launched nationwide demonstrations throughout Haiti on Sept. 30, 1998, the seventh anniversary of the 1991 coup d'état. Tens of thousands of demonstrators took to the streets. We have no illusions about the difficulty of the struggle before us. However, inspired by the example of our ancestors who fought against the greatest military power of their epoch, Napoleon's France, and by our heroic and resourceful neighbor to the west, Cuba, we are determined to continue our struggle. Surrender and resignation are not options.

Workers World, Dec. 24, 1998

Haitian Struggle for Freedom

Mumia Abu-Jamal

[from a radio column recorded 12/22/02]

The images of young, healthy, desperate Haitians, jumping overboard into the roiling Florida surf, burns itself into the American mind, evoking differing responses, depending on one's perspective.

To many Euro-Americans, the image is a terrible one, which seizes the heart in the icy grip of fear. To many African-Americans, however, the images evoke compassion, sorrow, and the shared feelings of loss for their Haitian cousins, who feel compelled to brave the terrible threats and dangers of the sea, to start a life of hope in America.

To them, the treatment of Haitians, who are routinely encaged in demeaning conditions of confinement in de facto prisons upon their arrival, contrasts sharply with the felicitous treatment accorded their Cuban neighbors, who are encouraged, nay—invited!—to brave the churning waters of the Caribbean Sea to make it to the southern tip of Florida. The U.S.-Cuban policy with its origins in the dark days of the Cold War is a remnant of the American determination to stick their finger in the eye of their perennial thorn-in-their-side, President Castro.

For Haitians, the flight to the shores of America must be bittersweet. Shortly after the Haitian Revolution ended, around 1804, Haiti was the proud historical inheritor of the distinction of a Revolution against tyranny, oppression and slavery, and emerged as the second independent nation in the Western hemisphere (after the United States), and the first people in history to stage a successful slave revolution. Their freedom came after the armies of Toussaint Louverture and General Henri Christophe defeated the French and English imperial armies in what was once called Saint Domingue (or San Domingo).

Indeed, when the Americans were fighting the British for their independence, they had help from Haitians, who fought on the side of the American revolutionaries. Indeed, Christophe, when a younger man, fought in the Battle of Savannah, in the regiment of Comte d'Estaing, and was slightly wounded.

After the Revolution, though, Haitians became victims of dreadfully 'bad press' by the Americans. Instead of being seen as a fellow member of the small confraternity of free nations, and welcomed, it was seen as a Terror, and shunned. That's because the U.S. was a 'free' nation, only in name, but a slave nation in the heart, and in fact.

The victory of the Haitians so dismayed the French imperial designs of Napoleon that he quickly sold the Louisiana Territory to the Americans for a song (thus doubling the size of the United States).

The Haitian Revolution sent shock waves throughout America, precisely because the U.S. was a slave society, that talked about freedom and liberty, but meant white freedom, and white liberty (and really only meant white men of means and wealth). It gave a spur and a spark to the anti-slavery movement on these shores, as the brilliant W.E.B. DuBois wrote in his *The Suppression of the African Slave Trade to the United States of America: 1638 to 1870*:

The role which the great Negro Toussaint, called Louverture, played in the history of the United States has seldom been fully appreciated. Representing the age of revolution in America, he rose to leadership through a bloody terror, which contrived a Negro "problem" for the Western Hemisphere, intensified and defined the anti-slavery movement, became one of the causes, and probably the prime one, which lead Napoleon to sell Louisiana for a song, and finally, through the interworking of all these efforts, rendered more certain the final prohibition of the slave-trade by the United States in 1807.

The grandsons and granddaughters of the 'Great Toussaint' are now the subject of mass media demonization in every report on Haiti. They are projected as the permanent 'Other,' those strange folk who believe in a strange religion, the very name of which has been the synonym for weirdness (remember Bush I's rant about "voodoo economics"?).

When they arrive on the shores of the nation that their ancestors helped free, they are thrown into Krome Correctional facility, or hauled back into the hells of a Haiti that has been economically choked to death.

Yet, the images haunt us, for they tell us how we are perceived in the eyes of our cousins.

Review of a Review
Answering recent distortions

March 12, 2003

Kim Ives

It is hard to know where to begin in dissecting Peter Dailey's pair of articles, "The Fall of the House of Aristide" and "Haiti's Betrayal" in the March 13 and March 27, 2003, issues of the *New York Review of Books*. Where do you start with an analyst who purports to be progressive but then portrays Washington's pressure on Haiti as that of the "international community," who sympathizes with "international lenders" who think that "Haiti today seems increasingly indistinguishable from any other third-world sinkhole," and who refers to anti-imperialist remarks as "anti-Americanism"?

Although he would have us believe he is an expert in Haitian affairs, Dailey mostly churns out, and perhaps relied upon, the same stereotypes, half-truths and misinformation seen in the mainstream media. His account is marked by historical distortions, glaring omissions, plagiarism, and outright falsehoods which belie his claim that "for most of the Lavalas years, I was a fairly regular visitor to Port-au-Prince."

Like a physicist's faulty mathematical theorem which omits an elementary factor such as, say, gravity, Dailey eliminates from his gloomy analysis of Haiti's recent history under the administrations of Presidents Jean Bertrand Aristide and René Préval the central role played by Washington in sabotaging Haiti's democratic movement and elected governments since the fall of dictator Jean-Claude Duvalier in 1986. This subversion is the flip side of U.S. support for Haitian dictators over decades before.

The article purports to be a review of Robert Fatton, Jr.'s book, *Haiti's Predatory Republic: The Unending Transition to Democracy*, which I have not read and which Dailey only occasionally cites in his review. Therefore I don't know how much of Dailey's argument was drawn from or inspired by Fatton, a Haitian-born professor of government and foreign affairs at the University of Virginia. But given the paucity of Dailey's referrals to the object of his review, I will treat the analysis as his.

Or perhaps I should say it is the analysis of the OPL (Organisation du Peuple en Lutte), Organization of Struggling People, the central component of the U.S.-backed Democratic Convergence opposition front. Headed by Gérard Pierre-Charles, a former leader of the Unified Haitian Communist Party (PUCH), the OPL is hailed by Dailey as "the social democratic constitutionalist wing of the Lavalas movement, the left-wing populist coalition that first brought Aristide to power, which was mobilized into opposition by the Aristide government's increasingly corrupt and authoritarian character." The less charitable characterization of the OPL's leaders would be boot-lickers of U.S. imperialism, who encouraged Aristide to break with Haiti's leftist popular organizations and return from exile in 1994 on the shoulders of 23,000 U.S. troops and who preach compliance and subservience to every U.S. dictate. Their Convergence front today receives millions of dollars funneled from Washington's National Endowment for Democracy to wreak political havoc in Haiti.

But for Dailey, this is "the social democratic constitutionalist left" which has sought "to consolidate and institutionalize Haiti's fragile democracy and to establish the concepts of pluralism and power-sharing integral to a modern political system" against Aristide's "authoritarian" power grabs. The OPL's role as Washington's collaborator in blocking three prime ministers proposed by Préval, in helping to privatize Haitian state industries, and in providing the excuse for the Bush Administration's blockage of $500 million in international aid and loans to Haiti reveals little that could be interpreted as "left" or "power-sharing."

Dailey makes ample use of tired clichés from the mainstream press. He refers to Préval as Aristide's "hand-picked successor," a common refrain in AP and Reuters dispatches. In reality, Préval was "handpicked" by the OPL in 1995 in opposition to the call by most Haitians for Aristide to serve out the three years that he spent in exile from his five-year term during the 1991-1994 coup d'état, a perfectly legitimate interpretation of Haiti's 1987 Constitution. But that wasn't Washington's interpretation, since Aristide was proving to be mercurial and uncooperative about privatizations and other neoliberal reforms.

The tension burst forth on Nov. 11, 1995, when Aristide verbally pilloried U.S. Ambassador William Swing and U.N. Haiti chief Lakhdar Brahimi at the National Cathedral during a funeral for one of the president's slain partisans (see Haïti Progrès, 11/15/1995). "The game of hypocrisy is over" Aristide exclaimed with a fire reminiscent of his sermons when a priest at St. Jean Bosco in the early 1980s. "We don't have two, or three heads of state, we have one."

Peeved and alarmed, Washington, whose troops still occupied the country, turned to the OPL to push Aristide out. Having no viable presidential candidates of their own, the OPL selected Préval, who had been Aristide's prime minister in 1991. The move galled Aristide, who didn't announce his support for Préval until the day before his Dec. 17, 1995, election.

Préval turned out to be his own man and gradually struck a course of growing independence from his OPL sponsors, starting with his refusal to name Gérard Pierre-Charles as prime minister, thus forcing a compromise on a lower level OPL cadre, Rosny Smarth.

Nor was Préval Aristide's "surrogate," as Dailey blithely asserts Although he did take account of Aristide's positions, their relationship was often prickly. Préval walked a line between the OPL, which controlled the Parliament, and Aristide, who formed his own party, the Fanmi Lavalas (FL), in November 1996.

Préval had to make a choice, however, in January 1999 when the terms of most OPL parliamentarians ran out due to the political gridlock they themselves had imposed. Préval refused to decree an unconstitutional extension of their terms, as they demanded, and the Parliament expired. Dailey is therefore wrong in parroting the mainstream press and OPL assertion that Préval was "shutting down the opposition-controlled Parliament," a step the OPL charged was "a coup against our democratic institutions." And also wrong for claiming "for the remainder of his term, together with a de facto government formed with his FL colleagues, [Préval] ruled by decree." The term "de facto government," used during the coup to characterize the military's puppets, was resuscitated by the OPL in an effort to demonize the Préval regime.

The comparison was ludicrous and generally Haitians applaud the way Préval ran the government and held elections after the obstructionist parliament self-destructed. (Préval held elections not because of "rising international protest," as Dailey asserts, but because the OPL could no longer block them). Furthermore, Préval was never a member of the FL, nor was his Prime Minister Jacques Alexis, nor were most of the ministers.

In the same vein, it is incorrect when Dailey says that "Aristide and his associates quit OPL to form the FL." Aristide was never an OPL member, nor were most of the FL founders.

In addition to the OPL, Dailey's references come from the regime's harshest foes. He regularly cites the National Coalition for Haitian Rights (NCHR), which he incorrectly says was "once [one of] Aristide's strongest supporters." NCHR, which like its cousin organization Americas Watch is supported by financier and currency-speculator George Soros, has had a thorny relationship with Aristide since his first administration in 1991.

Shortly after the Sept. 30, 1991, coup d'état, the NCHR abetted the first Bush administration by issuing a report, based in part on information and interpretations from the de facto prime minister Jean-Jacques Honorat, which portrayed the Aristide government as a human-rights abuser. The U.S. was thus able to posture that the coup was in some measure "justified." As a second Bush administration wars with Aristide, the NCHR continues to willingly provide the U.S. State Department with ammunition in the form of supposed Lavalas "human-rights violations" against the Convergence while ignoring repeated opposition attacks and abuses against Lavalas militants and the deadly campaign being carried out by neo-Duvalierist guerrillas who claim affinity with the opposition (see Haïti Progrès, 2/12/2003). The NCHR has thus perfected its knack of being in the wrong place at the right time.

Dailey also relies heavily on the Haiti Democracy Project, a Washington-based Convergence ally with a board full of U.S. State Department veterans and clients.

"Gross electoral fraud by the ruling party has deprived the entire political apparatus of legitimacy," Dailey writes, a silly charge that Convergence politicians regularly bark. "For most of this time attacks by government-sponsored and armed militants on opposition rallies made free assembly all but impossible." In reality, the Convergence regularly holds meetings, marches, and rallies, while its politicians dominate the Haitian airwaves and are often even interviewed on the government-run Haitian National Television. It even briefly and illegally set up a "parallel government" in Port-au-Prince until it collapsed under the weight of its own ridiculousness. Imagine state reaction if that happened in Washington or Paris.

"By 1999, it seemed to many Haitians that Aristide, who once personified Haitian aspirations for democracy, now represented Haitian democracy's biggest obstacle," Dailey continues. This phrase speaks volumes about Dailey's unground ax, because in 1999 Aristide had been out of office for four years and was making anti-neoliberal noises. The electoral wrangling of 2000 was still a year off. So who were the "many Haitians"? How was Aristide already "democracy's biggest obstacle"?

In fact, Aristide was an "obstacle" for the U.S. which feared his popularity and agenda and set out to engineer an "electoral coup d'état" in 2000. But that electoral coup was defeated by a massive popular mobilization and turn-out for the FL. Dailey completely omits any mention of U.S. meddling in Haiti's election and the people's response, pretending instead that the FL somehow engineered "gross electoral fraud," which even the Organization of American States (OAS) never charged. The FL was not in power for the 2000 elections and had no members on the Provisional Electoral Council (CEP) that presided over them. Half of the CEP members, however, were from the opposition.

Contrary to Dailey's mixed-up account, the OAS's dubious objection to the May 2000 parliamentary elections was that eight (not 14, as Dailey says) of the nineteen Senate races should have gone to a second round. (Seven of those eight senators voluntarily stepped down, one of the FL's early concessions.) The opposition, the U.S., and now Dailey have inflated this quibble over how run-offs were calculated to the point where the reviewer writes the "legitimacy of [Aristide's] government [is] very much in dispute." Deciding on which races required run-offs was solely in the CEP's jurisdiction and outside of OAS election observers' mandate. This charge is simply absurd, as is Dailey's charge that Préval was responsible for "forcing the resignation of Smarth" in June 1997, which "marks the end of the last legally constituted government Haiti has had to date." Smarth stepped down due to popular outcry over his OPL policies, and both of Aristide's governments since 2001 (Prime Ministers Jean-Marie Chérestal and Yvon Neptune) have been "legally constituted" and recognized by every government on the planet.

Dailey's assertion that the "Aristide government's increasingly authoritarian behavior has left it isolated and condemned by the international community, which has suspended crucial foreign aid to the point that today there is a total embargo apart from emergency humanitarian relief," is also laughable on several counts. The "international community," if defined as the majority of the world's nations, is sympathetic to the Haitian government and disapproving, at the very least, of the Bush administration's strong-arming. They have not "suspended crucial foreign aid." Only the U.S. and European powers have done that. (In fact, the U.S. has vetoed the disbursement of $140 million approved by the Inter-American Development Bank, a violation of the bank's internal rules against political meddling.) On the contrary, the majority of the OAS and CARICOM member states have pleaded for the release of the aid and loans to Haiti, held hostage only by Washington's hostility to Aristide.

Dailey's research is beyond sloppy. At one point he even lifts a quote of artist Edzer Pierre, uncredited, from another author's article and then changes Pierre's label from "former activist" to "former FL activist." When challenged about the plagiarism on an Internet Haiti discussion group, Dailey blamed the matter on an ill-informed New York editor.

The reviewer also champions Convergence spin-masters when he says that "the most plausible explanation" for the Dec. 17, 2001 commando attack on the National Palace (see Haïti Progrès, 12/19/2001) is that it was "a dispute between factions of the National Police, aided by their Dominican allies, over control of the drug trade." Is this explanation "most plausible" when similar commando raids by anti-Lavalas guerrillas based in the Dominican Republic both preceded and followed the attack, when people identifying themselves as its organizers laid out their plans to a prominent Haitian journalist in Miami weeks before it, when the attackers came with a 50-caliber machine gun bolted in the back of a pick-up, and when one of the attackers killed was a former Haitian soldier? Dailey does not mention (and perhaps did not know) that the "group of disgruntled officers of the Haitian National Police" who the Haitian government charges led the attack had been in exile for over a year, having fled when Préval's government claims to have caught them planning a coup. Dailey also states that "as everyone in Haiti knows," Aristide lives in Tabarre not the Palace. In truth, Aristide used to stay at the Palace and often returned there on Sunday night, when the attack took place. An assassination attempt against Aristide by the same neo-Duvalierist guerrillas operating in Haiti today appears a much more plausible explanation.

Dailey's analysis has a scientific veneer which might hold some allure to progressives unfamiliar with Haiti. But his use of long-discredited racist simplifications, like the mainstream notion that Haiti's ruling class is a "mulatto elite," reveal the weak and shallow nature of his "class analysis."

One could go on for at least the length of Dailey's two installments, ticking off their inaccuracies and fallacies. But the biggest problem lies in the reviewer's pro-Convergence premises.

Dailey eloquently describes many obvious problems currently besetting Haitian society: the destruction of agriculture, the resulting rural flight to the cities, the deterioration of education and infrastructure, and the rise of the state as the principal employer, all of which have brought terrible social distortions and strains. This is where Fatton got the notion of a "predatory democracy" in which "the Haitian government remains the primary route to power and wealth." The problem is not in enumeration of the symptoms, but in diagnosis of the disease. Dailey faults Aristide's "ecclesiastical authoritarianism," while progressives point to Haiti's past marked by colonialist rape, semifeudal obscurantism, comprador parasitism, and imperialist intervention and plunder.

It's sure that there are plenty of reasons to criticize Aristide. But the principal problem, for progressives, is not Aristide's "authoritarianism," as Dailey contends, but rather his half-measures, vagueness, and hesitation in defending the Haitian people's demands for radical change in Haiti, whether due to political cowardice, immaturity, miscalculation, or duplicity.

One might forgive someone's misconception or confusion about Haiti, but Dailey's white-washing of the U.S. role in undermining Haiti's democratic movement is inexcusable. He consistently misrepresents the dismay, alarm, or punitive actions of Washington or Paris as those of the "international community."

It is unfortunate that a publication like the *New York Review of Books* has become the vehicle for such unadulterated Convergence "dogma," as Dailey terms the defense of Aristide's government by "Lavalas parliamentarians and pro-Lavalas journalists as well as Aristide's more credulous foreign supporters."

Perhaps the biggest falsehood of all comes when Dailey asserts in his final paragraph that "increasingly" the Haitian people have "decided" to accept "acknowledgment of defeat," in Fatton's words, after the high hopes of 1990. But the majority of Haitians still appear to support Aristide, rightly or wrongly, as the agent of wealth redistribution in Haiti. They poured into the streets by the tens of thousands in December [2002] to denounce the Convergence's call for Aristide's overthrow. This seems to contradict Dailey's hopes that "political passions among the people appear to be spent."

Haïti-Progrès, March 12, 2003

The Struggle of Haitian Workers

—their alliance with Steelworkers Local 8751

Steve Gillis, President, USWA Local 8751
Frantz Mendes, Vice-President, USWA Local 8751

What follows comes from the scrapbook of the Boston School Bus Drivers Union, which is United Steel Workers of America Local 8751. This union has supported the struggles of the Haitian community in Boston since the mid '80s. The pictures are fuzzy copies of copies, but we are using them because they show how Local 8751 struggles.

We are very glad to have this contribution since it shows how Haitians have enriched and deepened the union movement in the United States.

— editors

The struggle that the Haitian working class in the diaspora has waged against racism and U.S. colonialism has been part and parcel of the daily activity of the Boston School Bus Drivers Union for nearly two decades. Currently, about 75% of the 800 bus drivers represented by the Local are immigrants from Haiti. They have been in the leadership and filled the ranks of the Local's battles over the years, battles which include nine strikes since the Local's founding in 1977.

The Local has been in the forefront in Boston in defense of the rights of Haitian workers.

In 1990, the Local's leadership and hundreds of its members helped organize mass marches, pickets and a boycott to protest the U.S. Food and Drug Administration and the Red Cross racist ban on Haitian blood donations. The union produced and distributed thousands of leaflets, reprinted by our members' families in Haiti, which condemned the U.S. government's scapegoating of Haitian immigrants and gay men for the AIDS epidemic. The leaflets called for massive government resources for scientific research and medical care to defeat the virus, like the billions the government spent on the Manhattan Project's nuclear weapons program during World War II.

During the late 1980s, the Local's members had joined tens of thousands in the streets of Boston—sometimes weekly, sometimes daily—in the popular upsurge, both in the U.S. and Haiti, that led to the overthrow of the U.S.-backed Duvalier dictatorship and swept the Lavalas movement into power in Haiti. Jean-Bertrand Aristide made several trips to Boston during that time. One of his rallies filled Boston City Hall Plaza with thousands of supporters. Many school bus drivers were on stage as part of his security. Union activists attended many of his lectures on campuses in the Boston area. They brought literature and his call for an "avalanche" to sweep away misery and repression in Haiti into the bus yards for daily discussion.

So when the CIA-backed military coup against President Aristide's new government shocked the world, Haitian unionists in Boston were among the first to hit the streets again. Mass marches and demonstrations rocked the streets around Boston's government center. The banners of Local 8751 always waved up front.

This momentum carried over into labor/management relations in the fall of 1991, when the school bus drivers launched a militant, close to six week strike against their private employer, who was trying to ram concessions and cutbacks down the throats of the drivers. Haitian workers did double duty, lighting the fire barrels on the strike line before the sun came up, battling wannabe scabs driving stretch limousines during the day, and hitting the bricks of government center in the evening with the thousands protesting the re-imposition of military death squad rule in their homeland.

To fight the fear which the military coup spread in the drivers' families, the local launched a campaign of solidarity with workers and their organizations in Haiti. The union participated in the boycott of Disney and other corporations who were using the coup as a chance to impose draconian labor conditions on their workers in Haiti. Local 8751 also sponsored meetings and tours of Haitian union leaders, many of whom were under threat from the military's death squads at home, such as the meeting with the Konfederasyon Jeneral Travayè (CGT) in the bus yards described below.

More recently, Local 8751 participated in mass pickets at Boston's JFK Federal Building demanding the immediate release of hundreds of Haitians locked up in federal detention from Boston to Miami during the FBI/INS mass roundups and detentions of Haitian and other immigrants in the U.S. following September 11.

And in an initiative which brought to the fore the alliance between the Haitian and progressive communities, the union movement and the anti-war movement in the U.S., Local 8751 launched a defense committee in February 2002 which got Haitian and Local 8751 activist Marcus Jean acquitted by jury in Boston District Court. Brother Jean had been framed up by the bankrupt Laidlaw management firm and the local district attorney's office on charges of "making terrorist threats." What he did was to stand up for his union rights against a racist boss hell-bent on utilizing discrimination and intimidation against the largely immigrant work force.

Local 8751 is honored to be asked by the editors of this book to contribute a chapter. We offer excerpts and photos from articles that first appeared in our Union's newsletters. We do so with a sense of urgency, as the political and economic crisis now developing in Haiti, due in large part to what the United States has done to Haiti since 1804, directly affects many of our loved ones. We also hope that others in the working class movement in the U.S. will see the need to broaden the scope of activity in our unions and organizing drives to include the struggle against racism, anti-immigrant scapegoating, U.S. colonialism and war. That is and must be an essential ingredient in the struggle to better the living standards of our members.

Lè nou ini nou pap jam fè bèk a tè!
United we can never be defeated!

Viv lit pou Haiti rété indépandan-an!
Long live the struggle begun by Haitian independence!

8,000 marchers denounce FDA's anti-Haitian racism

Ernst Merisier, shop steward USWA Local 8751 and
Stevan Kirschbaum, Vice-President USWA Local 8751

Boston, April 4, 1990

Today over 8,000 members of the Haitian community and their supporters converged on the JFK Federal Building here to protest Bush's and the Food and Drug Administration's new policy banning Haitians and Africans from donating blood....

In early February the FDA set out guidelines recommending that all Haitians be excluded from donating blood. The reason the FDA gave for this bigoted policy was to "slow the spread of AIDS."

The logic of this false reasoning flies in the face of all scientific data and smacks of the worst brand of racist scapegoating. AIDS activists have pointed out that barring Haitians and gay men, the other group banned, from blood donations stigmatizes groups where simply screening all blood would be the correct scientific approach....

Union participation

Many unionists participated in the demonstration, including hotel and restaurant workers, service workers, and teachers. Visible at the front speaker's area was the banner of the United Steelworkers of America, Local 8751- School Bus Drivers, which had a delegation of over 50 workers. Union stewards Ernst Merisier and John Accime played a leading role in coordination and security.

Local 8751, whose membership includes Haitian workers, distributed a statement entitled "Stop the Government's Racist Discrimination Against the Haitian Community." The statement called for a "massive Manhattan Project"-type full-scale coordinated scientific, medical campaign employing all available resources, initiated by the government to combat AIDS...

Haitian drivers do double picket duty

Steve Gillis, Executive Board USWA Local 8751

Boston, October 14, 1991

Many of Boston's school bus drivers are from Haiti. They've been most diligent in doing strike duty and then joining thousands of others from Boston's Haitian community to protest the right-wing coup d'etat in their homeland.

Hundreds of drivers rotate picket shifts between round-the-clock demonstrations at the JFK Federal Building in downtown Boston and the strike lines at ICBM [bus management company]. On October 1, the day after the coup, 7,000 marchers took over the streets chanting, "*Konplo sa'a pase.*" [This plot will fail.]

Ernst Merisier, Local 8751 Executive Board member, told Workers World, "Like the people struggling in Haiti, Haitians in the diaspora have fought too long for

the gains we have today. We're sending a message to both ICBM and the Tonton Macoutes that we are prepared to fight until justice is done."

Boston meeting salutes Haiti unionists

Ernst Merisier, Executive Board USWA Local 8751
and Stevan Kirschbaum, Vice-President, USWA Local 8751

November 29, 1993, Boston

On Nov. 29, Steel Workers Local 8751 School Bus Drivers and Monitors hosted a noon solidarity meeting with Cajuste Lexius and Porcenel Joachim, the general secretary and executive secretary respectively of the Konfederasyon Jeneral Travayè (CGT). The CGT is a Haitian trade-union federation formed in 1990.

The 22,000-member CGT has been a strong voice in the Lavalas movement. Lexius and Joachim went to Washington in early October at the request of ousted Haitian President Jean-Bertrand Aristide to help plan his return to Haiti.

Like Aristide, these union leaders have been unable to return to their country because the U.S.-supported fascist military continues to illegally hold power in Haiti.

The union leaders' visit to Boston is part of a campaign to build solidarity with the Haitian trade-union movement. While in Boston, Lexius and Joachim also met with the Hotel

Ernst Merisier, Local 8751 official, with Haitian trade unionists.

and Restaurant union and the Service Employees union.

The Local 8751 meeting was held in the drivers' room ... conducted in both Creole and English. Ernst Merisier of the Local's Executive Board and Philippe Geneus, a leading Haitian community activist, translated ...

In April 1987, while Joachim was president of the Haitian Steel Workers Union, the union went on strike for a decent contract. Not only did the workers have to face an intransigent steel company but they also squared off against five units of then-dictator Gen. Prosper Avril's military.

Despite these odds the 600 striking workers remained firm and eventually won a contract.

During the time of the Aristide government, unions for the first time were able to begin achieving some basic democratic rights to organize. The Lavalas movement fought to expand these rights and also mounted a struggle to raise the minimum wage in Haiti.

All these moves were met by openly hostile opposition by the international corporations in Haiti, most of them U.S.-based.

Since the coup, unions in Haiti function under extremely brutal conditions. Meetings, collecting dues, and other basics of organization must all be done clandestinely. Over 300 CGT leaders are currently in hiding.

Lexius ... a former president of the Public Transportation Union ... was en route to a radio interview in Port-au-Prince on April 23. He was kidnapped by the military, beaten and tortured to unconsciousness ... Finally, international protests won his release on May 21.

"You in the U.S. can play a key role in pressuring the U.S. government to end the Haitian crisis," said Lexius ... Joachim said in closing his remarks, "All workers everywhere have the same common interests!"

Boston's Haitian Community Protests Bush/INS Mass Detentions in Florida

Steve Gillis, Grievance Committee, USWA Local 8751

July 25, 2002

On July 25, 2002, hundreds from Boston's Haitian community rallied at the downtown Immigration and Naturalization Services office to demand the immediate release of over 250 Haitians including women and children locked up in Florida jails. 37 of them began a hunger strike on July 15.

These immigrants arrived by boat on Dec. 3, 2001, seeking political asylum from the U.S. and fleeing corporate-orchestrated violence and poverty on their island.

Within days, the Bush administration secretly changed its policy toward Haitian asylum seekers, singling out all Haitians for indefinite detention in maximum security Miami-area prisons. This is a significant change from the previous policy, which allowed the asylum-seekers to be released to the custody of friends, relatives or immigration advocates.

Many at today's spirited protest charged the INS with blatant racism and discrimination, pointing to the case of Cuban asylum seekers who are released from detention immediately following a preliminary hearing. In a statement from the Boston Haitian Reporter distributed at the action, publisher William J. Dorcena writes, "This is a Human Rights issue that all sectors must embrace. The Haitian community is under attack by the very leaders in the U.S. who ask us all to 'come together as a country in a time of war.' Well, the Bush administration is privately waging its own war, a very racist and ugly war against immigrants, specifically against Haitians."

Boston frame-up foiled:

Anti-war, labor unity wins victory for Marcus Jean

Steve Kirschbaum,
Boston Labor's ANSWER, member Steel Workers Local 8751

Boston, Nov. 21

On Thursday, Nov. 14th a jury in the West Roxbury Court returned its verdict of not guilty, after less than 30 minutes of deliberation, in the case of the Commonwealth of Massachusetts vs. Marcus Jean. This brings to a successful conclusion a critical phase in the struggle to win justice for Jean, a Boston School Bus driver and militant activist member of United Steelworkers of America (USWA), Local 8751. It also represents an important victory for the anti-war movement and the movement to defend labor's rights.

Rachel Nasca

Laidlaw, which is in Chapter 11 bankruptcy, had targeted Jean as part of their policy to weed out

Victory celebration on steps of courthouse, Nov. 21, 2002.

union militants that stand up to their plans to downsize, cutback wages and tighten their iron handed grip on the work force. Last January 30th Mr. Jean was involved in a minor disagreement with another driver concerning a bus parking spot. Jean and his union steward met with Readville Asst. Manager Diane Kelly and resolved the matter. No warning or discipline of any kind was issued. The following morning Readville Terminal Manger Rick McLaughlin, in a provocative and threatening manner tried to interrogate Mr. Jean about this same incident. Jean knew that this was a gross violation of his union rights and called McLaughlin on his racist discrimination and refused to submit to unjust management harassment…. That afternoon McLaughlin went to the police and claimed that Marcus Jean repeatedly threatened to blow up the building and that he posed a serious "terrorist" threat. ...

Government attacks on the labor movement are nothing new. The Teamsters, AFSCME, SEIU, the Steelworkers are just a few of the recent targets of this management tool. Injunctions during strikes, false "Rico" charges, and fraudulent persecution by the so-called Labor Department have become routine. However Bush's "enduring war" hysteria has qualitatively upped the ante on the attacks on labor. The Bush/Ashcroft "Homeland Security" machine clearly has the unions in its sights. The White House has given the green light to corporate America to use the war to declare war on union rights. When Homeland Security boss Tom Ridge recently called the president of the ILWU dock workers in California, under the guise of national security, to threaten the union if it took action in support of their rights the message was clear...

The March 2002 issue of the Unity Bulletin, the rank and file newsletter of Local 8751, explains that Marcus Jean's case is part of "a national wave of government directed anti-immigrant hysteria sweeping the country" which includes racist profiling, government detention of

Arab people without charges and racist violence against immigrant communities. It is in this context that the District Attorney for Massachusetts embarked on a ten-month prosecution of an innocent Haitian union activist based on the uncorroborated story of a racist Laidlaw boss.

Boston Labor's ANSWER leads struggle to defend Marcus Jean

It is regrettable that much of the leadership of the unions on a local and international level has been unable to respond to the corporate/ government attacks on the unions in the post 911-war climate. This was the case with Marcus Jean. However the rank and file members need and are ready to fight back. Boston Labor's ANSWER, made up of activists from the coalition Act Now to Stop War and End Racism (ANSWER), established the Marcus Jean Defense Committee. The Committee secured the top criminal attorney in the region, people's lawyer Barry Wilson, knowing that he would bring the struggle of the street into the courtroom.

ANSWER activists launched a full scale, all out defense campaign to mobilize support which included packing every court appearance, getting endorsers, holding picket lines and press conferences, speaking at churches and community meetings and spreading the word through the Internet. The Committee conducted a massive letter campaign to the DA demanding that the charges be dropped. Marcus Jean spoke at and marched on countless ANSWER protests against war in Iraq and in defense of Palestine. He was a featured speaker at the June 29th rally at FBI headquarters in Washington, D.C., against the Patriot Act. This campaign to defend Marcus Jean is a concrete expression of ANSWER's view that Bush's war has a domestic front. The anti-war movement must also fight on this front in order to build unity with the labor movement. This unity is key to a vital anti-war movement. ...

AUTHOR BIOGRAPHIES

MUMIA ABU-JAMAL is an African American political prisoner who has been falsely imprisoned on Pennsylvania's death row since 1982. A former member of the Black Panther Party, he is an renowned radio and print journalist with a worldwide audience. Mumia is called the "voice of the voiceless" by millions of people. An international movement is demanding his freedom.

PAT CHIN was born in Jamaica and has lived in the United States since the early 1960s. She has visited Haiti many times with political delegations. Chin has also traveled to Yugoslavia where she represented the International Action Center at an international war crimes tribunal on US/NATO aggression on Yugoslavia. Chin, who is also a photographer, frequently speaks and writes for Workers World newspaper on Caribbean issues and on anti-racist, anti-imperialist and women's struggles.

RAMSEY CLARK, the U.S. attorney-general in the Lyndon Johnson administration, is an international attorney and human-rights advocate. He has opposed U.S. military intervention all around the world. He is the founder of the International Action Center and author of *Crime in America* and *The Fire This Time*. He investigated the 1991 coup against Aristide as a member of the Haiti Commission.

EDWIDGE DANTICAT won the American Book Award for her 1998 novel, *The Farming of Bones*. She was born in Haiti in 1969 and immigrated to Brooklyn in 1981 to join her parents. While she was living in Haiti without her parents, she was raised by her aunt, for whom she has great affection. She currently lives in Miami.

FREDERICK DOUGLASS was a major African American orator, writer, and leader of the abolitionist movement in the 19th century. He was a significant political figure and the U.S.'s diplomatic representative to Haiti in the 1880s. Born enslaved, having taught himself to read, a crime then punishable by death, he fled to freedom.

GREG DUNKEL is a regular writer for Workers World and Haïti-Progrès. He is also a member of Haiti Support Network, has gone with HSN delegations to Haiti and is a delegate in his local union.

BEN DUPUY is the secretary general of Haiti's National Popular Party (PPN). He was ambassador-at-large for President Aristide's government from 1991-1993 and is editor-in-chief of Haïti-Progrès newspaper.

SARA FLOUNDERS is a co-director of the International Action Center. She writes and speaks frequently and co-edited seven books, including: *Hidden Agenda; NATO in the Balkans; Metal of Dishonor and Challenge to Genocide: Let Iraq Live; War in Columbia: Made in the U.S.* She has traveled to a number of countries under U.S. attack, including Iraq, Yugoslavia, Colombia, Cuba, Palestine.

STEVE GILLIS & FRANTZ MENDES are currently president and vice-president of United Steel Workers of America Local 8751, which represents the school bus drivers in Boston. They are both longtime union activists in the Boston area.

STAN GOFF is a retired Special Forces master sergeant, living in Raleigh. He is the author of *Hideous Dream: A Soldier's Memoir of the US Invasion of Haiti* (Soft Skull Press, 2000) and *Full Spectrum Disorder: The Military in the New American Century* (Soft Skull Press, 2003).

KIM IVES is a writer and editor at Haïti-Progrès newspaper and a documentary filmmaker who has worked on many films about Haiti (*Bitter Cane, The Coup Continues, Rezistans*). He is a member of the Haiti Support Network (HSN) and has led numerous delegations to Haiti. He frequently speaks about Haiti on Haitian and U.S. radio programs, most frequently at WBAI-FM in New York.

FLEURIMOND W. KERNS is a writer for Haïti-Progrès, based in Paris, who hosts a local Haitian radio program. He also organizes Haitian community events in France.

PAUL LARAQUE is a poet, author, and essayist on political and cultural affairs, in French and Creole. Born in Jérémie in 1920, he was exiled from Haiti in 1961. He was a founder and secretary general of Association of Haitian Writers Abroad (1979-86) and won Cuba's Casa de las Americas prize in 1979. A leading member of the Haitian Patriotic Action Movement in the late 1960s and early 1970s, he now lives in New York. His many works include *Fistibal* (1974), *Sòlda mawon* (1987), and *Open Gate* (2001), which he co-edited.

MAUDE LEBLANC is a co-director of Haïti-Progrès and a leader in the National Popular Party (PPN). She was also a founder of the Association of Haitian Workers (ATH), working among Haitian immigrants in New York in the 1980s.

SAM MARCY was a Marxist theoretician, organizer, and former trade unionist. He was the founder of Workers World Party and regularly contributed to its newspaper until his death in 1998. He wrote extensively on the problems of socialist and Third-World countries. His writings have been translated into a number of languages.

FÉLIX MORISSEAU-LEROY, the founder of modern Creole literature, was a lawyer, teacher, and journalist as well as a poet, playwright, and novelist, in French and Creole. Born in Grand Gosier in 1912, he was exiled from Haiti under the Duvalier dictatorship in 1959 and lived for 25 years in Africa, working in cultural affairs for the Ghanaian and Senegalese governments. He died in Miami in 1998.

JOHNNIE STEVENS is a co-director of the People's Video Network. He has traveled widely, including to the World Conference Against Racism in South Africa and Haiti and helped produce numerous videos on peoples' struggles in the U.S. and around the world. Stevens has also organized in support of Haitian popular organizations.

BIBLIOGRAPHY

These books and articles were referred to during the preparation of this book. They are also sources of further information. [Editors]

Barros, Jacques. *Haïti de 1804 à nos jours*. Paris: Editions l'Harmattan, 1984.

McFadyen, Deidre, and Pierre LaRamee. *Haiti: Dangerous Crossroads*. Boston, MA: South End Press, 1995.

Barthelemy, Gerard, and Christian Girault, eds. *La République haïtienne: État des lieux et perspectives*. Paris: Editions Karthala, 1993.

Dejean, Paul. *Haïti: alerte, on tue!* Montreal: CIDIHCA, 1993.

Dupuy, Alex. *Haiti in the New World Order: The Limits of the Democratic Revolution*. Boulder, CO: Westview Press, 1996.

Farmer, Paul. *The Uses of Haiti*. Monroe, ME: Common Courage Press, 1994.

Ferguson, James. *Papa Doc Baby Doc: Haiti and the Duvaliers*. New York: Basil Blackwell Inc., 1987.

Fick, Carolyn E. *The Making of Haiti: The Saint Domingue Revolution from Below*. Knoxville, TN: University of Tennessee Press, 1990.

Goff, Stan. *Hideous Dream: Racism and the U.S. Army in the Invasion of Haiti*. New York: Soft Skull Press, 2000.

Gutierrez, Carlos Maria. *The Dominican Republic: Rebellion and Repression*. New York: Monthly Review, 1972.

Haïti Progrès, various issues.

Hunt, Alfred N. *Haiti's Influence on Antebellum America: Slumbering Volcano in the Caribbean*. Baton Rouge, LA: Louisiana State University Press, 1988.

James, C.L.R. *The Black Jacobins: Toussaint L'Ouverture and the San Domingo Revolution*. New York: Vintage Books, 1963.

Landry, Harral E. "Slavery and the Slave Trade in Atlantic Diplomacy, 1850-1861." *The Journal of Southern History* XXVII, 2, 184-207.

Loewen, James W. *Lies My Teacher Told Me: Everything Your American History Textbook Got Wrong*. New York: Simon & Schuster, 1996.

Nicholls, David. *From Dessalines to Duvalier: Race, Colour and National Independence in Haiti*. New Brunswick, NJ: Rutgers University Press, 1996.

Padgett, James A. "Diplomats to Haiti and their Diplomacy." *The Journal of Negro History* XXV, 3, 265-330.

Plummer, Brenda Gayle. *Haiti and the Great Powers, 1902-1915*. Baton Rouge, LA: Louisiana State University Press, 1988.

___. *Haiti and the United States: The Psychological Moment*. Athens, GA: The University of Georgia Press, 1992.

Richardson, Bonham C. *The Caribbean in the Wider World, 1492-1992: A Regional Geography*. New York: Cambridge University Press, 1992.

Smith, Daniel M. "National Interest and American Intervention, 1917: An Historiographical Appraisal." *The Journal of American History* LII, 1, 5-24.

Trouillot, Michel-Rolph. *Haiti State against Nation: The Origins and Legacy of Duvalierism*. New York: Monthly Review Press, 1990.

Wesley, Charles H. "The Struggle for the Recognition of Haiti and Liberia as Independent Republics." *The Journal of Negro History* II, 4, 369-383.

Zevin, Robert. "An Interpretation of American Imperialism." *The Journal of Economic History* XXXII, 1, 316-360.

The following websites are useful for finding information about Haiti:

http://www.webster.edu/~corbetre/haiti/haiti.html —Bob Corbet's Haiti Page. Very comprehensive.

http://www.haiti-progres.com/—Haïti-Progrès Page contains selection from the week's issue and an archive to past issues. In French, Creole and English.

http://members.tripod.com/~davidco/#haiti—A list of links, useful but has annoying pop-ups.

http://www.haiti-usa.org/—A very attractive and informative page coming out of Trinity College in Washington, DC.

INDEX

Haiti Support Network (HSN)

In 1995, the Haiti Support Network was founded to raise material and political support for popular organizations and parties genuinely dedicated to Haiti's self-determination.

Much of our work has been in support of the National Popular Party (PPN), which in 1999 grew out of the National Popular Assembly (APN), a nationwide popular organization founded in 1987. The PPN, like the APN before it, is known for the professionalism and dedication of its militants, who are leaders formed by years of experience in the Haitian democratic struggle.

Over the years, the HSN has organized film premieres, public meetings, delegations to Haiti, demonstrations against police brutality, and fund-raising parties. We publish a yearly newsletter and periodically issue press releases about events in Haiti.

With the assistance and solidarity of the People's Video Network (PVN), the HSN has also produced a number of videotapes which have been shown and used for organizing in the U.S., Canada, and Haiti.

The HSN holds many of its meetings at the International Action Center (IAC), which has provided it with invaluable advice and solidarity.

For those who would like to know more about or work with the HSN, they can contact us at:

Haiti Support Network (HSN)
39 West 14th Street, Rm. 206, New York, NY 10011
Telephone: 212-633-6646; Fax: 212-633-2889
Email: HSNHaiti@hotmail.com
www.iacenter.org/haiti

We welcome contributions of any size. Tax deductible contributions of over $50 can be made out to the **People's Rights Fund** with a note that it is for the Haiti Support Network.

Contact information for other Haiti support organizations

Haiti Action Committee, PO Box 2218, Berkeley, CA 94702, USA
www.haitiaction.net
Haiti Support Group, PO Box 29623, London E9 7XU, United Kingdom, www.haitisupport.gn.apc.org
Quixote Center/Haiti Reborn, PO Box 5206, Hyattsville, MD 20782 USA, 301-699-0042, Fax: 301-864-2182
www.quixote.org/haitireborn

INTERNATIONAL *ACTION* CENTER

Former U.S. Attorney General Ramsey Clark and other anti-war activists founded the IAC in 1991. They had rallied hundreds of thousands of people in the United States to oppose the U.S./UN war against Iraq. It connects opposition to U.S. militarism and domination around the world to the struggle to end poverty, racism, sexism, and oppression of lesbian, gay, bisexual and transgendered people in the United States.

As part of the IAC's campaign to halt the intervention of U.S. imperialism in the Caribbean, it has sent delegations to conferences in Haiti of the National Popular Party, which grew out of the National Popular Assembly, a half dozen times since the late 1980s. It has also cooperated with the Haiti Support Network, organizing meetings and forums and now publishing this book.

The IAC has led delegations to Colombia, including attending the Tribunal Against the Violence of Coca Cola in December 2002. The IAC has fought against the blockade of Cuba and participated in the struggle to stop the U.S. Navy from using the island of Vieques, Puerto Rico.

It played a leading role in the struggle to end the death penalty in the United States and mobilizations to freed Black liberation fighter and death-row political prisoner Mumia Abu-Jamal.

After September 11, 2001, the IAC called immediately for anti-war protests and helped form the new coalition called International ANSWER, or Act Now to Stop War and End Racism. ANSWER drew tens of thousands of people to Washington, D.C., and San Francisco on September 29, 2001, to say no to the U.S. war drive. Since then, ANSWER, with IAC participation, has become the leading anti-war coalition in the U.S.

A major part of the IAC's work is to expose the intricate web of lies woven before, during and after each U.S. military intervention. It shows instead that U.S. intervention is dictated by the drive for profits and that as military funding expands, the money available for education, healthcare and needed social programs contracts. The IAC's popular web site, www.iacenter.org, has made the "top one percent of web sites" list for the thousands of sites that link to it.

The IAC is a volunteer activist organization, which relies totally on the donations and assistance of supporters around the country. To be a part of a growing network or to make a donation, request a speaker, to order books or videos, or volunteer your support, contact the IAC.

International Action Center
39 West 14th Street, Room 206, New York, N.Y. 10011 USA
Tel: 212-633-6646; fax 212-633-2889
Email: iacenter@action-mail.org
Web page: http://**www.iacenter.org**

CROWING ROOSTER ARTS

Crowing Rooster Arts has as its mission to produce films and videos which chronicle, analyze, and give life to Haiti's continuing struggle for democracy and self-determination. In the process, we hope to capture the beauty and valor of the Haitian people, the élan of their culture, as well as the drama of their unique history.

Our documentaries, such as the acclaimed "Haiti, Killing the Dream," have been broadcast internationally by public television as well as used by community groups, schools, churches, and researchers. They have been projected in venues ranging from prestigious international film festivals to basement meeting halls in New York City to peasant courtyards deep in the Haitian countryside.

We also produce audio tapes and CDs of music and poetry from some of Haiti's most renowned artists as well as work from those unknown. We have amassed and continue to catalogue an unparalleled archive of audio-visual material on Haiti which we know will be invaluable to future generations looking back on our historical period.

Through our work, we hope not just to reflect the social conflicts and changes underway in Haiti but also to show the beauty and complexity of the culture and, in some small way, to advance that country's emerging democracy.

Tel. (212) 334-6260   Fax. (212) 334-6263
www.crowingrooster.org   E-mail. crowingrooster@juno.com

BOOKS & VIDEOS *from the*
INTERNATIONAL ACTION CENTER

War in Colombia: Made in the U.S.A.

This book powerfully counters the Pentagon and media propaganda with facts about what's really happening in Colombia.

In these pages you will find the truth about the almost 40,000 Colombians who have died in the last several years, the more than 2.5 million who have been displaced, the broad sectors who are heroically fighting inhumane policies mandated by the multinational corporations like Coca-Cola.

This book is a compilation of voices that oppose Plan Colombia and express solidarity with the Colombian people. Authors include: Ramsey Clark, Fidel Castro, Teresa Gutierrez, James Petras, Rep. Cynthia McKinney, Javier Correa Suárez and Manuel Marulanda Vélez.

IAC, 2003. 300 pages, indexed, chronology, maps, softcover. $19.95

Plan Colombia: We Say No!   *Video*

This video documents the growing movement to stop U.S. war in Colombia. See footage from interviews with Raúl Reyes, other FARC-EP members, Wilson Borja, labor leaders, human rights activists and youth in Colombia. Also see excerpts from speeches by Ramsey Clark, Teresa Gutierrez and others.

Peoles Video Network VHS, 2000, 29 min. $20 individual $50 institutions

The Fire This Time   *U.S. War Crimes in the Gulf*
by Ramsey Clark

A book that tells the truth about the Gulf War tragedy — a sharp indictment of U.S. foreign policy that led to the Gulf War and its devastating human and environmental consequences. *The Fire This Time* stands out amid the deluge of self-congratulatory accounts which do injustice to history. Updated introduction since 9/11/01 by Sara Flounders and Brian Becker. "A strong indictment of conduct of the war and especially of the needless deaths of civilians caused by bombing." — New York Times "Not academic. ... Clark risked his life by traveling through Iraqi cities at a time when the U.S. was staging 3,000 bombings a day." — Los Angeles Times

IAC, 2002. 352 pages, indexed, pictures, softcover. $19.95

Hidden Agenda U.S. *NATO Takeover of Yugoslavia*

The International Action Center's second full-length book on the Balkans conflict exposes the illegal roots and procedures of the International Criminal Tribunal for the former Yugoslavia and its effort to stage a show trial of former Yugoslav President Slobodan Milosevic as an attempt to find the Serb and Yugoslav people guilty of resistance to NATO. Using evidence presented to dozens of popular international tribunal hearings in 1999 and 2000, it turns the tables on NATO by exposing and demonstrating the war crimes of Milosevic's accusers, including their decade-long conspiracy to wage war on Yugoslavia. With articles by Mumia Abu-Jamal, former Yugoslav President Slobodon Milosevic, Ramsey Clark, Michel Chossudovsky, Sara Flounders, Gloria La Riva, Michael Parenti, Michel Collon and other leading anti-war activists and analysts from many countries.

IAC, 2002. 400 pages, pictures, indexed, chronology, maps, softcover. $19.95

NATO in the Balkans *Voices of Dissent*

Confused about the REAL reasons the United States bombed Yugoslavia? This book, released in 1998, will give you the secret background and hidden role of the U.S. and Germany in the dismemberment of Yugoslavia. NATO in the Balkans shows how sophisticated, "Big Lie" war propaganda nearly silenced popular debate and opposition. Authors Ramsey Clark, Sean Gervasi, Sara Flounders, Thomas Deichmann, Gary Wilson, Richard Becker and Nadja Tesich will take you through the ins and outs, the framework and media lies that led to the series of bloody conflicts that have characterized central Europe in the last years of this century.

IAC, 1998. 230 pages, indexed, softcover. $15.95

War, Lies & Videotape *How media monopoly stifles truth*

What passes as news today has been predigested by a handful of megamedia corporations. In this book, hard-hitting media critics, journalists, and activists examine:
- The ever-increasing media monopoly that stifles dissent and information
- Links between the government, the media and the military
- War propaganda & NATO's expanding role in Yugoslavia
- Role of Big Oil, the Pentagon & the media in the Gulf
- How new technologies can help break through the media monopoly

Edited by Lenora Foerstel. Chapters by: Jean-Bertrand Aristide, Scott Armstrong, Ben Bagdikian, Brian Becker, Ramsey Clark, Thomas Deichmann, Nawal El Saadawi, Sara Flounders, Diana Johnstone, Michael Parenti and others.

IAC, 2000. 288 pages, indexed, softcover. $15.95

Metal of Dishonor–Depleted Uranium
How the Pentagon radiates soldiers & civilians with DU weapons

A devastating exposé of the Pentagon's new weapons comprised of depleted uranium. This is the book you've heard about, but won't see in most bookstores. Now in its second printing, Gulf War veterans, leaders of environmental, anti-nuclear, anti-military and community movements discuss: The connection of depleted uranium to Gulf War syndrome and a new generation of radioactive conventional weapons. Understand how the bizarre Pentagon recycling plans of nuclear waste creates a new global threat. Authors include former U.S. Attorney General Ramsey Clark, Dr. Michio Kaku, Dr. Helen Caldicott, Dr. Rosalie Bertell, Dr. Jay M. Gould, Dan Fahey, Sara Flounders, Manuel Pino and many others.

IAC, 1997, 2nd edition 1999, 272 pages, indexed, photos, tables, softcover. $12.95

Metal of Dishonor
Campanion Video

Interviews with noted scientists, doctors, and community activists explaining dangers of radioactive DU weapons. Explores consequences of DU from mining to production, testing, and combat use. Footage from Bikini and atomic war veterans.

PVN, VHS, 1998, 50 min. $20 individual $50 institutions PAL version for Europe $35

Challenge To Genocide *LET IRAQ LIVE*

Contains essays and detailed reports on the devastating effect of the economic sanctions on Iraq since the beginning of the Gulf War. It features "*Fire and Ice,*" a chapter by former U.S. Attorney General Ramsey Clark. Also included are personal memoirs from many who defied the sanctions and U.S. law by taking medicines to Baghdad as part of the May 1998 *"Iraq Sanctions Challenge."* Contributers include Ramsey Clark, Bishop Thomas Gumbleton, Rania Masri, Sara Flounders, Ahmed El-Sherif, Brian Becker, Barbara Nimri Aziz, Kathy Kelly, Monica Moorehead and Manzoor Ghori.

IAC, 1998. 264 pages, photos, indexed, resource lists, softcover. $12.95

Genocide By Sanctions
Video

Excellent for libraries, schools, and community groups and for cable-access television programs. This powerful video documents on a day-to-day, human level how sanctions kill. It contains an important historical perspective that explains why the United States is so determined to maintain the sanctions. An important tool in the educational and humanitarian "Medicine for Iraq" campaign to collect medicine while educating people so U.S. policy will be changed. This excellent video by Gloria La Riva took second prize at the San Luis Obispo International Film Festival.

PVN, VHS, 1998, 28 min. $20 individuals $50 institutions

The Children Are Dying
The Impact of Sanctions on Iraq

Report of the UN Food and Agriculture Organization, supporting documents, and articles by Ramsey Clark, Ahmed Ben Bella, Tony Benn, Margarita Papandreou, and other prominent international human rights figures. Shows the human face of those targeted by the weapon of sanctions. The UN FAO report showed with facts and statistics that over 500,000 Iraqi children under the age of five had died as a result of U.S./UN imposed sanctions. Photos and chapters define the social implications.

IAC, 1998. 170 pages, resource lists, photos, softcover. $10

Nowhere to Hide
Video

Traveling with Ramsey Clark in Iraq in 1991, award-winning video journalist Jon Alpert captured what it was like to be on the ground during the allied bombing. In dramatic, graphic scenes, *Nowhere to Hide* shows a different reality from what was on the nightly news. Tom Harpur wrote in the Toronto Star: "Only by knowing the true nature of 'Operation Desert Storm' can similar wars be prevented...send for the video."

PVN, VHS, 28 min. $20 individuals $50 institutions

Eyewitness Sudan
Video

An exposé of the 1998 U.S. bombing of El Shifa, the small factory that produced more than half the medicine for Sudan. The smoking ruins are skillfully juxtaposed to footage of Bill Clinton, Madeline Albright and Berger's charges. This documentary by Ellen Andors connects the years of sanctions to the cruise missiles sent against an African country.

PVN, VHS, 1998, 28 min., $20 individual $50 institutions

Mumia Speaks *An interview with Mumia Abu-Jamal*

by Mumia Abu-Jamal with forewards by Monica Moorehead, Larry Holmes and Teresa Gutierrez.

Political prisoner and award-winning journalist Mumia Abu-Jamal speaks from his cell on Pennsylvania's death row. In this far ranging interview, Mumia talks about prisons, capitalism, politics, revolution and solidarity. The pamphlet also includes two articles— *"The Oppressed Nations, the Poor and Prisons,"* by Monica Moorehead. and *"The Death Penalty and the Texas Killing Machine,"* by Teresa Gutierrez.

World View Forum, 2000, 33 pages, softcover. $3

The Prison Industrial Complex
Video
An interview with Mumia Abu-Jamal on death row

Censored journalist, political activist and death-row inmate Mumia Abu-Jamal, framed for his ideas, speaks about the current political scene in the United States. In an excellent interview Mumia discusses racism, prison labor in the United States, youth, elections, economics and the state of the world. See and hear the "Voice of the Voiceless" in this unique uncensored interview. Interview by Monica Moorehead and Larry Holmes.

PVN, VHS, 1996, 28 min. $20 individual $50 institutions

On A Move *The Story of Mumia Abu-Jamal*
By Terry Bisson

Covering Mumia Abu-Jamal's childhood in the North Philly projects, a turbulent youth in Oakland and New York, a promising career in radio journalism, and a fateful sidewalk altercation that changed everything, Bisson's colorful sketches tell the story of one of the stormiest periods in American history, and of a young rebel who came of age in its crucible. "The next time you see Mumia demonized in the mainstream media, pick up this book. It chronicles the evolution of an eloquent advocate for the damned."—Martin Espada, author, *Zapata's Disciple*

Plough Publishing, 2000, 240 pages, 36 photos, softcover. $12

TO ORDER: All mail orders must be pre-paid.
Bulk orders of 10 or more items available at 40% off cover price.
Include $5 U.S. shipping and handling for first item, $1.50 each additional item.
International shipping $12 for first item, $4 each additional item.

Send check or money order to: **INTERNATIONAL ACTION CENTER**
39 West 14th Street, Room. 206, New York, NY 10011
(212) 633-6646 email: iacenter@action-mail.org

To place individual CREDIT CARD orders (VISA & MC only),

order on-line at:

For bookstore and university invoice orders and discounts,
call the IAC in advance for specific information.

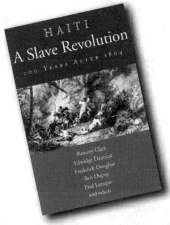

Haitians on Brooklyn Bridge protest U.S.-backed coup against Aristide, 1991.

Greg Dur